D1195763

WAGNER AT BAYREUTH

Parsifal, 1882: Zaubergarten
(design by Paul von Joukowsky [painting by Max Brückner])
Original: Richard Wagner-Gedenkstätte, Bayreuth

GEOFFREY SKELTON

WAGNER AT BAYREUTH

experiment and tradition

FOREWORD BY
WIELAND WAGNER

Barrie and Rockliff
London

© Geoffrey Skelton 1965
First published 1965 by
Barrie and Rockliff (Barrie Books Ltd)
2 Clement's Inn, London W.C.2
Printed in Great Britain by
Western Printing Services Ltd, Bristol

Contents

Illustrations

Colour Plates

Black and White Plates

6

Foreword

by WIELAND WAGNER

SOCIAL upheavals caused by wars and revolutions have always led to a reassessment of values. Everything that was once considered permanent has subsequently appeared questionable, outmoded or unfruitful. After 1945 it was widely felt that Wagner's work, as a vast compendium of nineteenth-century attitudes, had lost its significance. And so when it was reopened in 1951, in the year of its seventy-fifth anniversary, there hung over the Bayreuth Festival, the oldest festival of our time, a large question mark.

Wagner's works were of course still played in the immediate post-war years in other opera houses, in Germany as elsewhere. But the question remained whether they would stand the test of production in the place which the composer himself had created specially for them, before a festival public conditioned by the catastrophic shocks of the last war. As it happened, both Wagner and Bayreuth withstood the test, and their significance in the world of today has increased from year to year. Wagner is once again at work as a catalyst in the world, exerting an influence greater than ever before, as the composition of festival audiences clearly shows. Not even in the years before 1914 was it so strikingly international.

Bayreuth is no longer simply a national shrine. Since 1951 it has become the meeting-place of people from many nations, argumentative and for the most part young, who see Wagner not as a controversial representative of nineteenth-century Romanticism, but as a universal figure like Aeschylus, Shakespeare or Calderon. Wagner's modern champions have nothing more in common with those blind devotees of former times, the sect of Wagnerians whose tight bonds discouraged many of the 'uninitiated' from attempting to come to grips with Wagner at all. Nowadays there exists the basis for something like a free and uninhibited discussion across all frontiers, a living Wagner forum cleared of the dust and red plush of former days. In the work of such men as Ernest Newman, Theodor W. Adorno, Ernst Bloch, Willy Haas, C. G. Jung, Hans Mayer and Wolfgang Schadewaldt we can detect a new and more profound understanding of Wagner's dramatic genius.

The history of the festival, as presented to us by the author of this book, shows that Bayreuth has never entirely closed its mind to innovation, a fact that legitimizes the experimental nature of the new Bayreuth. It cannot of course be overlooked that the festival year of 1951 cut deeper than ever before. With this festival a line was drawn under much that had become dear to many in their conception of Wagner's works. The operation was necessary if these were not to become anachronistic in effect, appealing only to a backward-looking public. But it is precisely with this deeper incision that the Bayreuth of today believes it is paying its debt to tradition, to an extent that the orthodoxy of former guardians of tradition did not achieve.

A body of work that, like Shakespeare's and Calderon's, can be judged and experienced in so many different ways is of immediate topical concern to the family of nations which are today struggling so painfully towards one another. In it all the problems of social harmony and conflict are reflected, all the loneliness as well as the tragedy of human existence. Our task is to make Wagner's work accessible and familiar to everyone, with all the artistic and technical means at our disposal today and in full and constant awareness of our responsibility.

(*Translated from the German.*)

Introduction

THE festival theatre at Bayreuth was Richard Wagner's own creation—in every sense of the word. He sought the place for it, he earned or begged the money to build it, he designed it and, if he did not erect it with his own hands, he supervised its erection down to the smallest detail. For the first performances there of the *Ring* in 1876 he chose the singers, the *décor* and the costumes. He was the producer and, though not the conductor, he chose a man for that (Hans Richter) who could faithfully reproduce his ideas.

His hand was everywhere and, when seven years later he died, his spirit continued to exercise control through his widow Cosima and others who had been his close associates. Cosima was succeeded by their son Siegfried, Siegfried by his widow Winifred, Winifred by her sons Wieland and Wolfgang—an unbroken family succession covering three generations.

In the history of music Bayreuth is quite unique. Other composers have of course left widows and children and disciples behind, to claim, with more or less authority, a knowledge of the master's mind. Usually the result has been unrewarding and luckily short-lived. Composers truly worthy of immortality find no difficulty at all in withstanding the occasional misinterpretations and distortions to which their work may be subjected, both in and after their lifetime.

9

On the whole those without authorized or self-appointed guardians are the fortunate ones, for it has been shown time and time again that true works of art can be more easily killed by kindness than by occasional cruelty. Why this is so is not difficult to see. It is simply that there is really nothing absolute about a work of art. The creator himself knows (though he may not always say it) that what he has produced is seldom the whole of his inner vision, but only the nearest he can get to it. In music, what he writes down is only an approximation, since musical notation is notoriously rough and ready. And performance is again subject to the limitations, mental and technical, of the performer.

These are of course obvious facts, but facts worth mentioning because they have so much to do with the creation of the Wagner festival at Bayreuth and with its continuance. If Wagner's works—or at any rate the mature works from *Tristan und Isolde* to *Parsifal*—had not been revolutionary works Bayreuth would have been even in the composer's lifetime nothing but an expensive luxury: the works would have survived in the same way that the operas of Mozart and of Verdi have survived. But Wagner was right in thinking that these works were beyond the normal resources of his time, not only with regard to the production but even more to the interpretation. Bayreuth was in fact a necessity if all his ideas were to be realized in practice.

There was of course the danger that what Wagner did in his own specially built theatre would be regarded as the final word, that his successors at Bayreuth would see it as their duty simply to preserve what he had laid down and thus turn the festival theatre into a museum. There are many people who accuse Cosima Wagner of having attempted to do that, but this is to take a very superficial view of her achievements. In fact she inherited from Richard Wagner an imperfect tradition, mainly because he did not have the opportunity to put his theoretical ideas into practice except with two of his works. The 'Bayreuth style' which eventually emerged was far more

Cosima Wagner's creation than Richard Wagner's, and it was a necessary step on the way to a proper understanding of his works, as I hope in the course of this book to show.

Siegfried Wagner, inheriting the festival from his mother but obliged to administer it within the shadow of her strong personality, stood in far more danger than she of succumbing to the temptation simply to preserve— though in doing so he would have been preserving her ideas rather than his father's. In fact cautiously and perhaps somewhat belatedly he moved the festival along with his times.

The era of Winifred, Siegfried's widow, was characterized by a new danger, that of idolatry. It was not she who idolized, but Adolf Hitler. Hitler used Wagner for his own ends, probably both consciously and unconsciously. At any rate he seized on all those elements in Wagner which seemed to point to the supremacy of the Nordic races. That this was a distortion of Wagner is as easy to prove as to disprove. Like all great men Wagner can be looked at from very many aspects. And, quite apart from his music dramas, he expressed views on countless subjects, views which were not always consistent with one another. Thus by careful selection one can make him seem to be anything one wants.

In the story of Bayreuth the influence of Hitler is something that cannot be ignored. But it would be equally wrong to ignore the artistic achievements of the people who worked there in his time, in particular the producer Heinz Tietjen and the scenic designer Emil Preetorius, and in the chapters dealing with this period I shall try to sort out the artistic from the political implications.

However, none of this alters the fact that by his ostentatious devotion to Wagner Hitler almost wrecked Bayreuth. At the end of the Second World War the Germans seemed as ready to reject Wagner as they were to reject Hitler himself. Inevitably they could not. Wagner is far too great and significant a figure to be wished out of existence. His works continued to be performed, and it was obvious that in time Richard Wagner would be cleansed entirely of his

Nazi associations. It was not so obvious in the case of
Bayreuth, where Winifred Wagner, Hitler's friend, was
still by the terms of her husband's will in charge. It
seemed impossible that it should ever be able to recover
its old position as the Mecca of the Wagnerians.

In fact it has done so, far more effectively than anyone
would once have thought feasible. And that is the work of
Siegfried Wagner's sons, Richard Wagner's grandsons
Wieland and Wolfgang, to whom their mother transferred
the administration of the festival.

Their efforts to modernize the production of Wagner's
works have been just as fiercely condemned as they have
been praised. But they have achieved their object. Bayreuth is again at the centre of the Wagnerian world,
exercising its influence on Wagner productions everywhere. Possibly all other producers do not go as far as
Wagner's grandsons in their experimenting, but they all
bear some of the traces. It would be impossible nowadays
to find in any opera house a production that looks like the
popular conception of Wagner as he used to be.

Here I have stated in very broad outline the theme of
this book. It is not only a history of the festival at Bayreuth, but also an attempt to show how Bayreuth has, for
better or worse, spread its influence over the whole field of
Wagnerian production everywhere. And on top of that I
shall try to trace the line of development that has led—if
not in a straight line yet nevertheless in an understandably
coherent way—over the best part of a century from the
composer to his grandsons.

Nowadays one speaks of the 'new Bayreuth' as if the
grandsons had cut themselves entirely adrift from the
tradition they inherited. It is a view that they themselves
have not discouraged, since obviously it dissociates them
from the faults (if faults they were) of the past. But in fact
as time goes on and one is able to discern the artistic
impulses through the fading smokescreen of the political
ones, the idea of a completely new start begins to appear a
false one. Whatever differences one may see in the actual
achievements of Richard Wagner, of Cosima, Siegfried,

Winifred and the grandsons, they all of them go back to the same source: to the theories of the composer as expressed in his voluminous writings. And we will find them all doing approximately the same things and justifying them with the same reasons, though the results of their efforts may all look entirely different.

So there is really no old and new Bayreuth, no chain leading from Richard to Cosima to Siegfried to Winifred, the fracture of which encouraged the grandsons to begin anew. Rather there is a Bayreuth of each of these personalities, each Bayreuth reflecting something of the person at any one time in charge of it, but each stemming direct from the original source. Obviously each was in some way influenced by his predecessor, either positively or negatively. Obviously too, each was aware of the ideas of writers and producers outside Bayreuth and accepted them or rejected them as he thought fit. And for this reason I shall allow myself to wander occasionally outside Bayreuth, not only to see the effect of Bayreuth's influence on the outside world, but also to see the effect of the outside world on Bayreuth.

It is hardly necessary to point out that no performance of an opera is the work of one person alone. However powerful the person in charge may be, he is still dependent for the final results on the skill and goodwill of a host of other people. Bayreuth naturally owes much of its success within its own walls to the musicians and technicians who have worked there. For its success outside its own walls the debt is even greater, since it is these people —the conductors and singers particularly—who have been in a position to spread their Bayreuth experiences abroad. Here in fact lies the main distinction between Bayreuth and the other international festivals. Most festivals are built up on the star system, which essentially means that artists who have gained their skill and experience elsewhere pool their resources for an occasion which should provide benefit to the audience, none however (except in terms of finance and publicity) to the artists themselves. Bayreuth works on a different system. It does not live on stars: it makes them. There have of course been great Wagnerian singers and conductors who have never appeared at Bayreuth, but the number of singers and conductors who have been made into great Wagnerians by Bayreuth is very much larger. Many of them will be mentioned later in this book.

The fact that this is the story of a festival rather than of a family has necessarily dictated the form in which it has been told. It may therefore be helpful to give here a short continuous summary of the Wagner family history.

Richard Wagner's second wife Cosima, born in 1837 to Franz Liszt and the Comtesse d'Agoult, had five children: two by her first marriage to the conductor Hans von Bülow and three by Richard Wagner. Of these all but one played a part in the Bayreuth festival to a greater or lesser extent, the only exception being von Bülow's second daughter Blandine (1862–1941), who married the Italian Count Gravina and went to live in Italy. Of the daughters, the eldest, Daniela (1860–1940), was the most active, for she assisted her mother in the theatre wardrobe, designed the costumes for all the productions of her brother Siegfried and even produced *Parsifal* in the first festival following his death. Her marriage to the historian Henry Thode was dissolved, and Daniela lived at Wahnfried until her mother's death.

Cosima's third daughter Isolde (1865–1921) was in fact Richard Wagner's child, though she was born before Cosima separated from her lawful husband and was thus considered in the eyes of the law a von Bülow. She too assisted her mother with costumes until her marriage to the conductor Franz Beidler (with whom Siegfried was at loggerheads) disturbed the family unity. Relationships became even more strained when Isolde in 1914 brought a lawsuit against her mother, claiming a right of inheritance in Wagner's estate. She lost her case.

The fourth daughter Eva (1867–1942) was legally acknowledged as Wagner's child, though born before his marriage to Cosima. She took no direct part in the festival, but was Cosima's closest personal assistant throughout.

She was already in her forties when she married the English-born writer Stewart Houston Chamberlain (1855–1927), who was Cosima's close friend and neighbour in Bayreuth.

Siegfried, the youngest child and only son of Cosima, was born in 1869 and was thus only fourteen when his father died in 1883. He took over the management of the festival from his mother in 1907 and was in sole charge until he died in 1930, only a few months after Cosima.

Bayreuth was thus for the second time inherited by a widow. Siegfried had married the English-born Winifred Williams in 1915 and of their four children the eldest, Wieland, was only thirteen at the time of his father's death; his brother Wolfgang was eleven and his two sisters Friedelind and Verena twelve and ten. Winifred Wagner was the first to take charge of the festival who had not known the composer personally. Of the direct connections only Daniela and Eva remained in Bayreuth. Keenly conscious of their isolation, they withdrew to Villa Tribschen, the house in Switzerland in which Richard and Cosima Wagner had lived before they moved to Wahnfried.

Both Daniela and Eva were childless. Isolde had a son, for whose sake she claimed to have undertaken her lawsuit. Since she was unsuccessful, her son received no part in the Bayreuth heritage. Blandine, the Countess Gravina, also had a son, Count Gilbert Gravina, who now works as a stage manager in the Bayreuth of his much younger cousins Wieland and Wolfgang Wagner.

The Bayreuth festival was inaugurated in 1876 by Richard Wagner himself with three performances of the *Ring* cycle. The Festspielhaus, as the theatre was called, was closed until 1882, when *Parsifal* was first produced and performed sixteen times. In the year of Wagner's death and in the following year *Parsifal* was repeated. Cosima Wagner took over the active direction in 1885, in which year she prepared her production of *Tristan und Isolde,* launched in the following year, *Parsifal* also being played. There was no festival in 1887: Cosima was rehears-

ing *Die Meistersinger,* which was performed in 1888 and
1889.

From then on the regular Bayreuth pattern was established: that is to say, a year's rest while one of the works
was being newly prepared and then festivals in two successive years. *Parsifal* was performed at every festival
between 1882 and 1939 with the exception of 1896,
when the *Ring* was revived. From 1896 until 1942 the
Ring was also performed at every festival. The remaining
works, *Tannhäuser, Lohengrin* and *Der Fliegende Holländer,* had all been brought into the repertoire by 1901.
These three, together with *Tristan und Isolde* and *Die
Meistersinger,* are not, like the *Ring* and *Parsifal,* permanent features of the festival repertoire but succeed one
another at irregular intervals.

Cosima Wagner passed on the management of the
Festspielhaus to Siegfried after the festival of 1906. The
outbreak of the First World War interrupted the 1914
festival and for ten years the Festspielhaus was closed.
Siegfried reopened it in 1924 with a revival of pre-war
productions of *Parsifal,* the *Ring* and *Die Meistersinger.*
In 1927 he brought out a new production of *Tristan und
Isolde* and in 1930 (the year of his death) a new *Tannhäuser.*

The festival of 1931—the first under Winifred Wagner's
control—consisted of repeat performances of Siegfried's
Tristan und Isolde and *Tannhäuser.* In the succeeding
rest year she appointed Heinz Tietjen of the Berlin State
Opera as artistic director of the festival, and between
1933 and the outbreak of the Second World War all
Wagner's works from *Der Fliegende Holländer* onwards,
with the single exception of *Tannhäuser,* were given new
productions. Even *Parsifal,* which had remained virtually
untouched since the first production of 1882, received
new scenery: it was designed in 1934 by Alfred Roller of
Vienna and in 1937 by Wieland Wagner—his first contribution to the festival, though one showing no traces of
his subsequent scenic style.

From 1936 onwards the festival was held yearly at the

express wish of Hitler. It continued until 1944, though during the war years it lost its international character and was restricted in scope. In the three years 1940–2 only the *Ring* and *Der Fliegende Holländer* were presented, in 1943 and 1944 only *Die Meistersinger*, for which Wieland Wagner designed the scenery and costumes.

Since the reopening in 1951 Wieland Wagner and his brother Wolfgang have been in charge of the Festspielhaus and festivals have been held yearly. The traditional pattern, by which *Parsifal* and the *Ring* are presented in every festival, the other works successively, has been restored, and both Wagner's grandsons are active as producers, working not together but singly.

Acknowledgments

This book is the result of much personal observation of Wagner productions both in and outside Bayreuth over the past thirty years as well as of extensive reading of biographies, reminiscences and articles by a great number of singers, producers, scenic designers, music critics and so on. They are listed in the bibliography at the end of this book. To the authors and publishers of these works (and in the case of Bernard Shaw to the Public Trustee and the Society of Authors) I am indebted for permission to quote from them.

I have also had the benefit of personal conversations with many people in and outside Bayreuth who are or have been actively concerned with the festival. Chief among them have obviously been Herr Wieland Wagner and Herr Wolfgang Wagner and their mother Frau Winifred Wagner, to whom I express my deep gratitude for their ready help. To these I should like to add Professor Emil Preetorius who, though not a member of the Wagner family, has played a very important part in the story of the festival, as later pages will show.

Together with Christopher Sykes I made a number of broadcast features about the festival and in the preparation of these we came into contact with many people in Bayreuth, including Miss Friedelind Wagner and Count

Gilbert Gravina as well as conductors, singers and technicians. My thanks are due not only to these named and unnamed people but also to the British Broadcasting Corporation, which has allowed me to draw on material gathered in its service for the purposes of this book.

All photographic reproductions are (except where otherwise stated) by permission of the Bayreuther Festspielleitung, the Richard Wagner-Gedenkstätte and the Archiv des Hauses Wahnfried.

For practical help in research I am much indebted to Frau Margit Rostock, librarian of the *Deutsches Kulturinstitut* in London, to Frau Anna Schuster of Bayreuth and to Herr Eike Eberhard Unger of Nuremberg.

London, 1965   GEOFFREY SKELTON

One

The Beginnings

THE building of a festival theatre had been in Richard Wagner's mind for many years. The choice of Bayreuth for its site was almost an accident. The old court theatre in Bayreuth, completed in 1748, happened to possess the largest stage of any theatre in Germany. Since its huge dimensions seemed to be ideally suited to a production of the *Ring*, the composer and his wife went to inspect it.

They saw of course at once that it would not do for the *Ring*. The stage of this lovely old theatre, still in existence today, is indeed large, but it is larger than the auditorium, which was designed to accommodate at most a hundred people. Nevertheless the town of Bayreuth with its quiet classical beauty and its lovely surroundings of hills and woods seemed to Richard and Cosima Wagner to possess the features for which they were seeking, and they soon found influential people in the town who listened with willing ears to the proposal of Germany's leading operatic composer—for by now Richard Wagner undoubtedly was that—to build a festival theatre there for the performance of his own works.

Both artistic and practical considerations played a part in the composer's choice of Bayreuth for his theatre. He could have had it in Munich, the capital of his patron King Ludwig II of Bavaria. He could have had it in Berlin, the capital of the German empire, where he had powerful friends. He was offered facilities in some of the fashionable watering places. But all of these, the choice of any of which might have saved him immense trouble, anxiety and expense, he rejected in favour of Bayreuth.

In doing so he perhaps forgot the original purpose of his plan, which was to build a theatre for the people, dedicated to German art and independent of the princes and their court operas with all their artificial fashions and intrigues. This theatre for the people would not have been used for Wagner's works alone, as Bayreuth has been from the beginning and still is.

Perhaps, however, one should not take Wagner's plans for a people's theatre too seriously. He talked and wrote much about it, but it is fair to assume that all this was a cloak for the real intention, which was to have a stage on which he could himself produce his own works in his own way. It is understandable that he should have felt this need in view of his experiences during his lifetime. There had been only two productions which he could regard as relatively satisfactory, and both of these he owed to the support of the young King Ludwig, whose passionate devotion to Wagner is too well known to need further explanation here.

The first performances of *Tristan und Isolde* and of *Die Meistersinger* in Munich Wagner had supervised himself. Over the earlier works he had no control except in Munich. *Rienzi, Der Fliegende Holländer, Tannhäuser* and *Lohengrin* were being performed all over Germany and abroad, but usually in cut versions and certainly in the traditional old-fashioned way, to which they were to a certain extent amenable. *Tristan und Isolde* and *Die Meistersinger* were not, and even less so was the *Ring*. This work demanded a new approach not only on the artistic but also on the technical side.

Attempts by the impatient young king to produce *Rheingold* and *Die Walküre* in Munich in 1869–70 had ended in ridicule and failure, largely because Wagner was at odds with the Munich opera officials and refused to co-operate with them. But the failure confirmed his view that the *Ring* in order to make its effect needed a special theatre of his own design.

If Wagner had been by nature a more diplomatic man, he might have achieved in Munich what he wanted. Plans to build a special theatre there and an associated music school did in fact reach an advanced stage, only to founder on the scandal which arose through Wagner's association with Cosima, still at that time the wife of Hans von Bülow, who conducted the first performances of *Tristan und Isolde* and *Die Meistersinger*. The affair with Cosima and the subsequent divorce made it impossible for any of the three people involved to remain in Munich.

This explains why Wagner's festival theatre was not built in Munich. No doubt if he had waited a while for the scandal to die down he could have returned, now respectably married to Cosima, and continued where he had left off. But in the meantime he had conceived another objection to Munich which applied equally to Berlin, Baden-Baden and Darmstadt. They were all places in which other opportunities for diversion were to be had, and Wagner did not intend to have the attention of his audience distracted in any way from his own works.

Bayreuth had the advantage of possessing no regular theatre of its own or indeed anything in the way of public entertainment. Visitors would therefore be fresh and eager for the performances, which would begin in the afternoon and spread themselves over the rest of the day, allowing for long intervals between the acts, during which members of the audience could refresh themselves in quiet and idyllic surroundings. In fact, what Wagner wanted was exactly what audiences still enjoy today.

Another advantage of Bayreuth was its position more or less in the centre of Germany, yet within the borders of Bavaria. Though at the time he formed his plans Wagner's relations with King Ludwig were still somewhat cool on account of the liaison with Cosima, he knew well enough what he already owed to Ludwig's support and where, if things went wrong, his best hopes lay for the future.

It was as well that he put his faith in the king, for in the event it was Ludwig who extricated Wagner from the appalling financial difficulties into which he plunged himself with Bayreuth. The initial difficulties lay in his over-confident assumption that enough people could be found to share practically as well as theoretically in his festival dream. The choice of a comparatively inaccessible place such as Bayreuth (before the second festival in 1882 we find the festival committee putting in a plea for the improvement of the railway services) did not at first seem particularly rash, since Wagner did not visualize the public sale of tickets but evolved a patronage system whereby people would subscribe money in advance which would entitle them to attend festival performances. With this money the theatre was to be built and the perform-ances financed. By this means Wagner hoped to confine his audience to a number of genuine supporters who would not be put off by the necessity of a journey to an out-of-the-way spot.

It is one of the little ironies of life that the subscription scheme failed miserably and was abandoned by Wagner himself, whereas the inaccessibility of Bayreuth was to prove no obstacle to the ordinary members of the public in whom Wagner was reluctant at first to put his trust. Thus his original idea of a theatre for the people, abandoned in favour of an exclusive scheme for the chosen few, proved in the end to have been the sounder one.

Bayreuth was in any case a fortunate choice for Wagner in view of the solid and steadfast support he gained from a number of influential citizens. Men such as the banker Friedrich Feustel and the mayor Theodor Munker are nowadays remembered only by the streets in the town which bear their names, but it is in no small measure due to them that there is still a Wagner festival in Bayreuth. Feustel and Munker were in the first place responsible for persuading the town council to present Wagner with a site for the theatre free of charge. Incidentally, the present site of the theatre was the third to be picked on: the first proved impracticable for building purposes; and the

second was given up when a local business man protested
that a theatre would obstruct the water supply to his
factory. The present and in every respect ideal site owes
its existence rather to a series of lucky accidents than to
any sense of inevitability.

Having secured his site and received from King Ludwig
a sum of money towards building a house in Bayreuth for
himself and his family, Wagner set about raising the funds
for the erection of his theatre. Though he did not foresee
the financial difficulties—difficulties which were in the
ensuing years to cause him immense worry and work—
Wagner was by no means a hopelessly unrealistic visionary. From the very start he was conscious of the need for
economy. The theatre was to be a temporary structure,
based on designs which had already been prepared for
the original Munich project, a functional building in
which there would be no unnecessary pomp or superfluous
decoration. It was in fact the building almost exactly as it
stands today. The original plan to replace it with something more solid when the festival had proved itself
viable was never realized, a fact for which we have reason
to be grateful in view of the superb acoustics of the
Festspielhaus, which are due not only to the design of the
interior but also to the flimsy materials (mainly wood) of
which it is built. The *Prinzregententheater* in Munich,
built several years later more or less as a replica of the
Bayreuth theatre but with far more solid materials, shows
with its vastly inferior acoustics the danger of putting the
eye before the ear.

The efforts of Wagner and his associates (foremost
among them the Mannheim music publisher Emil Heckel
and Frau von Schleinitz) to raise money for the building of
the Festspielhaus and for the first performances of the *Ring*
consisted mainly in giving concerts and persuading people
to take out advance subscriptions. The building work was
however begun without waiting to see the results of these
efforts. Wagner himself laid the foundation stone on
22 May 1872 and followed the ceremony with a performance in the old court theatre of Beethoven's Ninth Sym-

phony. This was the origin of the custom, followed since 1951, of performing the Ninth Symphony at each yearly festival—the only music other than Wagner's own that has an official place in the festival programme.

For Wagner himself these years before the opening of the festival proved an almost intolerable strain. He was engaged at the time in writing *Götterdämmerung*, but had constantly to interrupt his work to travel all over the country, not only to give concerts but also to seek singers to take part in the first festival. This last task was by no means an easy one: it was not just a matter of picking the best of an available supply; there was literally no supply. The only singers who had proved themselves beyond a doubt to be true Wagnerian singers with the necessary stamina for the later music dramas were the original Tristan and Isolde, but Schnorr von Carolsfeld was dead and with his wife Malvina—now in any case too old— Wagner had quarrelled irreparably. *Die Meistersinger* makes less demands on stamina and therefore could not be regarded as a true test. Wagner did in fact engage Franz Betz, who had played Hans Sachs in the first production of *Die Meistersinger*, as Wotan, but a Siegfried and a Brünnhilde were still to be found. It was not only stamina he had to seek but also singers who were intelligent and humble enough to study with him new methods of interpretation and acting.

In May 1874 Wagner and his family left Tribschen in Switzerland and moved permanently to Bayreuth. In November of the same year he completed *Götterdämmerung* and with it the *Ring*, which had occupied him— with a long break for the composition of *Tristan und Isolde* and *Die Meistersinger*—for a full twenty years.

Now at last the huge work was ready for production. But the long struggle was by no means over. Subscriptions, in spite of all the efforts of Wagner and his associates, were still far below the level expected and the theatre, now complete but for the furnishings, was heavily in debt. Unless a large loan could be raised immediately, bankruptcy was inevitable. Ludwig had been approached before, but appeals to him had met with increasing resistance, and this time Wagner's urgent appeal was met with a blank refusal of further financial aid. Wagner turned to Bismarck in Berlin and, when that approach failed, to some of the ruling German princes. It was all in vain, and Wagner wrote to King Ludwig that the whole Bayreuth venture must be abandoned.

This was more than Ludwig could bear. He instructed the Bavarian state officials to negotiate a loan, and the Bayreuth theatre was saved. True, it was only a loan and had to be paid back within two years from the 'profits' of the first festival. It is difficult to believe that any of the persons concerned in this financial transaction really believed that the loan could be repaid. The only hope lay in the possibility that the princes and other influential persons who attended the first festival would be sufficiently impressed to extend their own aid and thus ensure its future.

They did not do so and thereby earned themselves the role of the villains of the piece in the eyes of posterity. Yet it is only fair to ask why in fact they should have helped. They had not asked Wagner to build his festival theatre. He had undertaken it because he wanted a place in which he could produce his works as he felt nobody else could produce them. The princes with their elaborate court theatres could not be expected to look kindly on a venture which usurped the functions of their own expensive institutions. They were willing to produce the works in their own theatres if the composer would permit it but, if he would not, that was his own affair. And in any case if Wagner's acknowledged patron, the king of Bavaria, preferred to spend fantastic sums of money in building one fairy-tale castle after another for himself instead of a festival theatre for Wagner, did this not suggest that he too regarded the Bayreuth venture as superfluous?

These were all perfectly sound arguments. Ludwig did indeed think Bayreuth superfluous and, though he did attend the first festival, he did so only because he knew that he could not hope to see the complete *Ring* cycle under any other circumstances. He did not attend the second festival in 1882. Bayreuth in fact offered poor Ludwig lamentable return for all his years of devotion to Wagner, for by its festival nature it forced him, being within his territory, to play the host to all the visiting princes and celebrities who might wish to attend. This was not Ludwig's idea at all: Wagner was not for him a means of social self-glorification, but a deep aesthetic necessity. He wanted to enjoy the works in privacy, as a man, not as a king, and to indulge this desire he had been willing not only to give Wagner the complete freedom of his court theatre in Munich but even to have the stage rebuilt to suit Wagner's requirements. Was Ludwig to blame if Wagner persisted in being at loggerheads with his theatre officials and in refusing to co-operate with them?

Considering Ludwig's difficulties, both public and personal, one must give him all the more credit for his generous support of a project that deprived him of what was nearest to his heart. When yet again Wagner had to appeal to him to rescue Bayreuth from its financial difficulties following the first festival, he was not refused. And this second financial arrangement not only made the 1882 festival possible, it also laid the foundations for a permanent festival in Bayreuth. By a fictional arrangement based on an assessment of the royalties which performances of Wagner's works in the Munich opera in the past might be reckoned to have produced, the unpaid loan was wiped out. The fiction lay in the fact that Wagner had already signed away the Munich rights of his work to the king in return for a yearly pension which, combined with large gifts of money for one reason or another, certainly represented a reasonable reward. But more important for the future was the undertaking to pay royalties for the future not only to Wagner himself but until twenty years after his death to his heirs. On this basis the continuation of Bayreuth was secured.

In the light of today's copyright laws this arrangement might not seem particularly generous. The law after all now recognizes the existence of a copyright until fifty years after death. Yet it was in fact far in advance of its time and much better than any other composer in Germany enjoyed.

Under the new arrangement made in 1878 the Munich opera undertook to place its whole company at Wagner's disposal free of charge during the usual summer vacation. Wagner should as far as possible make use of the Munich conductors and singers, but he was free to invite guest artists to take part in the festival if no suitable Munich singer was available. He for his part undertook to allow the Munich opera to perform the Bayreuth production of *Parsifal* exclusively in Munich. This might seem to have been a sacrifice on Wagner's part, since he had stated that *Parsifal* should be kept exclusively for Bayreuth and not staged elsewhere. But in fact he knew that Ludwig had too much respect for his wishes to allow advantage to be taken of this clause, which was meant solely to allow Ludwig to see and hear *Parsifal* in the privacy of his court. And under these circumstances a few private performances did take place in Munich for the king's benefit in the three years that elapsed between Wagner's death and Ludwig's.

Wagner had intended to run Bayreuth as a yearly festival and to stage there all his works from *Der Fliegende Holländer* onwards. In fact the financial obstacles prevented him in his lifetime from realizing more than two festivals, the first being devoted to the *Ring* and the second to *Parsifal*. It was left to his successors to complete the work of which he had laid the foundations.

Two

Richard Wagner's Artistic Ideas

RICHARD WAGNER'S main quarrel with opera as it existed in his time was that music occupied in it a too subservient position. An opera was basically simply a stage play with music. A story was unfolded, either by means of spoken dialogue or recitative, and at certain moments the action was halted so that a situation or emotion could be exploited in a set aria or ensemble. However good the music, it remained at the mercy of the dramatic action, so that it was impossible for an opera of this sort to have a musical shape in the sense that a symphony has a shape: it was simply a collection of assorted pieces which, divorced from their stage context, had no real connection with each other at all.

Wagner's ambition was not to make the music of paramount importance—for that would have been merely to turn opera into symphony—but to create a balance between music, words and action so that each could play its part in realizing the composer's conception of the work as a whole. This idea called in the first place for care in the choice of a subject. A strong dramatic action, in which a chain of situations lead to a climax and a denouement, was best left to the spoken drama; music drama should deal with ideas rather than actions, should be concerned rather with eternal truths than with individual human destinies.

One can perhaps best realize what Wagner was aiming

28

at in music drama by comparing *Lohengrin* with *Tristan und Isolde,* that is, a work written before he had fully clarified his aims and the work in which he realized them most effectively. As Wieland Wagner has pointed out, the theme of the two works is essentially the same: the nature of love between man and woman and the inexorable demands that it places on them. *Tristan und Isolde* is only superficially a version of the eternal triangle theme: fundamentally it is the story of a man and a woman in search of complete identity with one another and compelled to destroy themselves in order to achieve it.

In *Lohengrin* there is also more than the fairy-tale of the mysterious knightly rescuer and the innocent girl who is persuaded by her enemies to ask the fatal question that destroys her happiness. It is clear from the dialogue in the bridal chamber that Elsa is disturbed by the unreality of her relationship with Lohengrin. She feels the artificiality, the lack of trust implicit in a situation where she is not permitted to know the identity of the man she loves, and she is impelled to sacrifice her life with Lohengrin in order for one brief moment to know him completely.

Here then are two generally similar situations, both of them based on semi-historical stories, which Wagner treated in radically different ways. In *Lohengrin* the dramatic action which precedes and brings about the vital confrontation in the bridal chamber is realistically developed and occupies the first two acts of the opera. In *Tristan und Isolde* all the events which lead to the lovers' involvement with one another are simply related. It is clear from the very beginning of Act One that Tristan and Isolde are in love, and it would not really have mattered if Brangäne had given them plain water instead of the love philtre. The thought that they were about to die together was enough in itself to release their true emotions.

In the whole of *Tristan und Isolde* nobody matters except the two main characters, just as in the bridal chamber scene of *Lohengrin* nobody matters except Lohengrin and Elsa, and for that reason the attempt on Lohengrin's life by Telramund's confederates is as per-

functorily treated as the fight between Tristan and Melot.
Both are physical acts which are not in themselves
dramatically important but simply move us on to the next
stage in the spiritual drama which is the composer's main
concern.

In the third act of *Lohengrin*, written before his ideas
had reached full fruition, Wagner thus momentarily
achieves his music drama, just as he achieved it in
isolated passages of *Der Fliegende Holländer* and *Tannhäuser*. But for the rest he is writing opera in the old form,
if in a very advanced stage of that form. There are the
highlights of physical action: the summoning of Elsa's
champion, Lohengrin's arrival, the detailed fight with
Telramund, the vengeance duet of Ortrud and Telramund,
the wedding procession dramatically—and very operati-
cally—interrupted by the villainous pair. These are set
pieces in the usual tradition, though welded together with
such musical skill that one can almost overlook the fact.
But in *Tristan und Isolde* there is not one elaborate essay
of this sort, with the single exception perhaps of Marke's
monologue in Act Two—and one knows from experience
how easily this can lower the emotional temperature.

Having thus in *Tristan und Isolde* evolved a drama of
spiritual rather than physical action and reduced to a
minimum the succession of external situations which
constitute a normal dramatic framework, Wagner had to
invent a musical form to fit it. The music must not simply
heighten the emotional atmosphere of the spoken drama.
That would turn it into background music and give it too
subservient a function. Nor must it in turn impose its own
form on the spoken drama, forcing that into formality (as
happened for example with Handel). Words and music
must move together, enriching and reinforcing each other,
each a unity in itself yet each deferring to the other.

Wagner found the solution to his problem in the use of
short melodic and harmonic themes which were subsequently called (though not with his approval) *Leit-
motive*. Striking musical phrases identified with particular
people or particular emotions were of course not new.

Weber had made use of them and Wagner too in all his operas up to *Lohengrin*. Now however he was prepared to put such phrases to another use, to make them the whole stuff out of which his music evolved, just as Beethoven had built his symphonies out of scraps of themes capable of infinite variation. But whereas Beethoven had used his themes according to the dictates of symphonic design, Wagner's were to be ordered to dramatic design. (Incidentally it has been interestingly shown by Alfred Lorenz that dramatic design was not incompatible, consciously or unconsciously, with musical design.)

There must be no music-making just for its own sake. As Wagner wrote in his essay *Über die Anwendung der Musik auf das Drama* (The Use of Music in Drama), "It was for example impossible in the instrumental introduction to *Rheingold* to leave the basic chord, simply because I had no reason to alter it. A large part of the following scene between Alberich and the Rhinemaidens could be carried out by using only the most immediately related keys, since emotion is here revealing itself only in its most primitive simplicity."

This sentence gives the key to the musical structure of the *Ring*, which evolves out of that preliminary E flat chord, gathering new sustenance with each dramatic development, so that by the time *Götterdämmerung* is reached Wagner has an almost infinite number of musical threads to play with, each one of which has evolved from the preceding action.

This is of course only the theory, and it would be absurd to suggest that works of such tremendous depth and power as the *Ring* could have been written simply by slavish devotion to a formula, that Wagner could have taken just any dramatic story and by applying his evolution formula to it have created something equal to the *Ring* or *Parsifal*. The choice of a subject was naturally of great importance, but the real artistic impulse was an emotional one, an urge to express basic problems of human relationships.

In his very earliest works up to *Rienzi* Wagner like other composers had chosen his subjects simply because they offered dramatic possibilities: a perfectly legitimate way if the dramatic shape was to be determined by the events and not by the idea. But now he was working the other way round, and it was for this reason that he chose to seek his themes (with the single exception of *Die Meistersinger*) in mythology, not only because myths deal with the deepest human problems—they would not be myths if they did not—but because they freed him from the tyranny of historical fact, the weight of which was heaviest in *Lohengrin*. He could concentrate on the psychological rather than on the physical expression of his subject and thus achieve a genuine unity of form.

This is of course exactly the method of the classical Greek theatre with an added musical dimension. I call it a dimension since the musical accompaniment had not just to underline and intensify the emotional atmosphere as it did in the classical theatre: it had to give expression to the emotion, to interpret it, to anticipate it, to point out connections and significances and so on. It had in fact to take over the function of the spoken chorus in Greek drama.

This left the stage chorus itself very little to do, and in fact in all Wagner's works from *Tristan und Isolde* onwards (again with the exception of *Die Meistersinger*) the stage chorus plays a very minor part, being confined— where it is used at all—to providing background colour, as for example the sailors' song in *Tristan und Isolde*. One has only to ask oneself how any former composer, how even Wagner himself in his earlier days would have treated the end of Act Two in *Tristan und Isolde* to see what a vast change had here taken place in the use of the stage chorus.

If we accept that the Knights of the Grail and the Flower Maidens in *Parsifal* cannot be regarded as chorus at all in spite of their numbers and acknowledge that in *Die Meistersinger* the chorus functions as a true chorus only when it is singing church chorales and odes to Sachs, we are still left with the Gibichungs in Act Two of *Götterdämmerung*. This whole scene must indeed be regarded as a relapse on the composer's part back to the

Richard Wagner

The orchestra pit in the Festspielhaus

An aerial view of the Festspielhaus

V. Bouillon, Bayreuth

The *Ring*, 1876: Josef Hoffmann's design for *Siegfried*, Act III

Parsifal, 1882: Paul von Joukowsky's *Gralstempel*

state of development he had reached when he wrote the text directly after *Lohengrin*. He could certainly have re-written the scene if he had wished when he came to write down the music of *Götterdämmerung*, but at that stage he was far more interested in the practical task of getting the *Ring* finished for production at Bayreuth than in the theory of his music drama. Thus the second act of *Götterdämmerung* remains an anomaly, an exercise in grand opera with trios, ensembles and all, yet set so expertly to music in Wagner's mature style that it shines as an example to later composers, who, it must be said, have seemed to prefer old operatic traditions to Wagner's ideas.

Wagner also looked to classical Greece for the stage setting of his music dramas. The actual shape of the Festspielhaus, both of stage and auditorium, was as deliberately planned as the choice of remote Bayreuth for its site. Just as outside the theatre nothing was to divert the audience from complete dedication to Wagner's works, so inside it every distracting element must be removed. And just as in ancient Greece the theatre was a spiritual experience rather than a social occasion. The amphi-theatrical shape of the auditorium, every seat giving an uninterrupted view to the stage, was part of the process of persuading the audience to forget its social self. Equally so was the device, unknown at the time, of plunging the auditorium into darkness at curtain rise. All that the spectator could be permitted to see was the stage.

In this conception the idea of the invisible orchestra is of vital importance. The fact that this famous 'mystical chasm', as it has been named, plays a part in producing the marvellous and unique acoustical quality of the Festspiel-haus has perhaps led to the assumption that its acoustical function is its only one. In fact it has several. By conceal-ing the conductor and the orchestral players from the audience it shifts the emphasis of the whole production, concentrating attention on the drama rather than on the singer: the audience at Bayreuth is far less conscious of the fact that this soprano or that tenor is singing well or badly than of the fact that the character depicted is convincing or not convincing as the case may be. Even more important, the spectator, having no resting place for his eyes except on the stage, keeps them there and does not consciously take in the orchestral music at all. The orchestral sound works rather on the subconscious which, as Wagner was instinctively aware, responds directly and involuntarily to its emotional effect.

Yet another function of the invisible orchestra, or rather in this case the curved roof above it, is to deprive the audience of a standard of physical measurement. Simply because there is no visible conductor against whom the eye can measure them it is possible to make the figures on the stage, by positioning and by a scaling of the background scenery, look large or small as required. This is an important consideration in a work like the *Ring* which contains dwarfs and giants as well as gods and men.

The original creator of this deliberate optical illusion was the architect Gottfried Semper, though the idea was Wagner's own. Semper had been entrusted with the design of that projected Wagner festival theatre in Munich which was in fact never built, and Wagner made use of Semper's plans when he came to construct the Festspielhaus—legitimately enough, since most of the ideas were originally his. The actual construction was the work not of Semper but of the architect Otto Brückwald.

Every feature of the Festspielhaus auditorium is functional in the same way, including the pillars at each side, which are not real pillars at all but screens which play their part in the acoustic and visual properties of the theatre. As Wagner stated in a letter to Friedrich Feustel, "The theatre building must be regarded only as a temporary structure. I should be content if it were to be built entirely of wood like a gymnasium: no more solidity than is necessary to prevent it from falling down. So economise here—economise: no ornamentation. This building we intend simply as a sketch of an ideal and leave it to the nation to carry out as a monumental building. Technical facilities and stage decoration, everything bearing on the artistic ideal to be complete in every detail. Stint *nothing* here: everything to be designed for long wear, nothing temporary."

In making these stipulations Wagner was not only interested in saving money. He was well aware that there is no sure scientific method of measuring acoustics. It is simply a matter of trial and error, and the acoustics of the Festspielhaus as we still know them are measured by Richard Wagner's own ear. The 'monumental building' of which he spoke in his letter to Feustel has never material-ized—a fact for which we can be profoundly grateful when we consider how much the Festspielhaus owes not only to Wagner's ear but to the materials of which the theatre is built. The outer walls are lath and plaster, the pillars are hollow, the huge unsupported ceiling is sail-cloth. All these play their part, through resonance or absorption, in the acoustic miracle. Replace them with more solid materials, and the original acoustics would be lost for ever.

To return now to the music drama itself. In banishing the orchestra from sight it was not Wagner's aim to mini-mize its role but rather to integrate the visual part of the drama into the whole. This was to be achieved by careful attention to the movements of the actors, who must not be allowed to indulge in histrionic gestures but must in fact submerge their own personalities completely in their role. The purpose of the stage scenery was to supply what Wagner in a letter to King Ludwig called "an unobtru-sive practical background and framework."

Wagner's views on acting began to take shape when as a very young man he saw Wilhelmine Schröder-Devrient in a performance of *Fidelio*. Of that occasion he wrote in his autobiography, "If I look back on my life as a whole I can find no event that produced so profound an impression on me. Anyone who can remember that wonderful woman at this period of her life must to some extent have experienced the almost satanic ardour which the intensely human art of this incomparable actress poured into his veins. After the performance I rushed to a friend's house and wrote a short note to the singer, in which I briefly told her that from that moment my life had acquired its true significance, and that if in days to come she should ever hear my name praised in the world of art she must remember that she had that evening made me what I then swore it was my destiny to become. This note I left at her hotel and ran out into the night as if I were mad."

This passage for all its effusiveness speaks no more than the truth. Wagner's whole ambition became to make the 'intensely human art' of Schröder-Devrient the rule and not the exception in the operatic world. That it was not an easy task is shown by the remark of Schröder-Devrient herself, who sang Senta in the first production of *Der Fliegende Holländer* at Dresden in 1843. The Dutchman in that performance was, Wagner tells us, "utterly incapable of realizing the horror and supreme suffering of my mariner. His distressing corpulence, his broad fat face, the extraordinary movements of his arms and legs, which he managed to make look like mere stumps, drove my passionate Senta to despair. At one rehearsal, when in the great scene in Act Two she comes to him in the guise of a guardian angel to bring the message of salvation, she broke off to whisper despairingly in my ear, 'How can I say it when I look into those beady eyes?'" On that particular occasion Wagner solved the difficulty by arranging at the first performance that Schröder-Devrient's youthful lover of the day should sit in the audience in her path of vision.

Another complication that Wagner had to face was that many of the best singers of the day, including at times even Schröder-Devrient herself, saw no reason why they should put themselves out to intensify their performances when they pleased their audiences very well as they were. Of Joseph Tichatschek, the first Rienzi and Tannhäuser, Wagner relates, "He had never been able to lay aside his brilliant and heroic leading-tenor manners in order to render that gloomy demonic strain in Rienzi's temperament on which I had laid unmistakable stress at the critical points of the drama. In the fourth act, after the pronouncement of the curse, he fell on his knees in the

most melancholy fashion and abandoned himself to be-
wailing his fate in piteous tones. When I suggested to him
that Rienzi, though inwardly despairing, must take up an
attitude of statuesque firmness before the world, he pointed
out to me the great popularity which the end of this very
act had won as interpreted by himself, with an intimation
that he intended making no change in it."

Tichatschek's indignation at Wagner's demand that he
should express in his acting the meaning of the words he
was uttering may seem comic, but it was in fact the prevailing attitude—and is not unknown among singers even
today. Wagner, being young and relatively powerless in
his Dresden days, had to capitulate, but in Bayreuth he
was the master. There he could and did insist that singers
should read the text and get to know it thoroughly before
they even heard the music, maintaining that only in this
way could the singer grasp the musical line of his part,
which was shaped more by dramatic than purely musical
sense. Then, knowing exactly what he had to express, he
would naturally translate this into fitting gesture and
movement.

How this conception threatened later to become stereotyped into a so-called 'Bayreuth style', mainly because of a
too rigid application of it, will be discussed when we come
to Cosima Wagner's Bayreuth productions. Richard
Wagner was no stylist in this sense: in his view the singer
must physically express the feelings he wishes to convey in
a manner natural to himself. As long as it was a natural
gesture and not a thought-out one the composer was
satisfied.

Wagner himself had no difficulty in putting this simple
precept into effect, since he was by all contemporary
accounts a natural actor, as well able to work himself into
the part of Elisabeth in *Tannhäuser* as into Wotan or
Mime in the *Ring*. Nor did he remain entirely consistent in
his own demonstrations. Richard Fricke, whom Wagner
engaged to supervise movement in his first *Ring* production, relates in his reminiscences that the singers were
frequently confused by the composer's habit of showing a

way of doing things that conflicted with what they had
laboriously learnt the day before. What apparently seemed
to suggest uncertainty on the part of Wagner as producer
was in fact nothing of the sort: it was rather an unconscious testimony that there are as many ways of doing
things right as of doing them wrong.

Wagner himself early discovered the folly of trying to
drill people into a set way of doing things. Of the first
production of *Tannhäuser* at Dresden he writes, "I had
watched the young baritone Anton Mitterwurzer with
great interest and I had noticed that his delightfully mel-
low voice possessed the rare quality of bringing out the
inner note of the soul. To him I entrusted Wolfram, and I
had every reason to be satisfied with his zeal and with the
success of his studies . . .

"I began by going through the opening song of the
Sängerkrieg scene with him; but, after I had done my
utmost to make him understand how I wanted it done, I
was surprised to find how very difficult this particular
rendering of the music appeared to him. He was absolutely
incapable of repeating it after me, and with each renewed
effort his singing became so commonplace and so mechanical that I realized clearly that he had not understood this
piece to be anything more than a phrase in recitative
form, which he might render with any inflections of the
voice that happened to be prescribed, or which might be
sung either this way or that according to fancy, as was
usual in operatic pieces.

"He too was astonished at his own want of capacity, but
was so struck by the novelty and justice of my views that
he begged me not to try any more for the present, but to
leave him to find out for himself how best to become
familiar with this newly revealed world."

Wagner was wise enough to respond to this plea and
was rewarded with a performance by Mitterwurzer which
in his opinion saved *Tannhäuser* from complete failure.
Mitterwurzer had, as Wagner puts it, "utterly changed
himself in bearing, look and appearance in order to fit himself to the role of Wolfram."

Here is a striking example of a singer who, once set on the right path, was able to make his own way to the desired goal. But not all singers, however well they might have grasped Wagner's method of approach, were as successful as Mitterwurzer in finding their own solutions, and it was no doubt for the benefit of these that Wagner at rehearsals set himself up as a sort of salesman, displaying his wares in all sorts of varied ways so that his singers might take their choice. It is the method of his grandson Wieland too, who has inherited the composer's remarkable acting gifts.

Whether we nowadays would have capitulated as completely to Wagner's own methods of dramatic expression as his contemporary devotees can perhaps be measured against this description by Angelo Neumann of a production of *Lohengrin* in Vienna in 1875, supervised by the composer. For the wedding procession Wagner assumed Elsa's role. "With arms outstretched, the palms turned toward the audience, with uplifted countenance and radiant eyes—and never a glance at the steps he was to traverse—Wagner moved serenely down in stately progress, followed (at the interval prescribed by the flowing train and the pages who bore it) by four noble ladies in waiting and finally by Ortrud. So he proceeded, advancing nearly to the footlights; then, turning a wide circle, swept on to the left towards the Minster steps. Up to the instant when Elsa is about to mount the first stair and Ortrud rushes to bar her way, Wagner maintained that wonderful look of radiant exaltation, his whole progress a triumph of histrionic art."

For the end of the scene Wagner took Lohengrin's place and, "turning to Elsa, who stood on the step below, with radiant face turned up to him, he drew her tenderly to his level, till they stood together in fervent clasp—united before the Minster door. Then Elsa, still hanging on Lohengrin's look, turns her head for an instant to those below as if to testify to her people of her perfect ecstasy. At this moment resounds the 'Warning' motive, and Ortrud—withdrawn from the train and standing on the left opposite the Minster—raises her arm in sinister threat. Elsa in wildest panic hides her head on Lohengrin's breast, while he, drawing her backward, still wrapped in his close embrace, slowly mounts the stairs and approaches the portal of the church with face turned sternly towards the crowd below. The curtain falls as they slowly progress backwards up the stairs."

In this description Wagner's aim is throughout apparent: that the participants should play their part all the way, even when they are not singing. This procession must be more than just a ravishing spectacle—it must be seen to be from beginning to end a radical part of the drama. It is no wonder that his search for 'actors who are also singers' caused him so much trouble. Above all he needed people of intelligence who were able to grasp his new ideas and put them into effect. But intelligence and acting ability were then as now not always allied with beauty of voice, and if Wagner was forced to choose between a singer of intelligence and poor voice and one of less intelligence but better voice he was always inclined to pick the latter. It did not make matters easier for him of course, but it does give the lie to those who believe that beauty of tone is the least important asset of a Wagnerian singer.

Wagner not only considered that his parts should be sung, not declaimed, from beginning to end (as we have seen in the case of Mitterwurzer), but went to the greatest lengths in his matching of words with music to help the singer to achieve this vocal beauty. It was his contention that any failure to achieve it was due to the singer neglecting to observe exactly the value of each single note as written down, and he and his assistants spent endless hours drilling their singers in the art of exact and clear delivery, not only in the interests of all-important intelligibility, but in the interests of tonal beauty as well.

Here is what the composer had to say about this particular aspect of his ideas in an essay written after the first production of *Parsifal* (*Das Bühnenweihfestspiel in Bayreuth* 1882): "Above all we had to strive for the utmost clarity, in the first place of diction: a passionate phrase must prove confusing and can prove repellent if its logical content is not grasped. But in order that it can be easily taken in, the smallest part of each sentence must be capable of immediate comprehension: an omitted prefix, a swallowed suffix, a neglected conjunction destroys at once the necessary clarity of meaning. These same omissions also directly affect the melody, in which through the dis-appearance of the musical components only isolated accents remain. The more passionate the phrase, the more it is likely to culminate in mere vocal noises . . . When six years ago in the preliminary studies for the *Ring* singers were urged to pay more attention to the little than to the big notes, this was done in the interests of that clarity without which both drama and music, speech and melody all remain equally incomprehensible."

Considering all the many thousands of words that Wagner devoted to explaining his ideas on the music drama, it is surprising how little he found to say on the vital question of scenery. Whereas his writings on the function of words and music dwelt exhaustively on the practical application as well as the theory, his definition of the function of scenery and costume was kept in vague and general terms. At the centre of the drama, he writes in *Das Kunstwerk der Zukunft* (The Artwork of the Future) is the human being. But the human being is part of nature, and all that he thinks, feels and does is influenced by that fact. Therefore drama must show him in significant natural surroundings, and here it is that the visual arts must lend their aid, first of all by applying colour in meaningful order to the living human model, that is to say, by pro-viding characteristic costumes. "As the final and most com-plete means of expression in visual art, landscape painting will become the life-giving soul of the whole construction. It will teach us to build for the drama the stage on which it will itself represent the warm natural background for the living actor."

What this rather tortuously expressed idea led to in practice was seen in those productions of *Tristan und Isolde* and *Die Meistersinger* in Munich and the *Ring* and

Parsifal in Bayreuth which Wagner himself directed, and
it was the form of detailed naturalism practised by such
artists as Böcklin and Feuerbach—a naturalism far too
romantic in flavour to merit the name of realism. This
seems to confirm one's feeling that Wagner was as conservative in the field of art as he was original in the field of
music, though less perhaps in the thought than in the
execution. One can see that there may well be a wide gap
between the inner scenic vision and the practical realization of it, yet it cannot be denied that the detailed stage
directions which Wagner wrote for his works do seem to
point directly to a romantic form of realism. One may
legitimately wonder how his ships and castles, his river
bed and his rainbow, his trees and rocks and above all his
large menagerie of animals could be reconciled with his
conception of scenery as an unobtrusive practical background, as he defined it in his letter to King Ludwig.

On another occasion he confessed to a scenic designer
(Hoffmann) that he had perhaps been guilty in his stage
directions of thinking too much in terms of old theatrical
conventions, and elsewhere he let fall that he had after
Lohengrin deliberately turned away from the grand
historical subject in order to reduce the danger of too
much conventional spectacle. No doubt his disgust over
the first production of *Tannhäuser* in Dresden had something to do with his feelings here. He had indignantly
rejected the management's proposal that a set used for
Weber's *Oberon* would do very well for the second act
(the Wartburg) and had insisted on a new set being built
in Paris. Unfortunately this set did not arrive in time, and
so *Tannhäuser* was launched with the *Oberon* scenery
after all.

Whatever these isolated opinions and events might
amount to, one cannot say that they present a very clear
picture of Wagner's intentions. A further indication of his
basic uncertainty is seen in the letter which he wrote in
1872 to Professor Joseph Hoffmann, inviting him to
design the scenery for the *Ring* in Bayreuth. "I have come
to the conclusion," he wrote, "that nothing worthy of the

name German in its noblest sense will be achieved if I leave this task solely to the devices of our professional scene-painters. What I want is to be able to put in front of our most expert or experienced scene-painters sketches produced by real artists, in order thereby to stimulate them to nobler efforts. In this sense I have already made approaches to several artists (painters of historical subjects). Recently however I had my attention drawn most favourably to your work, which seems to me to come in character very close to my requirements. I am consequently permitting myself to ask you whether you would consider it worth your while as a first step so to familiarize yourself with my *Ring* text that you would feel able to prepare sketches for the principal scenes, taking into account the locale as well as the figures involved in each. These sketches could then serve as models for further consideration either by yourself, should you wish it, or by scene-painters and costumiers yet to be selected."

The elaborate sketches which Hoffmann produced as a result of this invitation (one of which will be found among the illustrations to this book) Wagner turned over to the brothers Brückner to work on, thereby offending Hoffmann, who had been willing to take on the task of realizing them in practice himself. It is strange to find Wagner, a strong believer in the ability of an artist to act as his own executant, adopting a very offhand tone when it came to Hoffmann claiming the same thing. "It is not my *wish*," he wrote in 1874, "that you should take no further part in the preparation of the scenery designed by you. I have made it clear to you that I set store on preserving good relations between you and the gentlemen to whom the execution of the work was directly entrusted in the interests of progress. This is not the place to explain the reasons that have now made the necessary good relations impossible ... My one genuine wish is that you and I, two honourable men, should—for now—part in peace ... As soon as the share of Messrs Brückner in the final preparation of the scenery can be established, I promise faithfully to consider in connection with the further use of the author's rights how you are to be compensated for your share in them up till now."

The task of designing costumes for the *Ring* production Wagner entrusted to Professor Emil Doepler of Berlin. Here too his commission was remarkably vague. In 1874 he wrote to Doepler, "The task must, I feel, be regarded as a rich field offering much scope for inventiveness. For what I am in fact demanding is nothing less than a characteristic picture by means of separate figures which will conjure up in all liveliness personal activities in a distant epoch of which nothing at all is known... Descriptions by Roman writers who came into contact with the Germanic peoples of their dress do not yet seem to have been successfully exploited. In my opinion the artist who is prepared to make his own my suggested line of approach will find himself confronted with a remarkable field both for intelligent research and for invention."

On the subject of costumes Wagner had been rather more explicit in his instructions for the first productions of *Rheingold* and *Die Walküre* in Munich. There, before deciding to give up the venture for lost and abandon its participants to their own devices, he had approved the costume for Loge: large dark eyes brightened by silver foil in a pale face, red hair flaring upward like flames. The gods must never change their appearance and Wotan must never be parted from his hat.

This is certainly more in line with Wagner's usual way of occupying himself with detailed as well as with overall effects, but it is only a tiny part of the whole huge conception and certainly not enough on which to build a clear picture of his visual ideals.

It is largely on account of his failure to convey this vital element of the music drama that the whole conception of Wagner production, as practised in Bayreuth or elsewhere, has remained elusive to this day. Only in *Parsifal*, on which Wagner worked in daily contact over a long period with his designer of scenery and costumes, Paul von Joukowsky, can we feel that he came anywhere near a solution. But against that we must put his plaint, made in a letter to King Ludwig in direct connection with the costumes of the Flower Maidens, that, having invented the invisible orchestra, he now wished that he could invent the invisible stage.

Parsifal gave Wagner his last chance to come to grips with his scenic problems. His intention that Joukowsky should provide under his supervision scenic sketches for all his works from *Der Fliegende Holländer* onwards was never fulfilled. And so, for all the works except *Parsifal*, it was left to his successors to seek a solution to the scenic problems.

Three

Richard Wagner as Producer

AGNER'S letter to Feustel, of which the beginning was quoted in the previous chapter, ends with these words: "Singers and musicians will receive from me only compensation, not 'payment.' Whoever will not come to me for the honour and out of enthusiasm can stay where he is. I do not give a jot for a singer who will only come to me for one of those fantastic fees. A creature like that could never live up to my artistic requirements. These, dear friend, are my miracles, by which I shall show the world how one sets about finding helpers for such a task."

It was indeed a herculean task, not however so much because singers were reluctant to accept the terms offered them (on the contrary, there were few who did not accept an invitation to Bayreuth with alacrity), but because opera managers proved on the whole unco-operative. Some refused to release their singers, whom they held under contract, under any conditions. Others saw an opportunity to strike bargains: they would allow a singer to appear at Bayreuth only if Wagner would grant them this or that right in his works. Vienna for instance released Wagner's first Brünnhilde, Amalie Materna, only in return for the right to produce *Die Walküre* in Vienna. Wagner, who was otherwise adamant that the *Ring* must be performed as a whole or not at all, yielded in this case since his need was great.

46

Some of the opera managers who refused to release their singers were inspired by personal dislike of the composer, others by genuine fear for the safety of their singers. Since the death of the first Tristan, Ludwig Schnorr von Carolsfeld, at the early age of twenty-nine rumours had been spread that the strain of singing Wagnerian roles was killing. When the first Vienna Beckmesser, Julius Campe, also died at a comparatively early age, this absurd contention gained even further in strength. It is true that Carolsfeld caught a cold while lying on a draughty stage in Munich during the third act of *Tristan und Isolde,* but whether his death a few weeks later was directly due to his cold or to typhoid, as others have claimed, has never been conclusively proved.

However, this was a definite obstacle with which Wagner had to contend in his search for helpers. But it was as nothing compared with the obstacle of his own high and on the whole uncompromising standards. If his exhausting trips around the opera houses of Germany in search of talent proved often in vain, they also brought the occasional reward, such as the discovery in Schwerin of the first Alberich, Karl Hill ("This man," Cosima noted during that visit to Schwerin, "is the most important of them all.")

From singers whom he knew and respected, such as Franz Betz, the original Hans Sachs in Munich, and the Berlin tenor Albert Niemann, Wagner was prepared to tolerate a certain amount of artistic temperament, though only because he knew that he could nowhere find a better Wotan or Siegmund. But in artistic matters he was as a rule inexorable. He wanted Heinrich Vogl, his first Loge, to sing Parsifal in 1882 but, since Vogl made it a condition of his consent that his wife should sing Kundry, Wagner let him drop without further argument—and that in spite of the fact that Therese Vogl was a very accomplished Brünnhilde (the first, incidentally, to be seen in London) and would have sung Sieglinde at Bayreuth in 1876 if she had not been expecting a child at the time. In his choice of a substitute Sieglinde, Wagner for once yielded to expediency, when it was hinted to him (erroneously, as it turned out) that Josephine Schefsky was a favourite of King Ludwig.

If the search for a Brünnhilde ended happily with Amalie Materna, Siegfried proved far more difficult. Niemann was as determined to have the role as Wagner was determined that he should not, but as one hopeful candidate after another fell by the wayside Wagner found it more and more difficult to resist Niemann's claims. It was entirely his artistic conscience that made him do so: it would have made for easier relations with Niemann if he had given in, but he felt that it was artistically wrong to allow the same singer to play both Siegmund and Siegfried in the same cycle.

Eventually he found in Georg Unger of the Mannheim opera a tenor who had the physical appearance for Siegfried and (he thought) enough intelligence to learn to sing it, even if his voice and his enunciation were suspect. Wagner went to enormous lengths to prepare Unger for the role. He persuaded him to leave the Mannheim opera and to spend many months studying singing with Julius Hey in Munich and acting with Wagner himself at Bayreuth. This meant great expense for Wagner at a time when money was very short, since Unger had to be compensated for loss of earnings at Mannheim. But Wagner was determined that he should be allowed no opportunity of falling back into his old bad habits. It is sad to relate that Unger, for all his willingness, did not fully come up to expectations, and both Wagner and Hey were constantly assailed by misgivings. It was certainly only the lack of other possible candidates that led them to persist with him, and Unger did in fact sing Siegfried in all three *Ring* cycles at the first Bayreuth festival. But thereafter his connection with Bayreuth ended.

For several other singers the first festival was only the beginning of a long association with Bayreuth. Eugen Gura (the first Sachs in London in 1882) sang Donner and Gunther: in later years he was to be seen as Amfortas, King Marke and Sachs. The first of the three Rhine-

Cosima Wagner

Cosima Wagner's daughters Daniela (*left*) and Isolde (*right*)

Der Fliegende Holländer, 1901: Max Brückner's design for Act III

maidens was Lilli Lehmann, the second her sister Marie: they owed their engagement in the first place to Wagner's friendship with their mother, who had herself been a singer. Lilli Lehmann later became one of the foremost of Wagnerian singers and in the 1896 revival of the *Ring* in Bayreuth sang Brünnhilde. By all accounts the supreme Wagnerian soprano of her time, Hedwig Reicher-Kindermann, who had not yet achieved recognition, sang in 1876 only a Valkyrie and substituted for Luise Jaide as Erda. Among the Valkyries was also Marianne Brandt, who sang Waltraute in *Götterdämmerung*. Though her personal relations with Wagner were somewhat uneasy, she was nevertheless engaged to sing Kundry at Bayreuth in 1882, and of her appearance in London and New York mention will later be made.

Chief of the Valkyries and the Norns was Wagner's own niece, Johanna Jachmann-Wagner, daughter of his brother Albert. She had sung Elisabeth in the first performance of *Tannhäuser* in Dresden while still in her teens. Later she lost her voice and became a dramatic actress. Wagner cannot however be accused of family loyalty in inviting her to Bayreuth. By that time she had recovered her singing voice sufficiently (Wagner would scarcely have entrusted her with a solo part in his performance of Beethoven's Ninth Symphony at the stone-laying ceremony if she had not), and her outstanding acting ability was of especial value to him.

In the circumstances Wagner could speak with justice of a miracle. Not only had he succeeded in assembling a cast of enormous collective talent without offering them any financial reward beyond their bare expenses, but he was able to bring them together for rehearsals for several weeks on end in the two years preceding the opening—and this in a period when the idea of 'production' in the modern sense of the term was unknown. Personal relations were not always smooth, but quarrels were invariably patched up: no singer, it seemed, was prepared to forgo the privilege of being in at the start of Wagner's great Bayreuth venture. Perhaps not all were entirely disinterested: Wagner did hold out the promise of a larger financial reward in the two ensuing years, in which he planned to repeat the *Ring* performances. This promise he was unable to fulfil owing to his dire financial difficulties, yet many of the same singers who had been disappointed gave their services again for *Parsifal* in the year 1882.

In these first years Wagner set the pattern for participation at Bayreuth which has been followed ever since. It is still the honour rather than the financial reward that compels artists to accept engagements there. Though obviously they now receive something more than their bare expenses, none of them gets an inflated celebrity fee.

Conductors, orchestral players and stage technicians were also called on by Wagner to sacrifice time and money in the realization of his ideas. Wagner himself confined his activities at Bayreuth to producing, and his sole appearance as a conductor was at the last performance of *Parsifal* in 1882 when owing to the sudden indisposition of the conductor Hermann Levi he himself took the baton for the last act. But he kept a strict eye on his conductors, even on Hans Richter, to whom he entrusted the first performances of the *Ring*.

Hans Richter owed his initial success to Wagner, however much he may later have improved it through his own merits. As a very young man he had been employed by Wagner to copy manuscripts during the composition of *Die Meistersinger* and subsequently Wagner secured for him a position as conductor at Munich—an engagement that came to an abrupt end when Richter refused to conduct the performances of *Rheingold* and *Die Walküre* which King Ludwig had ordered against Wagner's will.

Richter's devotion to Wagner on this occasion brought him his reward later in Bayreuth, but Wagner was by no means easy to work with. He insisted on treating Richter more as an extended arm than as an artist in his own right, and in a constant flow of notes gave him instructions not only on interpretation but also on baton technique. Richter was exhorted to attend all piano rehearsals "since otherwise you will not get to know my tempi". And after the first festival Wagner complained to Ludwig that Richter—although he held him to be the best conductor that he knew—had not always succeeded in getting things right. "Now and again something succeeds by chance, but true consciousness is not there." Harsh words, but spoken perhaps more by the idealistic composer than the practical producer. Richter was fortunately man enough to take such criticism and even in later years to admit that Wagner had been in all his strictures right.

Richter's subsequent work, above all in Vienna and in London, in preserving and spreading Wagner's own tradition is too well-known to need particular mention. His association with Bayreuth continued until 1912, and he lived there until his death in 1916. In these years he would not accept even his living expenses from Cosima Wagner. "The master taught me all I know," he said. "It would be a fine thing if I now expected to be paid for it."

Besides Richter, Wagner had with him at Bayreuth a number of young conductors who were content to act as quite humble amanuenses for the benefit of working in his company. The Rhinemaidens in *Rheingold*, swaying hither and thither in their swimming machine, were each allotted a conductor to direct their singing; at the first festival these were Anton Seidl, Franz Fischer and Felix Mottl, all of whom were later to carry the benefit of Wagner's teaching far beyond Bayreuth itself.

Here again, in this employment of talented young conductors for a variety of humble tasks, lie the beginnings of a tradition which has since been continually carried on. Among the lists of musical assistants in later years appear such names as Humperdinck, Weingartner, Kienzl, Richard Strauss and Max von Schillings, as well as of men who were later to become conductors at Bayreuth in their own right, such as Michael Balling, Franz Beidler and Willibald Kähler.

The Rhinemaidens' swimming machine called for the attention of more than just three singers and three conductors. In addition each singer had two stage hands to manipulate the machinery, and to devise the movements

there was a choreographer. This was Richard Fricke, who
had attracted Wagner's attention with a production of
Gluck's *Orfeo* in Dessau and who was then promptly
commandeered by Wagner to direct all movements on the
stage, whether of individual singers or of crowds.

In his diaries, published under the title *Bayreuth vor
dreissig Jahren,* Fricke has left a graphic picture of the
rehearsals for the first festival. He describes among much
else the first encounter of the Rhinemaidens with their
swimming machine. "The sisters Lilli and Marie Lehmann
and Fräulein Lammert arrived. Friendly exchange of
greetings. They saw the machines and the athletes swimming in them. 'No,' said Lilli, 'no one can expect that of
me, I won't do it under any circumstances. I have only
just risen from my sick-bed—and then my constant giddi-
ness . . .' Both the others were silent. 'Fräulein Marie,' I
said, 'be brave, try it once and I will bet your fright will
vanish and the pleasure of swimming will win the upper
hand.'

"The ladder is put in place, Brandt and I help her in.
Amid many 'Ohs' and 'Ahs', cries and squeaks we strap
her in firmly and the ride starts—very slowly. She begins
to lose her anxious expression, laughs and says it is going
quite nicely. Now Lilli decides also to make the attempt
and—what do you think?—within a few seconds she is the
more intrepid of the two.

"Now Fräulein Lammert joins them, and all three are
swimming amid delighted laughter. Wagner appears, the
whole scene is played right through. And on top of it the
three ladies sing their parts enchantingly. They move very
well. The feeling that came over me was indescribable.
Tears came into my eyes at the success of the thing, in
which all of us (except Wagner) had doubted, had indeed
been certain that the girls would not consent to it.

"The scene is in itself so strangely beautiful that one can
feel quite transported. Up till now only small young
athletes with awkward movements have lain in the
machines, and now these lovely figures—it was wonderful.
When the ladies left the machines Wagner thanked them

with tears of joy in his eyes and smothered them with kisses."

This was only one of the many technical problems with which Wagner and his helpers, particularly Karl Brandt who devised and built all the machinery and who helped Fricke to overcome the Rhinemaidens' fears, had to contend. Another was the handling of the Norns' rope in *Götterdämmerung*. Fricke tells of a conversation with Wagner.

"Before we parted I could not resist drawing his attention to the difficulty of the rope-throwing in the Norns' scene. I said, 'In reading a scene of such serious and solemn character our imagination works at full stretch, but as soon as the thing is done before our eyes, when all the other senses are alive, our imaginary picture can shrink into ridiculousness. In this scene, which in order to realize we must make visible to the eye and to our senses, the abyss in there. The rope must be long, golden and light, yet heavy enough to be thrown accurately. I fear the three ladies will not learn it.'

"'They must practise it until they can,' he exclaimed. 'But if they do not learn? How would it be if we moved the rope mechanically with wires invisible to the audience? If that cannot be done, I suggest we have no rope at all, but express it with gestures.' He blurted out, 'No, never with gestures—Well, we shall see.'"

Fricke's healthy scepticism was no doubt learnt in the humbler theatre at Dessau, where he had to do what he could with the resources at his disposal rather than go in pursuit of a limitless ideal, stinting nothing, as Wagner was doing at Bayreuth. It is not really surprising that in the excitement of the hour Wagner's artistic judgment tended at times to go awry. He was, as all contemporary accounts agree, a man of considerable humour and in less ecstatic circumstances would no doubt have seen that much of what he was trying to do verged on the ridiculous, not least the pantomime dragon in *Siegfried*. Fricke's instinct was to keep this creature completely out of sight, but in this case he evidently thought it wiser to keep his doubts to himself. After the festival was over and Wagner had seen some of his visions turn in practice into involuntary farce, his judgment reasserted itself and Fricke records him as saying, "We'll do it differently next time." Unfortunately the next time never arrived.

It is interesting to see that Wagner in a subsequent article ascribed all the inadequacies of his *Ring* production not to miscalculations but firstly to lack of money and secondly to accident. The lighting apparatus, for instance, was not ready until the very day of performance; the failure of the dragon's neck to arrive from England had necessitated last-minute improvisation; there had been insufficient time to rehearse the scenic transformation at the end of *Götterdämmerung*; and so on. He used excuses of this sort to defend the scenery of the brothers Brückner, which had been quite severely criticized: they had done their best under unfavourable circumstances. Unfortunately no authentic pictorial record exists of these original Brückner sets based on Hoffmann's designs, and the nearest one can get to them is in pictures of the sets used by Angelo Neumann in Leipzig, which were to a large extent copies.

In his article Wagner bestows far more effusive praise on Karl Brandt than on Hoffmann (who is dubbed 'very talented') or the brothers Brückner ('highly industrious'). Wagner had always shown far more interest in the machinery of his scenic devices than in the scenes themselves, and Brandt, the architect of them, was described as "my main support in the realization of the entire project", a man "as energetic as he was perceptive and inventive", with whom Wagner could work in complete sympathy. The same good relations did not exist between Brandt and the other experts on the visual side such as Fricke and Doepler, who found Brandt very unsympathetic to their problems when these conflicted with his machinery. On the subject of Doepler's costumes Wagner maintained a discreet silence. Perhaps Doepler had overdone Wagner's injunction to characterize the gods by including in their dress their special attributes, or perhaps he had yielded too easily to Wagner's criticism of his original designs. At any rate Cosima's final verdict, expressed privately, was devastating. "They look," she said, "like Red Indian chiefs."

The 1876 production of the *Ring* remained Wagner's only attempt at the work, but the experience he had gained in producing it he was able to put to good account in *Parsifal*, the only one of his works to be written after the Festspielhaus had become a reality. *Parsifal* was designed for production at Bayreuth and Wagner stipulated that it should be performed nowhere else. And in fact for many years it was not.

All contemporary accounts agree that the *Parsifal* production of 1882 was a vindication in all ways of Wagner's aims in creating his theatre in Bayreuth. It was made possible, as already described, by the generosity of King Ludwig who, magnanimous as always at the final count, did not take advantage of the rights which, for reasons of tact towards his own court officials, had been written into their agreement. Wagner had consented to make use of the conductor, singers and orchestral players of the Munich Court Opera for his production and to engage others from elsewhere only if suitable people could not be found in Munich. In fact Wagner exercised a completely free hand in his choice of singers, but he did not go to the length of disputing the ability of Munich's musical director to conduct *Parsifal* at Bayreuth. The only possible ground on which he could have objected to Hermann Levi was the fact that he was a Jew, and Wagner was well aware that the king had no sympathy with his anti-semitic views.

Indeed, Wagner was not very consistent in that matter himself, as his devotion to his musical assistant Joseph Rubinstein showed. And if he felt that it was somewhat odd to have a Jew in charge of his most directly Christian drama he certainly was not prepared to wreck his chances of staging the work at Bayreuth on that account. His treatment of Levi was not above reproach, since he did not conceal even to Levi's face that he deplored his racial origin. At one stage during rehearsals Levi felt himself so insulted that he left Bayreuth vowing never to return. Wagner hastily went in chase and the breach was healed. *Parsifal* was duly launched with Levi at the conductor's desk, and as the chief conductor of *Parsifal* in Bayreuth he remained until 1894.

The difficulties that Wagner had experienced in obtaining satisfactory scenery and costumes for the *Ring* were spared him in *Parsifal*. In Paul von Joukowsky, a young Russian painter of independent means whom he met in Naples in 1880, Wagner found an artist who was completely in sympathy with his ideas and able to devote endless time and to exercise exemplary patience in the painful search for perfection. The *Zaubergarten* scene, for instance, was redesigned seven times before Wagner was satisfied. The result fully justified the effort. Scenery and costumes made for the first performance in 1882 were kept intact until 1912, when Siegfried Wagner began to revise the second act. But Joukowsky's superb temple, based on the cathedral at Siena, survived unscathed until it was scrapped—in the face of much opposition—in 1934 for a new design by Alfred Roller.

The costumes of the Flower Maidens defeated even Joukowsky and have continued to present a virtually insoluble problem ever since. Not only the costumes but also the behaviour of the Flower Maidens caused difficulties. To preserve the innocent childlike naiveté at which Wagner aimed against the seductive quality of both words and music demand a high standard of acting as well as singing. Wagner, very conscious of the difficulties, invited Lilli Lehmann (his "Rhinemaiden directrice", as he called her) to find and train his Flower Maidens. She accepted the invitation but withdrew when, following the sudden death of Karl Brandt, Wagner appointed his son Fritz as technical director. Lilli Lehmann, who had had an unhappy love affair with Fritz Brandt, feared to re-open old wounds. The task of finding and training the singers fell to the musical assistant Heinrich Porges, and Wagner was delighted with the result. Lilli Lehmann however, who saw a performance of *Parsifal* in 1883 after Wagner's death, writes in her reminiscences, "It hurt me exceedingly to see the Flower Maiden scene, which I had imagined so ideally, played here with so much realism."

In the choice of his main singers Wagner had an easier task in 1882 than he had had in 1876. His own teaching efforts as well as those of his associates such as Richter, Seidl, Fischer, Hey and Fricke and the Leipzig director Angelo Neumann had by now begun to bear fruit, so that Wagner was able to allow himself the luxury of alternative castings. This brought new difficulties in the way of artistic jealousies, which Wagner however skilfully exploited to get his own way. Having rejected Vogl for the role of Parsifal, he gave it to three singers: Ferdinand Jäger (who had become his main protégé) as Siegfried in succession to the disappointing Unger, Hermann Winkelmann and Heinrich Gudehus. Gudehus and Therese Malten, whom he had seen in Dresden, Wagner regarded as potentially the ideal Tristan and Isolde, but since he could see no chance of using them in those roles he compensated them with roles in *Parsifal*. Therese Malten shared Kundry with two survivors from the 1876 *Ring* production: Marianne Brandt and Amalie Materna.

Other singers who took part in both the *Ring* and *Parsifal* were Karl Hill, who shared Klingsor with Anton Fuchs, and Gustav Siehr, the original Hagen, who was now rewarded with the role of Gurnemanz. But in this role he was eclipsed by the man whom Wagner had first wanted to sing Hagen, Emil Scaria. Scaria's refusal to accept Hagen except on payment of an inflated fee had aroused Wagner's anger so much that he subsequently threatened to veto a performance of the *Ring* in Berlin in which Scaria was to play Wotan. Angelo Neumann, who was in charge of that production, invited Wagner at least to hear Scaria at rehearsals. On Cosima's persuasion Wagner consented and was so overwhelmed that an immediate reconciliation took place. Scaria was invited to sing Gurnemanz, in which role, Lilli Lehmann says, "he will always remain in the memory of all who were fortunate enough to see and hear him."

With this production of *Parsifal* Wagner's life came to an end in a blaze of triumph. Within a further six months he was dead, leaving behind him not only a series of gigantic works, but also an ideal theatre to play them in, a voluminous amount of written instructions and a large group of people trained in his methods. These inheritors now had the task of preserving and developing his ideas, and they were to do so not only in Bayreuth but outside as well. The work outside Bayreuth had already begun in Wagner's lifetime and is worthy of a chapter to itself before we pass on to the period of Cosima.

Four

Spreading the Bayreuth Influence

FOR the vast majority of people Wagner's fame during his lifetime rested on the four works which we nowadays tend to regard as relatively youthful: *Rienzi, Der Fliegende Holländer, Tannhäuser* and *Lohengrin.* Not very many people even inside Germany could have seen a performance of *Tristan und Isolde,* though *Die Meistersinger* had enjoyed a more widespread popularity. Performances of the *Ring* as a complete cycle had been rare, and *Parsifal* was performed in Bayreuth only.

This situation was due not entirely to the obvious fact that the earlier works were closer in style to the traditional idea of opera and therefore could be considered better box-office attractions. Wagner did exercise a very strict control over performances of his later works. As a young composer fighting for recognition he had been in no position to hold a protecting hand over the earlier operas, and he naturally enough accepted what terms he could get to bring them to the stage at all. Since the laws of copyright in Germany had not reached anything like their present highly developed state, these terms were very unsatisfactory, giving only a meagre immediate financial reward with no royalties to follow and allowing theatres to hack the works about without the composer's consent. Wagner's disgust at the way his early works had been treated was directly responsible for his later strict attitude.

He owed his opportunity to King Ludwig, who provided

him with a regular income. Since Wagner was an extrava-
gant man, this income did not entirely remove the need to
earn money with his compositions, but it certainly lessened
it. In return Wagner legally surrendered his rights in his
subsequent compositions to the king, but it was a right of
which Ludwig generously took no advantage, except in
the case of those premature performances of *Rheingold*
and *Die Walküre* in Munich. Otherwise the king was
content to give Wagner a free hand in his negotiations for
performances of his works outside Munich.

In the main Wagner conducted such negotiations himself, and he used his powers to ensure that performances
were conducted and sung either by his own associates or
by people of whom he personally approved. His demands,
not surprisingly, met with resistance from the opera
directors, and the arrangements achieved were seldom
cordial and often enough the result of some mutual black-
mail.

There was in fact only one opera director in whom
Wagner ever showed any real confidence, and that was
Angelo Neumann. Neumann played so important a part
in the staging of Wagner's music dramas during and
immediately after the composer's lifetime that it is worth
while telling his story in some detail, though he never
worked at Bayreuth itself. But it was Neumann who with
Wagner's approval and support first brought the *Ring* to
the stage in many German cities and in Britain, Belgium,
Holland, Italy and Russia as well. In doing so he made use
of the singers and conductors and technicians whom
Wagner had trained and also discovered many others of
equal or even better status himself.

The full story of Neumann's association with Wagner is
told in a book of reminiscences which is still a delight to
read. They reveal Neumann as a man of incurable opti-
mism, good humour and resource, and it is not surprising
that Wagner once wrote to him, "If there were anything
on this earth that could still astonish me, it would be you.
Heavens, what energy, what faith and what courage!" It
is certainly true that Neumann had much to contend with

—not least from the composer's own impulsive and change-able nature.

They first met in Vienna in 1875, where Neumann was engaged as a singer. At rehearsals for *Lohengrin,* which Wagner was himself preparing, Neumann was in the position of an adoring slave, lost in admiration of Wagner's skill as a producer as well as in his genius as composer. When shortly afterwards he abandoned singing to become co-director of the Leipzig Opera, he had only one ambition: to present Wagner's works there in the way that he had seen Wagner present them in Vienna. Having seen the *Ring* at Bayreuth, he made up his mind that he would present this work at Leipzig and opened negotiations with Wagner at Bayreuth.

Wagner, seeing no chance of repeating the *Ring* at Bayreuth in the immediate future, was willing, after meeting and talking to Neumann (an interview in which Neumann did not withhold certain criticisms of the Bay-reuth performances) to sanction a production, though he made it a condition that his original Siegfried, Georg Unger, should be engaged by the Leipzig Opera. That Neumann's first bid ended in failure was not due to this condition but to the cautious attitude of his fellow director, August Förster, who held the *Ring*—with the possible exception of *Die Walküre*—to be unstageable outside Bayreuth. His evasive attitude eventually aroused Wag-ner's ire, and negotiations were broken off.

However, the impossibility of finding any other new opera worth doing very soon broke down Förster's opposi-tion, and he made no objection when Neumann proposed a second approach to Wagner. This time agreement was reached, and so in 1878 the *Ring* was brought to the stage in the composer's birthplace. Wagner was not present at the performance, but before the opening he sent Hans Richter and Anton Seidl to Leipzig to watch final rehearsals, giving them instructions to veto anything not in accordance with his own ideas.

According to Neumann, Seidl raised some objections, only to be overruled by Richter, whose judgment was that

Neumann had done wonders. This opinion was endorsed
after the performance by Liszt, who wrote to Wagner with
a tactlessness permissible perhaps only in a father-in-law,
"Neumann has managed the affair in some respects better
even than you did in Bayreuth." Seidl's doubts were
probably due more to the excessive devotion of a very
young man to his revered master than to any real disapproval of Neumann. They later became firm friends, and
in all Neumann's later triumphs Seidl was his main
associate.

The conductor of the first Leipzig performance was
Josef Sucher, a man to whom Wagner had no objection,
though he did later try to get him deposed in favour of
Seidl, in whom Wagner professed to have more confidence
than in any other conductor. Eventually, after Sucher had
accepted an engagement in Hamburg, Seidl was appointed
chief conductor at Leipzig. Shortly afterwards—again on
Wagner's instigation—Felix Mottl was taken on the
Leipzig conducting staff, to which another very young
man, Arthur Nikisch, also belonged. This remarkable
constellation lasted only a few months, since Mottl
accepted a higher appointment at Karlsruhe.

Added proof that the practical centre of Wagner activities was at that time Leipzig rather than Bayreuth can
be obtained from the cast list of the first *Ring* production
there, which included Otto Schelper as Wotan, Rosa
Sucher (the conductor's wife) as Sieglinde, Georg Lederer
as Siegmund and Katharina Klafsky as a Valkyrie and a
Norn. The Brünnhilde was Marie Widl of Vienna and the
Siegfried was Unger. Since those early negotiations, however, Wagner had withdrawn his support from Unger and
he now tried to persuade Neumann to engage his new
protégé Ferdinand Jäger. Neumann, having already
engaged Unger at Wagner's command, not unnaturally
refused.

Wagner's changeability with regard to singers and
particularly to tenors is most vividly in evidence in relation
to Unger and Jäger. For a subsequent performance of the
Ring in Berlin Neumann engaged Jäger as Siegfried. At

rehearsals he proved to be off form, and Neumann proposed that Friedrich Vogl should sing in his place. Wagner, who was present, angrily accused Neumann of having a grudge against Jäger. Neumann thereupon beat a tactful retreat. Jäger's performance in *Siegfried* was however so deplorable that Wagner himself now demanded that Vogl should take over. Here was Neumann's chance to turn the tables. He insisted that, as Jäger had sung in *Siegfried,* he must also sing in *Götterdämmerung.* And so it happened, much to Wagner's disgust.

Wagner's own grudging attitude to Vogl, his first and very successful Loge at Bayreuth, seems less excusable. Vogl was by all accounts a remarkable and intelligent singer, and in Neumann's ensemble he proved his versatility by singing all the main tenor roles (Loge, Siegmund and Siegfried) in one cycle of the *Ring*.

With his production of the *Ring* at Leipzig Neumann had triumphantly proved that the cycle could be done on a normal operatic stage, though certainly it had to be a large one, and Neumann had to close the opera house for a full three weeks in order to prepare it. Now, having won his point, he determined to take his production further afield. He hired the Viktoriatheater in Berlin, and there in 1881 the *Ring* was played four times with great success. At the end of the fourth cycle, at which the aged Kaiser Wilhelm I was present, an unfortunate incident almost led to a break between Wagner and Neumann. At the very moment that Neumann was paying tribute to the Kaiser in his curtain speech Wagner, who was standing beside him, left the stage. It looked like a deliberate demonstration. Wagner later explained that his action was due to a slight heart attack, but Neumann, who had suffered from the composer's impulsive rudenesses before, refused to believe him. For a while they were not on speaking terms and even after their reconciliation Neumann would not accept Wagner's excuse—an uncharacteristic failing on the part of this usually ebullient man which he bitterly regretted when two years later he heard of Wagner's death from a heart attack.

An interesting sequel to this episode was the criticism that it drew from Wagner about Neumann's production. In a letter to Förster he stipulated that for future performances Neumann should appoint "a new and competent stage manager who shall be thoroughly conversant with my methods". And he added, "The utter lack of style and finish in the staging of my *Ring* cycle has surprised me continually in view of my constant remonstrations on the subject, which Herr Neumann has seemed not to comprehend."

This letter brought from Förster a masterly lecture on the necessity for compromise. "Where shall we find this paragon of a manager?" he asked. "Who is he—this man who is so perfectly acquainted with the ins and outs of your works? I know only one such man, but he lives in Bayreuth and his name is Richard Wagner. If you are able and willing to unite the professions of poet and composer, impresario and stage manager and possibly—like Sophocles—be your own actor too, I think we should probably reach the ideal presentation of the Richard Wagner dramas. *Probably,* I say. For 'close packed our heads with seething thoughts, while deeds accomplished few and far between'."

It is more than likely that Wagner's criticism was due to pique, but it is equally likely that it did truly reflect his hitherto unstated feelings. After all, he had been dissatisfied with his own production of the *Ring*: why should he now be satisfied with Neumann's? Since Neumann was working on stages not built specially for the *Ring* and burdened additionally with all the cares of a normal nightly operatic repertoire, it was almost inevitable that his productions should have lacked finish. Great as Neumann's service was in Wagner's cause, it seems safe to assume that it lay rather in giving stage performances at all than in providing model productions. This was in itself a great feat. If Neumann had not provided the opportunities which Wagner was not at that time providing himself in Bayreuth, it is certain that the music dramas would not have established themselves as quickly as they did. One may

indeed wonder whether Bayreuth itself could have survived but for Neumann, since it was mainly through the
large sums earned by him and passed on to the composer
that Wagner was able to keep his festival theatre in
existence.

Neumann's next great service was the transportation of
his complete *Ring* production to London, where four
cycles were given in May and June of the year 1882.
Wagner had given the rights for the production of *Tristan
und Isolde* and *Die Meistersinger* in London to Pollini of
the Hamburg Opera, and by a coincidence these two
works were presented in German at Drury Lane Theatre
(with Richter conducting) at the same time that Neumann
was presenting the *Ring* in German at Her Majesty's
Theatre (with Seidl conducting). Neumann claims that he
gained considerably more attention than his rivals at
Drury Lane. If that was so, it was due rather to Neumann's
mastery of the then unacknowledged art of public relations
than to the artistic superiority of his productions over
those at Drury Lane. Neumann was fully aware of the
value of royal support and he lost no time in seeking an
audience of the Prince of Wales. The Prince at once
proclaimed the impossibility of himself and Princess
Alexandra attending a full cycle of the *Ring*: where could
he find four free consecutive evenings? However,
Neumann had come armed with a letter from the Kaiser's
son, Prince Friedrich, and the Prince of Wales was
reluctant to offend his brother-in-law. He told Neumann
that "he would see what he could do", and in fact he
eventually attended not only the first cycle of the *Ring*
but seven other performances as well.

London had the good fortune to meet Brünnhilde, after
the first performance by Therese Vogl, in the person of
Hedwig Reicher-Kindermann, whose voice according to
Weingartner was "magnificent, sumptuous—the most brilliant dramatic voice I have ever heard". With Niemann
as Siegmund, Vogl and Unger as Siegfried and Hill as
Alberich, it can be said that London's first acquaintance
with the *Ring* was certainly of the highest possible

quality, marred only in the first cycle by the mental breakdown of Emil Scaria during his performance of Wotan in *Die Walküre*. He had, according to Neumann's account, sung the second act magnificently. Then in the third act he entered from the wrong side, "creeping like a hunted soul with drooping shoulders and a trailing lance", and transposed his entire part. After the performance he seemed to remember nothing of the occasion and insisted on singing in *Siegfried*. But only with the constant help of the prompter and his fellow singers was he able to get through the performance: he had forgotten his part entirely. Neumann had to withdraw him, and his roles of Wotan and Hagen were taken by Otto Schelper and Theodor Reichmann in the succeeding cycles.

Considering London's previous scanty acquaintance with Wagner on the operatic stage—beginning with *Lohengrin* (in Italian) in 1868 all the early works had been done rather unsatisfactorily in either Italian or English—such performances of the *Ring, Tristan und Isolde* and *Die Meistersinger* simultaneously in 1882 must have had an almost stunning effect. The musician Hermann Klein was in fact more impressed by the Drury Lane performance than by Neumann's. Of these he says in his book *Thirty Years of Musical Life in London* that Seidl "at once won the high approval of connoisseurs by the skill which he displayed—with by no means first-rate material—in bringing out with clearness, refinement and intellectuality the beauties of Wagner's colossal score. It was through no fault of Seidl's that the representations were at many points open to criticism: nor, we may be equally sure, was he responsible for the number of extensive cuts which disfigured the last two of the four music dramas."

Of Drury Lane on the other hand Klein writes, "The rare excellence of these performances—doubly valuable in that they presented under perfect conditions difficult operas mostly new or unfamiliar to English audiences—has never been forgotten by any who witnessed them ... Henceforward we were to understand what was signified by Wagnerian declamation and diction superimposed upon a correct vocal method, as distinguished from mere shouting and a persistent sacrifice either of the word to the tone or of the tone to the word. . . . Imagine the advantage of hearing *Tristan und Isolde* and *Die Meistersinger* for the first time with such a noble singer and actress as Rosa Sucher as Isolde and Eva; with such a glorious Tristan and Walther as Winkelmann; with the famous Marianne Brandt as Brangäne; with that fine baritone Gura as König Marke and Hans Sachs! . . . How these operas were conducted by Hans Richter I need hardly say. Enough that the ensemble was superb and the *mise en scène,* generally speaking, beyond reproach."

Neumann's London season was the first step in the realization of his ambition to create a "travelling Wagner theatre". For this, Wagner consented to give him the complete rights of presentation of the *Ring* both in Germany and abroad for the period of his tour. The extent of Wagner's trust is clearly seen in a letter which he wrote at this time to the director of the opera house in Königsberg, who had shown some annoyance at being expected to give his stage to Neumann's company before being allowed to present the *Ring* himself.

Asserting that all opera houses except Leipzig had failed to present the *Ring* adequately, Wagner continued, "This, as well as his recent signal success in Berlin, has led me to entrust Neumann with the further production of my entire cycle in those German cities which have not yet had the opportunity of hearing them, giving him my support and full power of attorney within certain time limits. While I give the public of such towns the advantage of hearing my works in their entirety—and given in a superior manner—at the same time I give the directors an added advantage. For when their audiences are acquainted with my works as a whole, so that the production of a single opera would be understood and appreciated, I should gladly dispose of the rights for a single performance, which could then make a successful run in the regular theatre repertoire.

"I now ask you to weigh this advantage well and, instead of considering it an insult that I should send you a model production of the *Ring* for your stage, rather take it as a genuine assistance which, far from injuring your enterprise, will be of inestimable benefit; as I will then gladly turn over the rights for a single performance—for you to rival the original *if you can!*"

There is no need here to follow in detail the triumphant course of Neumann's travelling company, of which he writes most entertainingly in his own reminiscences. It is enough to say that the company of 134 people, including an orchestra of sixty and a chorus, toured through Germany, Holland, Belgium, Italy, Hungary and Austria, taking scenery and musical instruments with them in five railway wagons. The singers included Hedwig Reicher-Kindermann, Heinrich and Therese Vogl, Georg Unger, Emil Scaria (now recovered from his breakdown) and Otto Schelper. In Danzig, Neumann gave the part of Sieglinde to a young and untried singer, Katharina Klafsky, who was later to achieve fame throughout the world in the dramatic roles. She was only too soon to have the opportunity of replacing in these roles Hedwig Reicher-Kindermann, who during the tour died at Trieste at the age of twenty-nine.

The tour ended at Graz in Austria in the summer of 1883. It had triumphantly fulfilled its mission: all the cities in which the *Ring* had been performed were now presenting the work on their own account. Now Neumann could lay down his burden and turn his attention to a less strenuous field of activity. He assumed the management of the opera house in Bremen, where he continued to work in Wagner's cause. After three years there he moved to Prague, where he founded a permanent German opera.

But his days of touring were not yet over. In 1889 he was invited to introduce the *Ring* to Russia. There were on this occasion notable differences in his company. Seidl, now busy in America, was not available as conductor, and so Neumann took with him from Prague a man who was later to become one of Bayreuth's most distinguished conductors, Karl Muck. Vogl was still able to sing Siegfried, if not with the same splendour as before, but his wife was no longer up to her former roles and Therese Malten took her place.

Now, however, we have got a little ahead of the story. But it is a point from which we can see how the seeds planted by the composer in Bayreuth were thriving. Not only was the Festspielhaus in full bloom but Wagner's direct assistants, and their assistants in turn, were established in influential positions throughout Europe and America. At the beginning of the Nineties Richter was in Vienna, making frequent excursions to England; Mottl was in Karlsruhe; Levi and Fischer in Munich; Zumpe in Stuttgart; Neumann in Prague and among his assistants not only Muck (soon to go to Berlin) but also Gustav Mahler, who was to become a leading Wagnerian conductor in Budapest, Hamburg and in Vienna, though he never worked in Bayreuth. Seidl was in America, spreading the Bayreuth tradition there. But to him and his work we will return later.

Five

Cosima Wagner

THROUGH all the difficulties of creating the Fest-spielhaus in Bayreuth and launching first the *Ring* and then *Parsifal* Richard Wagner had had his wife Cosima by his side. She had been more than just the mother of his children and his stepchildren, more than the capable manager of his household: she had also been his closest assistant in all the events leading to the opening of the festival, had smoothed the way with King Ludwig and his officials, had travelled with her husband in search of artists, intervened and advised. She had even thrown her own personal financial resources into the venture when bankruptcy threatened it after the first production of the *Ring*.

Yet never with one word did Richard Wagner suggest that in the event of his death his wife might assume the directorship of the festival. In his more optimistic moments he saw himself surviving long enough to produce all his works from *Der Fliegende Holländer* onwards, after which his son Siegfried would be of an age to take over from him. In more pessimistic mood, he once wrote to Neumann that he feared the festival must die with him, since he knew no one capable of carrying it on in the spirit he desired.

However, Richard Wagner was not alone in being oblivious of his wife's artistic potentialities: Cosima seemed at first to be unconscious of them herself. At his death she had no thought but to die with him. It was not the needs of the festival but the needs of her young children that prevented her from taking her own life. For more than a year after her husband's death she lived for her children alone, shut up in Wahnfried and receiving nobody.

The festival meanwhile went on. There were performances of *Parsifal* in the two years following Wagner's death, carried out by the artists and assistants who had worked with the composer, Scaria assuming artistic control in the one year and Fuchs (the Klingsor) in the other. It needed a written note from one of the musical assistants, Julius Kniese, conveyed to her through her elder daughters, to rouse Cosima to the consciousness that Richard Wagner's work at Bayreuth was in danger of falling apart. The singers, Kniese warned her, were slowly but surely, freed of all control, relapsing into their old operatic ways.

Even then she hesitated to assume open control of the festival. She found a solution in the construction of a curtained box off the stage of the Festspielhaus from which she could watch rehearsals without herself being seen. From there she would despatch little notes to the persons concerned, reminding them of what they appeared to be forgetting. Hermann Levi at the conductor's desk received many of these notes and kept them. Only long afterwards did they come to light, to show what a detailed knowledge Cosima Wagner had of her husband's works and how determined she was that not the slightest deviation from his instructions should go unchallenged.

This was to be the spirit in which she administered the festival even after in 1886 she assumed open control with a production of *Tristan und Isolde*. But it was a spirit which did not hinder the unfolding of her own formidable personality. Nietzsche's sister wrote, "Cosima has for me always been the personification of will and a longing for power in the noblest sense of the word. As long as Wagner was alive she exercised this power through him. Not that she dominated him: his art, his greatness and his omnipotence were her power. But I think it was only after his death that her real and quite outstanding gifts as a leader showed themselves."

The extent of her outstanding gifts in this direction can be seen not only in her remarkable achievement in gradually extending the Bayreuth repertoire to cover the whole of Wagner's output from *Der Fliegende Holländer* onwards, but also in the almost religious atmosphere with which she managed to surround herself. Wahnfried became a sort of temple, with herself as its priestess, her daughters as her handmaidens and at her feet a host of adoring disciples such as Ernst von Wolzogen, who had worked with her in Wagner's lifetime in the creation of the periodical *Bayreuther Blätter* and now, freed from the master's occasional scepticism, could work unhindered on furthering the Wagnerian myth.

To the bands of adorers came a young Englishman, Stewart Houston Chamberlain, who later married one of the Wagner daughters and who put his pen almost entirely at the service of Cosima's and von Wolzogen's myth. In the *Bayreuther Blätter* he once wrote, looking back on Cosima's achievements, "Among us closer associates it is regarded as a pious rule that we should not in public speak the name of the person who from now on placed not half but her entire strength in the service of the festival. The reasons for this attitude lie embedded in the heart, in the soul, and permit of no discussion. I should be the last who would wish to transgress such a reverent duty. Indeed for my part I would raise no objection if in a history of Bayreuth not a single name were to be mentioned; for the more each was prepared to submit to the will of the creative genius and exactly to fulfil his guiding rules, the more complete was the achievement. And since in this particular case compliance was so exemplary, as only the most highly endowed can make it, silence (the naming of no names) denotes the greatest reverence of all. However, one thing must naturally not remain unsaid: that the immediate rise in the standard of the festival was due first and foremost to the circumstance that from now on an intelligence was shaping and ordering it which reflected the will of the artistic creator as no other in the whole world. I shall not return to this matter again."

The rather comic awe that emanates from this passage was no doubt acceptable to Cosima, for otherwise she would have vetoed it. On the contrary, she did all she could to emphasize both her difference from other mortals and her unique connection with Wagner, for whom she remained in mourning for the rest of her long life. She was always dressed in unadorned black, even when conducting rehearsals on the stage of the Festspielhaus, and in public she cultivated a distant air which could prove disconcerting even to her admirers. Albert Schweitzer says of a meeting with her in 1904, "Her manner of receiving people was lacking in simplicity and naturalness. She did not have the gift of putting people at their ease; she liked them to approach her with the reverence due to a princess."

Later, however, Schweitzer came to know her better and realized, as he says, "what a delicate and vital soul there was in this woman, at first approach so distant". More important still was his discovery, after he had talked to her at length about Richard Wagner's struggles to achieve his ambitions, that Cosima even at the time when Wagner's work had finally triumphed "was haunted by the idea that the master's enemies remained active and formidable".

Here no doubt we find the real clue to Cosima Wagner's distant behaviour, her determination to impose her will on everybody and everything and her hostility towards new ideas. Bitter experience had taught her during the composer's lifetime that not even friends could be entirely trusted to do exactly what was required of them. Not even Richter, not Mottl nor Seidl had fully satisfied the composer, let alone the singers, a source of constant friction and disappointment. If Richard Wagner had not entirely trusted them, how could she? She had worked closest with him, she had shared his disillusionment and known his wishes, and so it was on her own memories alone that she was willing to rely. If Richard Wagner's battle was

already over, if he had finally triumphed her own battle
was not—the battle in which she had to convince friends
as well as enemies that she was competent to carry Bayreuth on in the spirit of her husband.

Her difficulties were in fact enormous, not only because
as immediate successor to Richard Wagner she had to
bear the full brunt of that instinctive resentment which is
inevitably aroused in such circumstances. She had other
disadvantages which she could not help, but for which
she was nevertheless criticized. First of all, she was not
German, but a mixture of French and Hungarian, and
she was accused on that account of ignoring German
singers in favour of foreign ones. Secondly, she was a
woman. At a time when producers in the modern sense
were still in any case a rarity, how startling must it have
seemed that a woman should actually physically direct
rehearsals on stage. Schweitzer tells of conversations
with members of the Bayreuth orchestra who "were not
unanimous in their opinion that it was a real advantage
to have a woman of such an imperious will as Madame
Cosima directing the performances". Since it appears unlikely that a woman of weaker will would have been
capable of directing them, one can assume that the real
objection here was simply to the fact that Cosima was a
woman.

Though Cosima's psychological secret might have been
divined by so acute an observer as Schweitzer, she took
great care that it should not be openly recognized, neither
by her enemies nor her friends, not even in fact by Cosima
herself. She had a very effective way of dealing with all
attacks on her authority, of which there were inevitably
many: she simply refused to acknowledge their existence.

One of the most virulent of her critics was Felix
Weingartner, whom Cosima had engaged on the recom-
mendation of Levi as a musical assistant in 1886. Weingartner formed the opinion that Cosima in her production
of *Tristan und Isolde* was following her own rather than
the composer's ideas. When during that festival Cosima's
father and Weingartner's revered teacher Liszt died in

Bayreuth and no official notice was taken of the occasion, Weingartner vowed never to enter Wahnfried again, and asked Cosima to release him from his Bayreuth engagement. A few years later, after Weingartner had expressed his hostile views on Cosima's Bayreuth in a famous pamphlet, he was advised by friends to do something to heal the breach. As he relates in his autobiography, Weingartner organized a concert of Wagner's works in Mannheim, to which he invited Cosima. Not only did she attend it, but afterwards she took Weingartner in her arms and kissed him "as a mother kisses her son". But she never invited him to Bayreuth again.

Another who beat in vain against Cosima's imperturbable outward show of rightness was Wagner's "Rhinemaiden directrice" Lilli Lehmann, who sang Brünnhilde in the first revival of the *Ring* since the opening of the festival twenty years earlier. She tells in her reminiscences of her dismay at the extent of the changes that Cosima was making in Wagner's original production. Cosima, however, would counter any questioning of her decisions with a remark addressed to her son, "That was how the master did it, don't you remember, Siegfried?" To which Siegfried would reply, "I believe you are right, mama." Lilli Lehmann remarks tartly that Siegfried had rarely been present at the *Ring* rehearsals in 1876 and in any case had been barely seven years old at the time. If further challenged, Cosima had another answer ready. "This was a decision the master came to after the original production", she would say. Here, as Lilli Lehmann ruefully admits, Cosima was in an impregnable position, since nobody could possibly prove her a liar.

Lilli Lehmann was of course not unbiased. She had been wounded, when, for the 1886 production of *Tristan und Isolde,* she had been passed over for the title role and offered Brangäne instead (which she refused). This led Lilli to adopt an unusually mercenary attitude when asked ten years later to sing Brünnhilde, and she received a dignified reproach from Cosima. However, as Lilli admits, none of this affected Cosima's professional attitude: she was kindness and consideration itself and full of praise for the performance, so that Lilli's carefully planned gesture—in which she subscribed all of her Bayreuth fee plus some money of her own to endow a bed for aged singers in a charitable institution—fell, as a demonstration against Cosima, somewhat flat.

In the matter of Cosima's faithfulness to the composer's instructions one should not of course take the hostile evidence of Weingartner and Lilli Lehmann too seriously. They were pitting their memory of the master's intentions against hers and giving her no credit for the fact that she was faced with the practical task of getting the works on the stage, where dreams of a vanished glory had to give way to present necessities. From this point of view the evidence of Bernard Shaw carries more weight. "I need hardly add," he wrote after a visit to Bayreuth in 1894, "that the supernatural powers of control attributed to Madame Wagner do not exist. Prima donnas and tenors are as unmanageable at Bayreuth as anywhere else . . . On the other hand, if we leave the vagaries of the stars out of account, we may safely expect always that in thoroughness of preparation of the chief work of the season, in strenuous artistic pretentiousness, in pious conviction that the work is of such enormous importance as to be worth doing well at all costs, the Bayreuth performances will deserve their reputation."

One would certainly expect, as Shaw suggests, that within the Festspielhaus itself a less priest-like attitude than in Wahnfried and Bayreuth as a whole would have prevailed. Yet Cosima's relations with her artists, of which more will be said in the next chapter, were governed by the same sort of awe. Descriptions of her at rehearsal are made in the same sort of religious phrases of which Stewart Houston Chamberlain was such a master, and only rarely does the picture of a human being emerge out of them. Anna Bahr-Mildenburg, the great Kundry of her time, writes, "I never heard Frau Wagner speak with a raised voice, let alone shout. Force and energy she expressed only with her eyes, which she could bring to rest on people with such wonderful tranquillity, so penetrating and attentive, as if she would not trust the words alone but wished first to seek the truth behind them. And when she had come to that, these eyes would put up defensive barriers, become cold, hard and indifferent. Or they would assume a soft lustre, and her heart would bid a welcome in a shining warm gaze. And then she could suddenly break out in merriness and humour, arousing in me the feeling that she would make fun of the whole world."

One of Cosima's biographers, Walther Siegfried, speaks of the peculiar quality of her voice, "this unusually deep, musical voice which in normal conversation sounded completely feminine but in argument, in vigorous assertion and defence, took on a masculine energy, and in the striking mouth there would suddenly appear something of the startling demonism of her father Liszt".

This, though more human, is still all formidable enough and reveals how completely Cosima managed to impress on the world the image of herself which she chose to present. Successful in all she undertook, she was defeated in the end by one thing only: by ill-health, and even then we are left with the question whether she did not manage to turn even that to good account. By 1901 she had brought all of Wagner's works from *Der Fliegende Holländer* onwards to the Festspielhaus stage, exactly as he had planned to do, and with her productions of the early works in particular had triumphantly proved that Bayreuth was a necessity not only for the *Ring* and *Parsifal* but also for the proper appreciation of all Wagner's works. She had in fact established Bayreuth beyond all shadow of a doubt, and now there was nothing left to do but to repeat and refine the performances.

So she could yield to her failing eyesight and physical exhaustion, conscious of her duty done both to her husband and to her son who now, at the age of thirty-seven, took over from her. She was herself sixty-nine and was still to live for a further twenty-two years. She remained in Wahnfried, ministered to by her daughters

Daniela and Eva, and in constant communication with her son and successor, with whose administration of the festival she never openly interfered. And so—fitting end for a high priestess—she became a legend in her own lifetime: not (one feels) against her will.

Six

The Bayreuth Style

IF with her productions of *Tristan und Isolde* in 1886 and of *Die Meistersinger* in 1888 Cosima Wagner did no more than faithfully recreate Richard Wagner's own first productions, with *Tannhäuser* she found herself on much more difficult ground. First of all, it lacked a definitive form. Wagner himself had said that he owed the world a proper *Tannhäuser*, but he had never made good his debt. There was the original Dresden version, with which the composer himself was dissatisfied, there was his more elaborate Paris version which had caused a scandal, and in between these, all sorts of other versions, prepared either by Wagner himself (like that for Vienna) or by opera managers all over Germany to suit their own purposes, as was the way at that time. Secondly, in whatever form it was played, it had now become one of Wagner's most widely performed and popular works. Consequently everybody had his own conception of *Tannhäuser* and, whatever Cosima might do with it at Bayreuth (she chose in fact the Paris version), she was bound to arouse on some sides a fury of opposition.

Cosima herself was fully conscious of this fact. "I knew," she wrote afterwards in a letter to Davidsohn, the publisher of the *Berliner Börsen-Kurier,* "that we had set ourselves the Bayreuth task *par excellence* ... If we were to make an operatic production (even in the best sense of the word), it was inevitable that the musical riches of the

79

first scene would make not only the following scene but also the second and third acts appear pale and flat ... Whereas, if we could succeed in bringing to realization the characters with their tragic destiny and the life of the Middle Ages, the musical riches I spoke of would be seen as part of Venus's magic wiles and the simpler means would appear as the natural expression of the other way of life.

"The warmth in the welcoming of Tannhäuser (in Act One), the utmost simplicity and clarity in the enunciation of the words, the avoidance in positioning, expression, tempo, etc. of everything that could remind one of a septet —this was our one endeavour." Great care was taken that the chorus should sing clearly and appear to be an integral part of the drama. "It was due to this chorus that the usual ineffective ending of the whole work became what it was meant to be: the proclamation of salvation and the tragedy of life."

Cosima goes on to speak of her casting problems. She rejected the usual operatic Elisabeth in favour of "a child-like virginal figure whose first terrible experience makes her a saint at the cost of her life. The contrast with Venus, in whom we see woman personified in all her demonic bewitching power, could not be too much stressed." And Wolfram, "that musically so richly endowed figure", was urged to keep his significance in the drama constantly in mind.

When Cosima eventually achieved her ambition of presenting *Tannhäuser* at Bayreuth in 1891, the result of her new approach was startling. "The opera *Tannhäuser*", the young Richard Strauss wrote, "has been resurrected as a drama", and he leaped to a spirited defence of Cosima's production in the *Bayreuther Blätter*. His defence was in fact not particularly necessary, for all but the most conservative soon realized the significance of Cosima's deed, which had given *Tannhäuser* a new dimension. She had conclusively proved that Wagner's dramatic ideas were as relevant to his so-called early works (as he had always insisted) as to the later ones. With *Lohengrin* in

Siegfried Wagner

Lohengrin, 1908: Max Brückner's set
for Act I

Tristan und Isolde, 1927: Kurt Söhnlein's set for Act I

Parsifal, 1928: Kurt Söhnlein's set for the *Zaubergarten*

1894 (regarded by Stewart Houston Chamberlain as Cosima's greatest achievement of all) and with *Der Fliegende Holländer,* which she presented in 1901 in one continuous act as the composer had originally written it, she went on to consolidate her victory. All her productions, including the 1896 revival of the *Ring,* were characterized by a strict subservience to dramatic form, and this disciplined approach led to the evolution of a method which eventually became known as the "Bayreuth style".

The "Bayreuth style" is worth examining in detail—and not only the style but also Cosima's way of achieving it—since it affected not only Bayreuth but countless productions outside; and in the eyes of many people it put a straitjacket on Wagner which was eventually to do him more harm than good.

The definition that Karl Kittel, a musical assistant from 1904 and Bayreuth's chief musical coach from 1912 to 1939, finds for the "Bayreuth style" looks harmless enough. "In Wagner's works", he wrote, "melody is and has always been the lifeblood of the drama, and the complete integration of dramatic impulses with musical expression forms the basis of the "Bayreuth style.'" Daniela Thode described it as the complete fusion of the actions on the stage with the sounds of the music. "No theme, no melodic phrase which has not to be given visual expression through gesture, movement, positioning and mime."

In these two definitions one already sees the difference between an idea and the practical application of it. What began as a general artistic principle has been brought down to the level of a recipe. Cosima Wagner, in applying her husband's interpretative ideas with religious devotion, may have lost sight of the quality of improvisation which Richard Wagner prized above all. His efforts were directed towards ensuring that the singer fully understood and therefore could give complete expression to the character he was depicting. Hers took the process a stage further and imposed on the singer the very actions with which he should depict the character, thus destroying his spontaneity.

It was this preoccupation with detail that gave Cosima Wagner's productions that quality of mechanical precision of which not only her enemies but many of her friends, including Albert Schweitzer, complained. Yet it was not due to any lack of artistic perception on the part of Cosima herself. For all her devotion to Wagner's ideas she was no narrow-minded pedant but by all accounts a very great natural actress who could depict as expertly and convincingly as her husband her conception of a role. The tenor Alfred von Bary tells of a rehearsal of the second act of *Tristan und Isolde* at which only he, Cosima and Felix Mottl (at the piano) were present. Since the singer of Isolde was indisposed, Cosima herself took the role, speaking and not singing her part.

Bary writes, "Hardly had the music begun when I perceived in the stance and in the features of the noble lady an almost indescribable change. The tall slim body stood raised in elastic tension, the intellectual head thrown slightly back, proud and passionate. The delicate and yet so expressive features trembled slightly ... The surging music at this point is like a great wave swelling as it advances on the towering rock, breaks and draws back into the infinite wideness of the sea. This Isolde trembled in all her body, the lines of the figure and the black silk enclosing it flowed harmoniously with the waves. Then suddenly there was a moment of stillness, and I gazed in astonishment at a picture of quiet resolution and profound simplicity ... I do not know what I myself sang and did in the whole scene. I know only that I absorbed these changing pictures into myself helplessly, in a spirit of intoxication, unconscious of myself and yet intuitively aware that I should never again experience so tremendous a spectacle ... It was the finest *Tristan* rehearsal of my whole life. Again and again I recall it to my mind and feel sad at the thought that so much tragic beauty and power was never seen depicted in all its glory, but lived on only in the too often inadequate rendering of others."

Anna Bahr-Mildenburg writes in a similar strain. "Many times Frau Wagner sat down and read to me the poem of

Parsifal . . . Her voice remained soft and restrained, yet no change of mood and tension was lost. And when she would suddenly lay her hand on mine, so gently that I was scarcely aware of her touch, I could feel in her hand a quivering and vibrating which told me that this woman sitting quietly before me, her lips scarcely moving, was at this moment someone quite different, transformed mysteriously into Kundry."

Descriptions such as these are sufficient to dispose of any suspicion that Cosima was a cold martinet, imposing a series of drilled movements on reluctant singers. But not all her singers were able to see beyond the drill to the inner intention, to feel—as Anna Bahr-Mildenburg puts it—that "nothing could be achieved through simple imitation of these movements unless I could make them my own inner property." She goes on to say, "What appeared so natural and inevitable in Frau Wagner seemed often forced in the copy. Animation of the outward form from within was lacking in the imitation. For that many singers had neither the aptitude nor the understanding often too, neither the good will nor the earnestness. It was after all so easy to give nothing of one's own, to submit simply to the yoke."

For an artist in sympathy with her one can see what profit was to be had from Cosima, yet even to her devotees she could prove a harsh and pitiless teacher. Luise Reuss-Belce relates that after a rehearsal in the role of Fricka she received a note from Cosima saying simply, "Dear child, in what language were you singing today?" No wonder that all but her most determined adherents took refuge in an unquestioning imitation of her example in order to escape that searing tongue. No wonder either that such imitations sometimes—no doubt through a sub-conscious defence mechanism—assumed the aspect of a caricature. The tenor Max Alvary for instance delighted to tell of the 'minuet' which he as Tannhäuser was obliged by Cosima to execute at one point with Wolfram.

But none of this can alter the fact that in matters of technique Cosima was almost invariably stylistically right.

Some of her principles seem indeed so obvious that one wonders how they could ever have appeared novel: the insistence, for example, that the physical expression of an emotion should precede the verbal expression of it. This is in fact so instinctive a reaction that one can scarcely conceive that it ever had to be taught. However, one must not lose sight of the historical perspective. Wagner had been fighting a tradition which, nowadays completely forgotten, was in his own time the usual thing: a tradition of histrionic attitudinizing and prescribed gesture which was rather, as far as singers were concerned, a comfortable substitute for acting than acting itself.

The composer's instruction that singers must look at each other and not at the audience, which led Cosima to evolve a rigid system of profile positions, was in fact initially a preventive measure directed against singers who considered themselves more important than the roles they were playing. It was a necessary precaution as we know from the experience of Jean de Reszke, who after a performance of *Lohengrin* in New York was reproached by the critics for turning his back too often on the audience. What de Reszke had in fact been doing was to stand in the way of his Elsa (Melba) so that she could not rush forward to sing her "arias" at the footlights.

All Cosima's efforts in connection with movement and positioning were directed towards this one stylistic principle, to preserve the drama intact; and it was important in this respect that the actors on the stage should show no consciousness of the audience. This is of course the normal law of realistic drama, and it caused singers no particular difficulty once realism had become the usual form of operatic presentation, as it did after Wagner's own lifetime. In our own time, however, we find the difficulty recurring as realism gives way to a deliberate non-realism: under the influence of Brecht and others the audience is encouraged to preserve its awareness that it is watching not life itself but a representation of life. How impossible it is to present Wagner's works in this particular way can be seen in occasional misguided attempts to do it.

In a recent production of *Rheingold,* for example, I saw Loge come to the very front of the stage to confide directly to the audience, like some male Zerbinetta, his shame at having to associate himself with Wotan and the other gods. The inevitable result of this stylistic blunder was to make the gods look ridiculous and reduce their entry into Valhalla to the level of an ingenious pantomime.

What fault there may have been in Cosima's approach lay not in the principle but in her over-laboured efforts to achieve a set pattern. Kittel writes, "Frau Wagner possessed a purposeful control over her body, and with very few exceptions could demonstrate her wishes. The movements of her arms (Brünnhilde's awakening in *Siegfried,* Act Three), of her hands (Kundry in *Parsifal,* Act Two), of her head (Isolde) revealed an exceptionally well disciplined body, with which she could express an infinite amount with a single gesture.

"Cosima Wagner laid great stress on the use of the palms of the hands, particularly in the female roles. They had to be held in a cupped position: she would never allow the palms to be held up straight towards the audience. The movement of warding off (Brünnhilde in *Götterdämmerung* in the scene of the seizure of the ring) had to be done towards the side, the upper part of the body being turned . . .

"Loge's swaying, dancing walk, the springy play of his arms and his empty hands—these Cosima Wagner could demonstrate as unforgettably as the heavy stamping stride of the two giants, their clumsy play with their great clubs (which had to be thrown in wild rage from one hand to the other while the shafts remained firmly on the ground) . . .

"Great significance was attached also to the facial expression and the play of the eyes (as mirror of the soul). This refinement of acting—the conscious control of the eyelids—had to be practised in three stages: (1) the gaze is directed at a point on the ground at a distance of five or six yards: the lids then almost cover the whole eye; (2) the gaze is slowly raised to eye-level: the eyelids are now raised; (3) the gaze is widened by a drawing back of the eyelids. In this way one achieves looks of weariness, of longing and of recognition."

This is only one example of Cosima's exhaustive efforts to train her singers, efforts which—as Kittel says—she would not give up until the whole scene down to the movement of each single finger could be played through without a mistake. One can only sympathize with Mime, who according to Kittel had to express his despair at his inability to forge Siegfried's sword in the following way: "After the cry *'Könnt' ichs dem Kühnen schmieden, meiner Schmach erlangt' ich da Lohn'* he lowers his head reflectively and (at the first entry of the two bassoons) places the finger-tips of both hands pressed together on his forehead; then (on the repeat of the phrase) he raises his head thoughtfully, so that the stiffly held hands touch the pursed mouth and (at the entry of the tubas) turn into clenched fists."

Cosima's efforts were directed towards intimacy rather than largeness of gesture, and it is reported that she even went on one occasion to the length of having weights secretly sewn into the sleeves of Elisabeth's costume in *Tannhäuser* so that she could not fling up her arms to greet *dich, teure Halle* in the second act. There is, after all, truth in Richard Wagner's injunction, "Reticence in the movement of arms and hands. The more economy one here employs, the more impressive will the few gestures be that one uses on the stage."

How deeply Cosima Wagner had taken to heart her husband's views on gesture is revealed in a letter to Hermann Levi concerning a production of *Tristan und Isolde*. "Repetitions in the music intensify and deepen the experience; the repetition of a gesture is simply a repetition and consequently as a rule weakens the effect ... Here in my opinion lie the tremendous difficulties in the staging of *Tristan,* in which the most intricate drama of the soul revealed in the music scarcely allows of a corresponding gesture without absurdity, and scarcely any facial expression can match the power of the music ... I believe that a certain well-meaning realism is quite out of place, whereas a static pose, which may at the same time be regarded as the shell in which the emotion portrayed by the orchestra lies hidden, is at least harmless, if by no means really adequate ... We must banish everything that is commonly conventional, everything realistic, and make room for a noble convention, for style."

It is rather startling to find Cosima speaking here in almost the same terms as her grandsons, though the solution at which she aimed—the establishment of a "noble convention" was, as we shall later see, the very opposite of that sought by Wieland and Wolfgang Wagner. However, it is clear that she was trying to steer a course between naturalism and the artificial convention of the normal opera house. We see this again in her views on the behaviour of the chorus in *Die Meistersinger*: "If the chorus has nothing to do, it should remain still; when it has a part in the action, the movements should be as individual as possible. The so-called liveliness and naturalness of the chorus, the stereotyped exchanging of glances, signs, etc. I consider bad, a debased and false form of realism." (Here again we get a distinct whiff of Wieland Wagner.)

Gesture was only one aspect of the Bayreuth style, and it is only because it is the one that strikes the eye rather than the generally less perceptive ear that it has received more attention than the other aspects. Kittel writes, "Cosima Wagner's working method had three distinct divisions. Once the musical line was fixed—and it had to be exact in rhythm and clarity—the words, in certain ways the most important element, were dealt with. The acting instructions came only after that.

"Cosima Wagner, in common with Julius Kniese and also the other conductors and musical assistants, took the piano rehearsals with the soloists. She would often arrive unannounced, would seat herself by the piano—always with her back to the window—and follow the work closely, paying attention to every single detail, but in particular to the enunciation, to the sound content of the words, and in this connection the singer was made to take great care with the consonants (which might really be regarded as the skeleton, the bony framework of the words, while the vowels constitute the living marrow within).

"For minutes on end Cosima Wagner would dilate on the tonal significance of the double consonants such as ll, mm, nn, ff, pp, rr, tt and so on. Tirelessly she would demonstrate to the singers, giving them all sorts of practical hints. The difficulties in achieving proper understanding and execution lay in the fact that the singers had always to keep in mind the characters they were playing. Fricative and hissing consonants such as rr, ff, ss, ch, sch, z had to be pronounced for instance by Alberich, Mime, Loge, Hagen, Klingsor, Kundry (Act One) and Beckmesser in a completely different way from Wotan, Siegfried, Brünnhilde, Gurnemanz, Parsifal and Amfortas.

"What longing and desire lay—to take just one example —in the profoundly conscious enunciation of the consonant w (Amfortas, Tristan, Wolfram, Dutchman) as Cosima Wagner spoke it and demanded it from her singers."

The purpose of all this unwearying and for the singers no doubt often irritating insistence on detail was less to make the words understandable to the audience (though this was of course desirable) than to convey character. As Kittel says, there is and must be a difference between the enunciation of an Alberich and a Wotan, a Klingsor and an Amfortas, if the differences of their characters is to be conveyed to the audience. Wagner himself did much with the style of his music to emphasize character differences, but the effect of his music is obviously minimized if Alberich, for example, sings with the same noble roundness of tone as Wotan. Wagner does use words as pure sound and not only as instruments of understanding, and the vocal line is designed consciously to bring out the tonal value of each word. It was not vanity or pedantry that led him in his "last request" to his singers on the eve of his *Ring* production to write, "The big notes will look after themselves: the little notes and their text are the main

Tristan und Isolde, 1886: Act III
(painting by Max Brückner)
Original: Richard Wagner-Gedenkstätte, Bayreuth

thing." He was simply reminding his singers that every note in every musical passage has its own carefully calculated function. Failure to observe note values, phrasing and enunciation might not very noticeably disturb the overall musical effect, but it undoubtedly weakens the dramatic impact.

Intent on correctness in this respect as in all others, Cosima insisted that singers should use full voice at all rehearsals, but she would sternly repress any attempt to achieve an effect through sheer power. "Power lies in the expression," she would say, "and not in the volume of a sound."

With her stage settings and costumes Cosima continued to work strictly along the lines laid down by her husband, refusing absolutely to consider the new ideas of Adolphe Appia, warmly as these had been recommended to her by her friend Chamberlain. It is evident however, at least as far as the *Ring* was concerned, that she found Wagner's actual achievements unsatisfactory, for in 1896 she had the *Ring* scenery completely redesigned by Max Brückner and the costumes by the artist Hans Thoma.

Brückner's designs may have solved isolated practical problems of staging, but they did not escape the reproach of a general pedestrianism even from Cosima's deepest admirers. Chamberlain rather unkindly wrote to a friend of Brückner's "familiar stuff, without a trace of invention or imagination". And he added, "Frau Wagner and her son can do a lot, but they cannot inject talent into that man". Harsh words and, to judge from the painted sketches of *Der Fliegende Holländer* and *Lohengrin* reproduced in this book, certainly undeserved. But of course between the original intention and the practical application of it to the stage there may—as we already saw in the composer's time—be a very large gap.

Thoma's new costumes appear to have been more successful. What chiefly distinguished them from the Doepler designs of twenty years earlier was an increased simplicity, an absence of ornamentation and a more unified use of colour. The costumes were no longer variegated in colour

like Doepler's, but generally each character wore a dress
of one colour, chosen to correspond to his own character-
istics.

For *Parsifal* Cosima retained Joukowsky's designs, and
in her productions of *Tristan und Isolde* in 1886 and *Die
Meistersinger* in 1888 she did no more than recreate with
the help of Max Brückner as stage and Josef Flüggen as
costume designer, her husband's original Munich productions. With the three earlier works *Tannhäuser, Lohengrin*
and *Der Fliegende Holländer* she was obliged to rely
more on her own ideas, since there was no actual production of the composer's to build on. The works of course had
one feature in common: they were all historically based,
and Cosima, working as she was in the realistic tradition,
felt no need to look beyond the contemporary records of
the relevant period for her visual ideas. This was in itself
a considerable advance on the normal opera house custom
of her time, which was content to recreate history only
in a conventionally modified form of its own contemporary
romantic realism.

Daniela Thode, who helped her mother with research
for the production of *Lohengrin,* writes of the result: "The
historical framework—how King Heinrich wins over an
unwilling German tribe, the Brabantines, for the military
forces of the empire, the contrast between paganism and
Christianity—emerged in a clear light. Ortrud was transformed from a jealous plot-spinner and wicked magician
to the representative of the submerging Germanic faith,
that is to say, to the custodian of a great conception which
she could defend only through cunning. King Heinrich's
emblem was the flag of St Michael, not the eagle which
was first used in the thirteenth century."

Whether any of this has much to do with what Wagner
was trying to express in his works may of course be
questioned. Cosima Wagner, who was well aware of the
spiritual impulse behind Wagner's work, certainly never
stopped to consider whether such extraneous detail
obscured or clarified the intention. Nor, to be fair, did
Wagner himself in his capacity of producer. But to say

that is perhaps simply to be wise after the event. It can be and in fact is still strongly argued by many Wagnerians that the balance at which Wagner aimed can only be achieved by a strict adherence to his visual as well as to his musical instructions, and, if this is so, obviously complete historical accuracy in the matter of scenery and costumes (where it is possible to achieve it) could only be considered a gain. But, whatever one may feel about this argument, it remains undeniable that a conscientious application of realistic detail was infinitely preferable to the perfunctory conventions prevailing generally in opera houses of the composer's and Cosima's times, and was in fact a necessary and inevitable stage in the pursuit of an ideal method of presentation.

As a witness for this contention we can quote Bernard Shaw: "What I feel bound to record concerning the Bayreuth *Lohengrin*—remember that this is the first time the work has been done there, and probably the first time it has ever been thoroughly done at all, if we except the earliest attempt under Liszt at Weimar—is that its stage framework is immensely more entertaining, convincing and natural than it has ever seemed before. This is mainly because the stage management is so good, especially with regard to the chorus . . .

"One example of this will suffice. Those who know the score of *Lohengrin* are aware that in the finale to the first act there is a section, usually omitted in performance, in which the whole movement is somewhat unexpectedly repeated in a strongly contrasted key, the modulation being unaccountable from the point of view of the absolute musician, as it is not at all needed as a relief to the principal key. At Bayreuth its purpose is made clear. After the combat with Telramund and the solo for Elsa which serves musically as the exposition of the theme of the finale, the men, greatly excited and enthusiastic over the victory of the strange knight, range themselves in a sort of wheel formation, of which Lohengrin is the centre, and march round him as they take up the finale from Elsa in the principal key. When the modulation comes, the women, in their white robes, break into this triumphal circle, displace the men, and march round Elsa in the same way, the striking change of key being thus accompanied by a correspondingly striking change on the stage, one of the incidents of which is a particularly remarkable kaleidoscoping of the scheme of colour produced by the dresses.

"Here you have a piece of stage management of the true Wagnerian kind, combining into one stroke a dramatic effect, a scenic effect, and a musical effect, the total result being a popular effect the value of which was proved by the roar of excitement which burst forth as the curtains closed in."

Seven

Cosima's Assistants

BAYREUTH in Cosima Wagner's time had not only to set an example in the production of Wagner's works but also to establish itself both financially and artistically, so that when the inevitable relaxation of control over the works came about, it would be able to survive on merit alone. In the struggle to maintain its unique position Cosima owed much to the Bayreuth banker Adolf von Gross, who had been one of Richard Wagner's closest associates in building the Festspielhaus and in launching the festival. He was executor of the composer's estate and legal guardian of his children, and it was his practical sense of values that often proved an effective curb on Cosima's sense of divine mission. In fact he was probably the only man who by virtue of his responsibilities was able openly to remind Cosima of her human limitations. He discouraged her from holding the festivals yearly, since audiences could not yet be found to keep the Festspielhaus filled, and he resolutely opposed her wish to follow the *Tristan und Isolde* of 1886 with *Tannhäuser*, maintaining that what Bayreuth needed now was a real box office attraction, and that could only be *Die Meistersinger*. Cosima very reluctantly consented, and von Gross was proved right. *Die Meistersinger* of 1888 was an enormous success both artistically and financially, and Cosima was able to follow it in 1891 with that revolutionary *Tannhäuser* production on which she had set her heart.

Von Gross showed great foresight in insisting that the festival should pay for itself out of its takings, the money arising from royalties on performances of Wagner's works outside Bayreuth being devoted to the upkeep of the family and to the building up of capital to provide a personal income when copyright should expire and royalty payments cease. He was well aware of the vulnerability of the Festspielhaus and indeed, following King Ludwig's death in 1886, soon found himself fighting in defence of its existence.

He was summoned to Munich and informed by the minister Graf Crailsheim that the rights in all Wagner's works including *Parsifal* belonged by the terms of the composer's agreement to the Munich Opera. There was thus nothing to stop the Munich Opera from producing *Parsifal*. Von Gross produced the letter in which King Ludwig had given Wagner the assurance that *Parsifal* belonged to Bayreuth alone. Crailsheim said that this was invalid, since the king had been declared insane and therefore was not responsible for his actions. Thereupon Gross declared that, since the king had appointed Crailsheim minister in the year after he had written the letter to Wagner, it must be assumed that Crailsheim's appointment was also invalid: perhaps the point should be left to the law courts to decide. Faced with this embarrassing situation, the Bavarian ministers decided that there was room for negotiation, and from these talks Gross emerged the triumphant victor. Under the new agreement Munich undertook to regard the composer's heirs as sole copyright owners of all the works from *Rienzi* onwards. Bayreuth's exclusive right to *Parsifal* was recognized, the only stipulation being that, if its production were ever to be allowed outside, Munich should be given the first chance to do it. For all these valuable concessions Gross yielded something to the Munich Opera in return: the complete rights in Wagner's two youthful operas *Die Feen* and *Das Liebesverbot!*

But Munich had another surprise in store. A few years later a special festival theatre—the still existent *Prinz-*

regententheater—was erected there for the performance of Wagner's works. A rival festival in Munich was of course not at all to Bayreuth's liking, but, if it could not be prevented entirely, at least something could be done. Gross reminded the Bavarian authorities that Munich's licence to perform all Wagner's works with the exception of *Parsifal* was confined specifically to the Court Opera itself and did not cover the newly built *Prinzregententheater*. Armed with this watertight legal argument he was able to establish a *modus vivendi*. Munich undertook to confine its festival to the works which were not being presented at Bayreuth in the same year. Furthermore, singers engaged by Bayreuth would not be invited to sing at the *Prinz-regententheater* and vice versa. It was an arrangement that did no serious harm to either festival and benefited the public, which now had the choice between two Wagner festivals.

Munich was by no means the only artistic centre to cast covetous eyes on Bayreuth and to seek ways of circumventing Cosima's tight hold. In many countries of the world there was a growing interest in Wagner and with it an increasing resentment that his last work of all should be withheld from all who were unable or unwilling to journey to Bayreuth to see it. Some satisfaction had been found in concert performances of *Parsifal*: London heard it this way in 1884 in a performance by the Royal Choral Society conducted by Joseph Barnby with Heinrich Gudehus, Therese Malten and Emil Scaria (all members of the original Bayreuth cast); New York in 1886 in a performance conducted by Walter Damrosch with Marianne Brandt as Kundry; and in Amsterdam the work had even been presented on the stage, though in a private performance for members of the Wagner Society only.

Since European copyright did not operate in the United States of America, there was nothing to prevent managements there from defying Cosima's ban on performances of *Parsifal*. Lilli Lehmann relates that Edmund Stanton, the manager of the Metropolitan Opera in New York, contemplated producing it as early as 1887, but abandoned the idea out of consideration for Cosima Wagner. Heinrich Conried, a later manager of the Metropolitan, was made of sterner stuff and put *Parsifal* on the stage there in 1903, an act which earned him the opprobrium of all European opera managers: rather unfairly, one feels, since as soon as the European copyright in *Parsifal* expired in 1913 they themselves all rushed to produce it.

However, a performance of *Parsifal* in distant New York could do no serious damage to Bayreuth, and in fact the only sufferers from this breach of Wagner's own wishes were the singers of Parsifal and Gurnemanz, Alois Burgstaller and Anton van Rooy, who were banished from Bayreuth without further ado. The rival festival in Munich was of course pleased to take them over.

Nothing could better illustrate Cosima Wagner's sense of divine rightness than this ruthless sacrifice of two of her most valuable singers for an offence which they did not voluntarily commit. Conried had astutely engaged them for a Wagner season in New York without specifying the roles they were to sing, and a refusal to take part in *Parsifal* would under those circumstances have been for them a costly breach of contract. However, this argument moved Cosima not at all.

Burgstaller's treachery (as she regarded it) must have been all the harder to bear since he was as a singer Cosima's own creation, a product of the short-lived music school which she had founded in Bayreuth in 1892. It had always been Richard Wagner's ambition to have his own training establishment, since he felt that the only way to eradicate what he considered to be the false operatic tradition in Germany was to start again from the beginning. His first attempt to found a school having come to grief in Munich owing to intrigues and other causes, he had tried again at Bayreuth without success to raise support for it.

Cosima therefore, in founding a music school in Bayreuth under the direction of Julius Kniese, was here as in all else simply fulfilling her husband's wish. But by now it was apparently too late. There was no rush to join the

Two designs by Adolphe Appia. *Above: Die Walküre*, 1892 (not staged);
below: Tristan und Isolde, 1923 (La Scala, Milan)
Fondation Adolphe Appia, Berne

Die Meistersinger, 1933: Emil Preetorius's set for Act II

Winifred Wagner

school with its austere curriculum based on the writings of the master and its emphasis on physical training. But in Alois Burgstaller, a former farmworker, the school did produce a Siegfried of some status and in Hans Breuer one of the most successful Mimes of all. Burgstaller went straight from the school (after a few small parts in the festival of 1894) to the role of Siegfried in the 1896 revival of the *Ring,* and considering his age (he was not yet twenty-five) it was not surprising that he shone more effectively in *Siegfried* than in *Götterdämmerung.* In the ensuing years up to 1902 Burgstaller also sang the roles of Siegmund and Parsifal, and it is pleasant to recall that Siegfried Wagner subsequently forgave him his lapse from grace and recalled him to Bayreuth to sing Siegfried in 1908 and Siegmund in 1909.

Cosima's attitude towards her singers was not always entirely consistent. Though she had resented, perhaps even more than her husband, the occasional fits of temperament of his first group of singers, she remained loyal to them even after they had passed beyond their prime. It was on her insistence that Franz Betz, whom she had once slightingly called a matador on account of his great opinion of himself, was invited to sing Hans Sachs, the role which he had created in 1868, when *Die Meistersinger* was presented at Bayreuth for the first time twenty years later. Gustav Siehr and Eugen Gura were others from the original *Ring* production whom she invited to sing such roles as König Marke and Hans Sachs. Vogl, the original Loge, was given even more to do: he continued to appear at Bayreuth until 1897, singing Parsifal and Tristan in addition to Loge. By that time all but Theodor Reichmann, the original Amfortas, had dropped out. Gudehus made his last appearance at Bayreuth in 1889, Amalie Materna in 1891 and Therese Malten in 1894.

It was by no means only advancing years that severed these long-standing connections. Of Lilli Lehmann's uneasy relations with Cosima I have already written. Cosima did in fact eventually make up for her tactlessness in passing Lilli Lehmann over as Isolde by giving her Brünnhilde in the revival of the *Ring*. But even here Lilli Lehmann had to share the role with the then unknown Ellen Gulbranson, who made such a success of it that poor Lilli was put right in the shade.

However, Lilli Lehmann continued her career as a Wagnerian singer triumphantly enough outside Bayreuth, notably in New York and in London, as also did Marianne Brandt, whose connection with Bayreuth did not survive Richard Wagner's death. Bayreuth in fact no longer had an undisputed first call on the eminent singers of the day. New York in particular, where Wagner's old associate Anton Seidl was active, proved a strong counter-attraction, not only financially but also as an escape from Cosima's obsessive insistence on a uniform style.

New York's interest in Wagner's music dramas dated back to 1884, in which year Leopold Damrosch conducted *Die Walküre* and *Lohengrin* at the Metropolitan, with Amalie Materna and Marianne Brandt among his singers. Walter Damrosch, his son (whose mother incidentally had sung Ortrud in the first performances of *Lohengrin* in Weimar) inherited his interest and brought Seidl to New York together with Lilli Lehmann, Max Alvary and other prominent singers from Europe. Ten years later Walter Damrosch emulated Angelo Neumann with a travelling opera company which, after a season in New York, toured the United States as far afield as Kansas City with a repertoire consisting of the *Ring, Tristan und Isolde, Die Meistersinger, Lohengrin* and *Tannhäuser*. His singers included Rosa Sucher, Johanna Gadski, Emil Fischer, Max Alvary and Marie Brema.

Of these great names only two can be said to have been genuine products of Bayreuth: Rosa Sucher and Marie Brema, of whom more will be said when we return to Cosima Wagner. Johanna Gadski and Max Alvary did make isolated appearances in Cosima's Bayreuth, as did other distinguished singers of the New York and London Wagner seasons, such as Milka Ternina, Lilian Nordica and Dmitri Popovici. But there were others who never sang at Bayreuth at all, among them Katherina Klafsky and the de Reszke brothers.

On one of these—Jean de Reszke—Cosima did indeed turn covetous eyes, and both she and Kniese tried hard to persuade him to sing Siegfried in Bayreuth. Jean de Reszke's refusal was, it appears, not due to any unwillingness to sing there: he voluntarily travelled to Bayreuth to study the role exhaustively with Cosima and Kniese. It is said that the Princess of Wales (later Queen Alexandra) was responsible for his abstention, since she did not wish to share her favourite tenor with her royal cousins in Berlin.

Cosima Wagner was no longer in a position to pick and choose among the leading singers of the time as Richard Wagner had done, secure in the knowledge that he had only to knock and the door would be opened to him. But she could—and did—find her own singers and train them in the way she wanted them to be, and the evidence is that this was the way she really preferred and with which she achieved considerable success. Only with Burgstaller and Breuer could she perhaps be credited with educating her singers from the very beginning, but in the smaller German opera houses or even in the larger ones she found others who had not yet succumbed to bad operatic habits and were eager or intelligent enough to place themselves in her hands.

One of the finest of these was Rosa Sucher, the wife of the man who had first conducted the *Ring* in Leipzig for Angelo Neumann. She made her Bayreuth debut in the role of Isolde, after long and arduous drilling by Cosima which did not apparently stifle her own considerable personality. And after this success she went on in the next ten years to sing at Bayreuth the roles of Eva, Venus, Kundry and Sieglinde.

Cosima's anxiety to avoid an operatic Elisabeth in her production of *Tannhäuser* led her to choose two young and inexperienced singers who could, she felt, supply the innocent childlike quality at which she aimed. With Pauline de Ahna (later Richard Strauss's wife) and the

Norwegian singer Elisa Wiborg, who had had only a year's experience at the relatively minor opera house at Schwerin, she took a risk which succeeded brilliantly. Equally successful was her choice of Marie Brema, an English-born singer of German parentage whose stage experience was of the slightest when she was chosen to sing Ortrud and Kundry at Bayreuth in 1894. Marie Brema returned to Bayreuth in 1896 and 1897 to sing Fricka in Cosima's new production of the *Ring* in addition to Kundry.

Marie Brema was one of the substantial numbers of foreign singers who were invited to Bayreuth in Cosima Wagner's time, much to the chagrin of the champions of German nationalism at that period. But in fact, though Cosima was blamed for this disloyalty, the real culprit was Julius Kniese, who, though known officially as the Bayreuth chorus master, was in fact far more than that in Cosima's Bayreuth up to his death in 1905. Kniese first appears in the Bayreuth records in 1882, when he was one of the musical assistants at the first production of *Parsifal*. Purist that he was (he is reported to have replied to Levi at a *Parsifal* rehearsal when asked for his tempo of a certain choral passage, "Not my tempo, not your tempo— *the* tempo"), it was Kniese, as we have seen, who persuaded Cosima after Wagner's death to take active control of the festival in order to correct its falling standards. And, once established, he not only helped vigorously in the search for new singers, he also worked hard to train them.

One of his most notable successes was the Flemish tenor Ernest van Dyck, whose command of German was dangerously weak when he was engaged to sing Parsifal in 1888. As Hey struggled with Unger, so did Kniese struggle now with van Dyck and brought forth a Parsifal who is still remembered in Bayreuth with awe.

Another foreign discovery was Ellen Gulbranson, who in 1896 came straight from Stockholm to the role of Brünnhilde, which except in the first year, when she shared it with Lilli Lehmann, became her sole property in all successive years until 1914. Ellen Gulbranson is still remembered by the older generation at Bayreuth with veneration, not only for her singing but also for her ability (not surprising in someone who was a farmer when she was not singing) to manage her horse Grane on the stage. However, it was not this qualification which was likely to have impressed Cosima particularly: Lilli Lehmann relates that when she once extolled the prowess of an earlier Brünnhilde (Therese Vogl) in mounting Grane while the horse was in motion and dashing with it into the flames Cosima remarked contemptuously, "Circus tricks!"

"A large woman", wrote Albert von Puttkamer in his book *50 Jahre Bayreuth,* "Ellen Gulbranson possessed a massive voice which overcame with complete ease the greatest exertions from beginning to end and poured forth in glorious brilliance. Though not an actress of any great talent, she had an inward sincerity of expression which was very affecting. Stage affectation of any sort was foreign to her nature. If she thus appeared somewhat amateurish and revealed rather too clearly in many places the directions she had received from Frau Wagner— because she lacked the art of making them a part of herself—her performance gained for that very reason a very consistent style of its own."

Part of Cosima's boldness in her choice of untried singers was certainly due to the knowledge that she had on the conductors' side associates on whom she could rely implicitly. Richter, Levi and Mottl were for years at her side, and for occasional performances two other of Richard Wagner's former associates, Seidl and Fischer, could be called on. Gradually however through retirement, death or other causes these great men began to drop out, and in the early years of the twentieth century only Richter remained. By this time Siegfried Wagner had established himself as a conductor and, though opinions differed about his prowess, he was obviously there to stay.

However, Bayreuth with its now extensive repertoire needed more than two conductors. In the festival of 1904 the new pattern began to emerge. Beside Richter and Siegfried Wagner appear the names of Karl Muck,

Michael Balling and Franz Beidler. The first two of these were destined to dominate the Bayreuth scene for many years. Muck, the protégé of Angelo Neumann, made his first Bayreuth appearance in 1901, when he took over *Parsifal*. From then until 1930, the year in which both Cosima and Siegfried died, he conducted *Parsifal* at every festival and occasionally some of the other works. Muck, undoubtedly one of the foremost musicians of his day, conducted the Boston Symphony Orchestra for several years up to the First World War.

Michael Balling, conductor of both *Parsifal* and the *Ring* from 1904 to 1925, was first associated with Bayreuth as a viola player in the orchestra and then became one of the musical assistants on the stage. It was during this period that he went to New Zealand where, in addition to founding a school of music at Nelson, he did much towards establishing a musical tradition in that still very young country. Later he established ties with England, being chosen to succeed Hans Richter as conductor of the Hallé Orchestra in Manchester.

Franz Beidler, like Balling, came to the conductor's desk after a few seasons as musical assistant at Bayreuth. He also became a member of the Wagner family by marrying Cosima's daughter Isolde. But this was not to save him from family displeasure, which was summed up by Siegfried in a pained letter in which Beidler was accused of caring nothing for the spirit and aims of Bayreuth: he was not even familiar with the collected written works of the composer. With Siegfried's accession to the directorship, Beidler's name disappears from the list of Bayreuth conductors.

The fate of Beidler illustrates vividly the spirit of fanaticism which prevailed in Bayreuth throughout the twenty years of Cosima's directorship. And who can say that it was not at that time a very necessary quality? Even Wagner's immense reputation had not been enough during his lifetime to persuade the opera managers of his day that his works needed a new approach. Once he was dead, having had only scant opportunity to show his ideas in practical form, it may be assumed that even less attention would have been paid to these ideas than ever before, if his widow had not at Bayreuth insisted on the strictest observance.

It was a time at which Wagner's popularity stood at its height, and productions of the later music dramas as well as of the early ones were being made in opera houses all over the world. The direct control of Bayreuth was consequently in a physical sense weakened, and Cosima's only effective method of imposing her will outside its walls lay through her conductors and singers. The number of these who passed at least once through her hands, whether or not they ever took part in a performance at Bayreuth, was immense. Beside the singers already mentioned there were others of equal eminence who appeared in opera houses all over the world, such as Theodor Bertram, Luise Reuss-Belce, Ernestine Schumann-Heink, Erik Schmedes, Emmy Destinn, Karl Perron, Richard Mayr and Frieda Hempel. Some of them may have been critical of Cosima's methods. But, to take just one example, would Jean de Reszke, playing Lohengrin in New York, have felt it quite so necessary to field his Elsa from the footlights if he had not been conscious of the watching eye in Bayreuth thousands of miles away?

Eight

Siegfried Wagner

SIEGFRIED WAGNER was thirty-eight when he took over the directorship of the Festspielhaus from his mother in 1907. The first festival under his direction took place in the following year, when to *Parsifal* and the *Ring* he added *Lohengrin*, which had not been given since 1894. He did not attempt an entirely new production, though he modified certain details in Cosima's very successful presentation, and he himself conducted all five performances.

Siegfried was by this time well versed in festival affairs. He had been assisting his mother in work of ever increasing responsibility over the previous sixteen years. When the *Ring* was produced by Cosima Wagner in 1896 he shared the conducting duties with Richter and Mottl, with whom he had studied conducting extensively beforehand. And in 1901 he had produced *Der Fliegende Holländer*—the first time this work was played in the Festspielhaus. Outside Bayreuth Siegfried was already established as a composer in his own right. By 1907 four of his operas had been performed in major opera houses in Germany with considerable success.

One would have thought that all this would have enabled Siegfried to confute the malicious suggestions that he was simply the small son of a great man. It did not entirely do that, and even today there is a tendency to regard Siegfried as the weak link in the family chain,

sandwiched between a domineering mother, whom he
outlived by only a few months, and an equally strong-
willed wife. Here is an example of the sort of thing that
was written about him: "Richard Wagner had a clear idea
of Siegfried's capabilities. He intended him to become an
architect, since this high art embraces many humble
offices. With concentration and hard work he would be
able to manage a reasonably fitting door, if not a respect-
able window, for windows are difficult. But that Cosima
as mistress of Bayreuth would one day push him forward
as a composer, 'manage' him as an operatic star and by
truly terroristic methods force his stillborn works on German conductors—with such appalling irreverence Wagner
would never in his most sober moments have credited her."

This supreme example of female cattiness, penned by
the German writer Annette Kolb, is obviously directed
less at Siegfried than at Cosima, whom Annette Kolb
hated for reasons of her own. It was a favourite way of
paying back old scores against Cosima in which many
others also indulged: but it is obviously unfair to Siegfried.

No doubt it would have been better for him if he had
shown the independent spirit, which he undoubtedly
possessed, earlier and more clearly. Lilli Lehmann tells
gleefully in her reminiscences of the gaffe of a mutual
friend who once dared to suggest that the young Siegfried
should accept an engagement as a conductor in a small
German opera house in order to learn operatic routine.
This proposal brought the wrath of Wahnfried on the
head of its unfortunate author. The only person who
apparently took it in good part was Siegfried himself.
But he did not follow the proffered advice.

Siegfried was admittedly built on a more modest—and
for that reason more approachably human scale than either
of his parents: he was more tolerant, more liberal, and
his aristocracy, if he had any, was far more artistic than
social. Artistically he knew very well what he wanted, but
he pursued his convictions unobtrusively. His method of
selecting singers, as described by his daughter Friedelind,
reveals much of his character. He abhorred the pomp of

auditions and preferred, when he had heard of a likely
singer, to slip unknown into the opera house at which that
singer was appearing. Then, if not impressed, he could go
away without anyone knowing that he had ever been there.
Albert Schweitzer admired Siegfried deeply. "I have
rarely met anyone so natural, kind and generous-hearted,"
he once wrote. "As a producer he was magnificent. He
took great pains about every detail of the staging as well
as the singing; he could do more than instruct the cast, he
could inspire them. He did not expect more of them than
they could give, but he would try to develop and to
deepen the idea which they themselves had of their parts.
I shall never forget the production of Der Fliegende
Holländer which Siegfried staged and directed. He was a
workmanlike and sensitive conductor who knew how to
carry his instrumentalists along with him."

Another admirer of Siegfried Wagner as a conductor
was Bernard Shaw, who, after hearing him conduct a
concert of Wagner and Liszt in London, spoke of "his rare
combination of insight and innocence and his purity and
delicacy of sentiment, not to mention complete technical
knowledge of his business and a first-rate standard of
orchestral execution".

These tributes from two eminent men who obviously
had no axe to grind sufficiently dispose of any suspicion
that Bayreuth under Siegfried's direction simply kept
going on the impetus given it by his father and his mother.
A clue to his own conception of Bayreuth can be found in
his compositions, in which he applied the technique of
Wagnerian music drama to subjects of humbler scope—
to fairy tales in fact. He was not the only composer to
do so: another Bayreuth assistant of earlier times, Engel-
bert Humperdinck, pursued the same idea and created in
Hänsel und Gretel a Wagnerian fairy tale opera of
inexhaustible skill and charm. Humperdinck of course had
the great advantage that his name was not Wagner even if
his methods were Wagnerian: he did not have to stand
comparison with his own father. Whether he was in fact a
more inspired composer than Siegfried need not be inves-

tigated here. The important point affecting Bayreuth is that Siegfried Wagner wanted to show, both in his compositions and in his productions at Bayreuth, that Richard Wagner was not only a towering genius but also a practical musician who had pointed the way for the future development of opera and had provided in Bayreuth a place where his methods could be studied as well as applied. There was thus a radical difference in the approach of Cosima, who was interested only in the towering genius and concerned to show him to the best advantage, even if she had to dragoon singers and conductors to do it; and the approach of Siegfried, who was more concerned to allow these ideas to develop naturally than to preserve them artificially. To Richard Wagner's famous injunction, *"Kinder, schafft Neues!"* (Do something new), he added his own rider: "But the new things must be better than the old."

It was perhaps a rather cautious statement, quite in keeping with Siegfried's own modest character, but it did not prevent him from being violently attacked by all who regard moderation as a suspect quality. The traditionalists saw every cautious innovation as a betrayal of his father's (or his mother's) trust, whereas the progressives accused him of being tied to his mother's apron-strings. The attacks often showed a curious ignorance of the considerations that moved him. In his early years, for instance, he unwittingly raised a storm when in a letter to a friend he stated that the orchestral conductor at Bayreuth occupied a position secondary to the producer. This was taken as a sign of marked ingratitude on Siegfried's part towards such men as Levi, Richter and Mottl who had taught him all he knew of the art of conducting. But in fact Siegfried had simply been echoing his father's view that producing is a full-time task—a view that had still not gained general acceptance. Siegfried himself again demonstrated the truth of it when he followed his father's example and gave up conducting at Beyreuth—much to the benefit of his producing.

The composer Hans Pfitzner characterized clearly if

not very cordially the nature of Siegfried Wagner's position in his book *Werk und Wiedergabe*, published in 1929: "I do not doubt that the present festival administration is fired by the best and noblest intentions to fulfil its task of preserving Bayreuth. But I doubt very strongly whether it is keeping to the right path. In respect of its scenic obligations it is treading the path of vacillating half-concessions. It does not go to the length, in the fashion of certain Leftist theatres (one cannot nowadays avoid the use of political expressions in discussing art), of stylizing to the point of idiocy, it does not yet build the second act of *Die Walküre* with cubes, but neither does it have the courage consciously and undeterred to keep firmly to the basic demands of the work itself. A part of the press naturally sees to it that this path is not made easy. When Bayreuth brings out sensible, beautiful scenic designs, one can read in newspapers and even in illustrated periodicals that Bayreuth still stands where it was in 1896 and does not move with the times; that Richard Wagner had been 'a child of his own time in the matter of stage directions' and Wagner 'would have done' this or that. I should not care a damn about such judgments if I were the head of Bayreuth."

However, Siegfried Wagner was not made of the stern stuff of which his two sons Wieland and Wolfgang are and presumably Hans Pfitzner (though in the opposite direction) was made. That he regarded his father's writings as sacrosanct is evident from his treatment of his brother-in-law Franz Beidler. Nevertheless, he claimed the priest's right to interpret the canonical laws in the light of later events. Pfitzner's historical purism did not impress him at all. Though he would not go all the way with Appia or the experimenters of his own day, he did adopt the idea of three-dimensional stage sets to replace the painted scenery of his father's and mother's time and extended the back area of the Festspielhaus stage in order to make room for them. He also modernized the lighting system.

One might feel that some of his production ideas verged towards cheapness, such as his device in the third act of

Der Fliegende Holländer of quelling the mockery of the
ghostly crew with a held-up crucifix, or his little quirk in
the third act of *Die Meistersinger* when David, told by
Sachs to shut up shop, pulled the stage curtain across the
cobbler's shop with his own hand: a piece of self-conscious
audience communication which a shocked Hans Pfitzner
described as "like playing a zither solo between the
movements of a Beethoven symphony."

These are of course only minor details, which incidentally found their admirers as well as their detractors. More
important as a sign of independence was Siegfried's
decision in the *Ring* production of 1928 to provide a
separate setting for the Norns in *Götterdämmerung* and to
lower the curtain for the transition to Brünnhilde's rock
—a deliberate flouting of the composer's directions which
was later paralleled by Wieland Wagner in the second act
of his *Lohengrin* production, when he lowered the curtain
to effect a scene change during the dawn transformation
music. Siegfried's innovation met with little support and
was dropped after his death.

If the picture of Siegfried Wagner so far drawn suggests
a very cautious, perhaps even rather uncertain figure,
this must now be corrected by putting it against its
historical background. From a sociological point of view
the First World War represented a change far profounder
than the Second, and Siegfried Wagner's directorship of
Bayreuth falls into two equal halves, one each side of
this dividing line between the old world and the new.
That the transition from Siegfried Wagner to Heinz
Tietjen was not an abrupt one, that in fact Siegfried
Wagner can be said to have paved the way for his own
successor, shows that during his period of management
Bayreuth had kept far nearer to the changing artistic
atmosphere than is generally supposed. The *Tristan und
Isolde* production of 1927 and the *Tannhäuser* of 1930,
both of them associated with Arturo Toscanini as conductor
and with singers such as Melchior, Kipnis and Maria
Müller, belong securely to our own times and cannot be
regarded as museum pieces.

In revealing his capabilities Siegfried Wagner was certainly hampered as much by financial difficulties as he was by family loyalties. In the year 1913 the copyright in Richard Wagner's works expired, and this obviously meant a drastic reduction in financial means. It also meant that the exclusive right to produce *Parsifal* at Bayreuth now rested on an ethical and no longer on a legal basis, and it was of course not long before that broke down. Up to this period, the festival, securely established by Cosima Wagner, was able to finance its own upkeep. But when the outbreak of war in 1914 put an end to all performances it was doubtful indeed whether it would ever be able to open again. During this period Felix Weingartner put forward a proposal that opera houses throughout the world should voluntarily grant a small royalty to Bayreuth on all their performances of Wagner's works. He managed to persuade his own theatre, the Volksoper in Vienna, to take this step. But its example was not widely followed.

Though it has always been insisted that the income derived from the festival does not go to maintain the Wagner family in Bayreuth but is ploughed back into the festival funds, the strain on Siegfried in the war years and immediately after of having not only to maintain his family and the empty Festspielhaus but also to accumulate funds if possible for the reopening was a heavy one. Family expenses were large: not only had Siegfried his mother and his sister Daniela to care for, but he had married Winifred Klindworth-Williams in 1915 and their four children arrived in quick succession during the years 1917 to 1920. Siegfried's main source of income during these years came from his own operas, of which he wrote several while the festival was in abeyance. He also brought out a short autobiography, which makes disappointing reading today, since a large part of it is devoted to a detailed account of a journey made to the Far East when he was in his twenties. This journey was significant only in that it enabled him, away for the first time from the surroundings of Bayreuth and the influence of his mother, to make up his mind about his own future. He decided to abandon his ambition to become an architect and to dedicate his life to composition and to the continuance of the Bayreuth festival. "I must make it quite clear", Siegfried wrote, "that my mother had never directly expressed to me her wish that I should become a musician. She watched my development without any attempt to influence me. Consequently the accusation that I was forced by her into a musical career can only have been made by somebody who did not know her."

Siegfried Wagner always insisted that Cosima, once she had decided to give the management of the festival over to him entirely, made no attempt to influence him in any way. During the pre-war years, however, it is undeniable that he was very conscious of her continual presence in Bayreuth. The somewhat lyrical words of the Austrian writer Hermann Bahr, husband of Anna Bahr-Mildenburg, written in 1911, provide a fair summing up: "For years one has known that he has treated his heritage, the style created by his father and effected by his mother, not as a faithful treasurer but rather in the manner of a gardener to whom tree and bush, mysteriously growing and fulfilling themselves over the years, bring ever new blossoms, ever new fruits."

True though this may have been of the pre-1914 Siegfried, it no longer adequately expresses his attitude in the second part of his directorship. Certainly those permanent qualities of his character—his warm-heartedness, his humour, his loyalty, in general his ability to inspire affection in all with whom he came into contact—helped him greatly in the enormous task of restarting the festival, but from an artistic point of view the Siegfried Wagner of the second phase was virtually a different and more independent one, though one still hampered by financial difficulties, from doing exactly what he wanted.

He managed to restart the festival in 1924 by persuading people to subscribe to a new foundation, and he proved more successful than his father had been in gaining the necessary support. Some five thousand contributions, each valued at one thousand marks, were received, and the donors included the ex-Kaiser, the former king of Bavaria (Ludwig III), King Ferdinand of Bulgaria, the dramatist Gerhard Hauptmann, the conductor Arthur Nikisch and the painter Max Slevogt. The contributions came mainly from within Germany, but there were more than two hundred donors abroad.

The funds thus assembled would under normal circumstances have provided the festival with a healthy capital, but growing inflation in Germany severely diminished its usefulness. Once the necessary repairs and improvements to the Festspielhaus had been carried out and the expenses of rehearsals in the two years preceding the reopening defrayed, Siegfried found himself virtually dependent on box office takings for the continuance of the festival. He had to make use of the pre-war sets for all productions until the festival of 1927, when he brought out his new *Tristan und Isolde.* Yet even this production was in the nature of a stopgap, a cheaper substitute for the planned revival of *Tannhäuser,* which finally reached the stage in 1930. His hopes of eventually doing justice to the *Ring* in particular were not to be fulfilled. In 1930, a few months after his mother's death, he collapsed on the stage during a rehearsal of *Götterdämmerung.* The first performance of his new *Tannhäuser* took place as he lay in hospital, and before the festival of that year ended he was dead.

Though he was sixty when he died the reputation he left behind him was scarcely more than tentative. Force of circumstances rather than lack of ideas can be held responsible. Perhaps a less easy-going, less common-sensical man would have made more of his chances than Siegfried Wagner actually did, but one can doubt whether circumstances, if he had lived longer, would have been any kinder to him in the future than they had been in the past. His liberal views, his scorn for any sort of racial discrimination, his deep conviction that as far as Bayreuth was concerned only artistic considerations counted, would have equipped him poorly to deal with the Nazi regime which was at the time of his death within sight of power.

Lohengrin, 1894: Act II
(painting by Max Brückner)
Original: Richard Wagner-Gedenkstätte, Bayreuth

One cannot know of course what would have happened. Siegfried, for all his liberalism, shared the Wahnfried philosophy of German supremacy. Hitler, as a close friend of his young wife Winifred, was a frequent guest in his house, and there is no evidence that Siegfried disapproved of him. Equally there is no evidence that Siegfried realized exactly what Hitler would eventually become or that he, any more than his father, would have approved in practice what seemed good in theory. One knows from a much quoted letter written in the Twenties to a fanatical German nationalist that Siegfried vigorously refused to countenance the idea of excluding Jewish artists from Bayreuth, where for him only artistic rules applied. However, this is less a proof of political conscience than an indication of complete indifference towards politics.

Anna Bahr-Mildenburg paints a sympathetic picture of Siegfried, dressed in his knee-breeches and yellow stockings, coming to the door of the Festspielhaus to summon his singers to rehearsal with a clap of the hands and the cheerful call, "Come along, children, it's time." He wrote out the daily rehearsal schedule in his own hand on a blackboard and would embellish it with facetious remarks such as "Unfortunately the orchestra has a day off yet again", and perhaps a plea for help in the recovery of his lost umbrella. But in rehearsal, Anna Bahr-Mildenburg tells us, he worked harder than anybody, with complete dedication. And when during the breaks he went outside to eat his sandwiches, his sister Eva would be at his side to see that in his mood of preoccupation he did not bolt them.

It is an intimate domestic picture, recalling the happy dedicated days of Richard Wagner and his artists on the eve of the very first festival, a return to relaxed informality after the rarified religious atmosphere of Cosima. With Siegfried's death the idyll vanished, but one feels that it must have vanished even if he had lived on, since it was quite out of tune with the grim fervour of the Nazi days.

There remains the memory of a warmhearted and very talented man whose innate modesty prevented him from pushing himself forward and whose self-effacement obscured the actual size of his achievement. As a composer he was certainly nowhere near the equal of his father, though that is not to say that his thirteen operas, for which he wrote the texts himself, are negligible. However, even in his own consciousness, composing seems to have been a secondary occupation. His main duty was to his father's creation, and he accepted it without complaint.

Writing in his reminiscences of Cosima's breakdown in health in 1906, he remarks, "Trustfully this incomparably great woman laid her office in my hands. In this moment, as once before when I first stood at the conductor's desk in the Festspielhaus, I was clearly conscious of a higher power at work and I felt how fortunate I was to have been born into the world with a mission to fulfil. Siegfried was the name my parents gave me. Well, I have smashed no anvils, killed no dragons and waded through no seas of flame. All the same, I hope to have been not unworthy of my name, for at least I am not given to fear."

There was much else in his operatic namesake that Siegfried Wagner was not, and perhaps for that very reason he seems all the more human and endearing. One is tempted to suggest that his parents would have been nearer the mark if they had named him Siegmund, with whom he had both in character and destiny more in common—except that, unlike Siegmund, he was not given to the weakness of self-pity.

Nine

Siegfried's Assistants

THE first period of Siegfried Wagner's directorship up to 1914 was to all intents and purposes, as already pointed out, an almost imperceptible continuation of Cosima Wagner's regime. Though Cosima herself was no longer active, she had in Luise Reuss-Belce a successor fully versed in her methods. For Luise Reuss-Belce, still in the middle of her distinguished singing career (she continued to sing Fricka at Bayreuth until 1912) the new post of dramatic coach was created in 1908. She held it until 1933, when it was abolished. In this long period all singers at Bayreuth passed through her hands, to be drilled in the art of movement and dramatic interpretation. She was active not only in Bayreuth but also in Berlin and Dresden, where she passed on her methods to a large body of singers besides those who actually appeared on the stage of the Festspielhaus.

Although in this first period Siegfried used the existing stage sets with only very slight modification, he did not stick slavishly to the established production pattern. Puttkamer describes the performances of *Lohengrin* in the festivals of 1908 and 1909 as "possibly the greatest yet achieved at Bayreuth". He goes on, "During the prayer (in Act One) Siegfried Wagner produced something quite new. The king did not place himself in the usual way in front of the prompt-box, Elsa and Lohengrin to his left, Telramund and Ortrud to his right, everything tidily according to the old operatic plan. In place of that we were shown to the left of the stage an old sacrificial stone, crowned with a cross as a sign of the triumph of Christianity over the heathen customs represented by Ortrud. Facing this and kneeling down before it, the king sang his prayer, all the participants in the scene singing into the wings. Thus the whole scene gave the impression of an exciting dramatic episode, all operatic effect being obliterated."

Puttkamer describes Alfred von Bary, who sang Lohengrin, as comparable only to the most distinguished of his Wagnerian predecessors, Schnorr von Carolsfeld (the original Tristan) and Albert Niemann (the first Siegmund). Bary, a discovery of Nikisch, had already made a great impression in Cosima's day with his Parsifal and Siegmund and above all with his Tristan, and he remained the foremost heroic tenor at Bayreuth, singing all these roles and also Siegfried, until 1914. He retired from the stage in 1918 and returned to his former profession as doctor of medicine.

In the cast of that much praised *Lohengrin* of 1908–9 appear the names of three Americans: Gertrude Rennyson, who sang Elsa, also sang small roles in *Parsifal* and the *Ring* in 1909 and 1911; Edyth Walker (Ortrud) sang Kundry in 1908; and Allen Hinckley (King Heinrich) sang Hagen in 1906 and Hunding in 1908.

The 1909 performances of *Lohengrin* are also interesting for marking the return to Bayreuth of Anna Bahr-Mildenburg. In spite of her close association with both Cosima and Siegfried Wagner this great Viennese singer appeared in only two roles at Bayreuth: as Kundry in 1897 and again from 1911 to 1914 and as Ortrud in 1909. Anna Bahr-Mildenburg, who learned her Wagner under Gustav Mahler (another great Wagnerian who in fact never conducted at Bayreuth), did not accept the Bayreuth teaching entirely without protest. She prepared her own costume for Kundry's seduction scene, feeling that the red costume offered her at Bayreuth was out of keeping with the purpose of the scene. Her conception of the character of Kundry seems in fact greatly in advance of her time. This scene, she wrote in her reminiscences, deals with "a seduction of truly demonic force, supernaturally enlarged. Not a banal seduction with obvious sensual weapons, but a purely spiritual seduction working on the man's deepest and purest feelings. And for that the burning red of the usual stage demonism seems to me to be quite wrong, though or perhaps in fact just because it is exactly what the public expects."

In the field of dramatic sopranos Siegfried Wagner had for Brünnhilde the great Ellen Gulbranson. For Sieglinde and as an alternative Kundry he had the American-born singer Minnie Saltzmann-Stevens, who was a pupil of Jean de Reszke and with her wide range of three and a half octaves was a celebrated exponent of the dramatic roles, singing Brünnhilde and Isolde at Covent Garden and in other opera houses throughout the world.

Cosima Wagner's great Wotan, the Dutch singer Theodon Bertram (who succeeded the disgraced van Rooy), had taken his own life in Bayreuth in the year before Siegfried Wagner's first festival, but in Walter Soomer a successor was found whom Kurt Mey, in his reminiscences, describes as the ideal Wotan. "Dominating the other gods even in size," he writes, "he possesses a voice of which one could praise equally the power, the range, the suppleness and the beauty. And in addition Soomer is a quite exceptionally talented actor ... In *Die Walküre* he is at his height. Here we see the profoundly tragic nature of Wotan's character; here we realize that the great Wotan scene in the second act is the core of the whole *Ring* tragedy." Soomer, who was the sole Wotan at Bayreuth between the years 1908 and 1914, was only thirty when he took on the role. In Siegfried Wagner's first period he also sang Amfortas and Hans Sachs and returned in 1924 and 1925 to sing Hagen and Gurnemanz.

Another discovery of Siegfried's first period was Heinrich Schultz, who was chosen to be the successor of the famous Fritz Friedrichs in the role of Beckmesser. Schultz was quite unknown as a singer until he was discovered

in Weimar and coached carefully before making his Bayreuth debut. Beckmesser was the only role in which he
sang at Bayreuth, but he sang all performances between
the years 1911 and 1925.

On the orchestral and technical side Siegfried Wagner
took over almost everything from Cosima. The conductor's
duties he shared himself with Richter, Muck and Balling.
As technical director Friedrich Kranich, who had taken
over from Fritz Brandt in 1886, continued in charge of
stage machinery. The invaluable Julius Kniese had died
in 1905 and was replaced during Cosima's last festival by
Karl Müller as chief coach and as chorus master by Hugo
Rüdel, whose Bayreuth career was to last until 1934.
Even today the chorus still rehearses in the building to
one side of the Festspielhaus which is known as Rüdels-
heim, and in which the paternally strict Rüdel not only
trained his choruses but also lived. The building serves
during festivals nowadays as a restaurant.

Cosima's retirement gave an opportunity to Siegfried's
half-sister Daniela. "For costumes," Siegfried said, "I
need Lulu [Lulu was the family name for Daniela]. I have
nobody else with anything approaching her taste." He
had in fact his sister Isolde, who had been in charge of
the wardrobe in Cosima's day and whose "bold genius",
as Daniela once modestly wrote, "I shall never achieve."
But between Siegfried and Isolde there was a coolness
arising from his disapproval of her husband Franz Beidler,
to whom as a good wife she remained loyal. Daniela,
whom Weingartner described as "vivacious and intelligent", seems to have inherited the volatile temperament
of her father, Hans von Bülow, whom in later life she
came much to resemble. Also in character she was the
same mixture of forcefulness and vulnerability.

She began her work modestly enough, as she confessed
in a letter to a friend published in the *Bayreuther Festspielführer* of 1931. "Very hesitant at first, I altered nothing of
what was in existence and simply tried to modify certain
details. That included an attempt, unfortunately in vain,
to force another hair shade—a blonde Frisian one—on a

very famous singer who was playing Ortrud. For the years
1911 and 1912 a production of *Die Meistersinger* was
planned. Here I found myself on historical territory and
could base myself on the works of German artists of the
Renaissance period. I faithfully copied portraits of Dürer,
Holbein, Wohlgemuth and others in the cut of the clothes,
colours and hairstyles. Of course I could not follow the
example of the great Duke of Meiningen, who was concerned with the spoken drama and could virtually copy
reality down to the smallest detail. We, however, were
confronted with the music drama of the master, were
therefore in an aesthetically enhanced world of ideas and
had to produce ideal figures. So if you ask me for the
aesthetic basis for my work, seek it in the attempt to
dematerialize the material in order that costume should
also become music in the works of our master. If you ask
me for the ethical basis, without which no work can be
blessed, my answer is service and freedom."

In this pious spirit Daniela created the costumes for all
her brother's new productions: *Die Meistersinger* in 1911,
Der Fliegende Holländer in 1914, *Tristan und Isolde* in
1927 and *Tannhäuser* in 1930.

It was not until the year following the resumption of the
festival in 1924 that Siegfried Wagner made a serious
attempt to replace the flat painted scenery of his father's
and mother's time with solid three-dimensional sets. His
main assistants in this task were the designer Kurt
Söhnlein and Friedrich Kranich the younger, who had
succeeded his father as technical director in 1924.

Söhnlein, who was scenic designer at Schwerin and
subsequently at Hanover, summarized his work in a manu-
script report which lies in the Richard Wagner-Gedenkstätte in Bayreuth. This gives, in spite of its sober
telegraphic style, a clear picture of Siegfried Wagner's
efforts during the six remaining years of his life. In 1924
Söhnlein was a stage assistant at Bayreuth. "During these
weeks the reconstruction of the *Gibichungenhalle* was
carried out according to the plans of Siegfried Wagner
and Friedrich Kranich, by which the former Brückner

decorations were transformed in exactly the previous visual form from canvas flats to fully rounded pillars and beams with a complicated collapse mechanism. At the same time the two main front columns of the old *Grals-tempel* were built up in plastic form... I received my first commission: to work out a new design for Klingsor's tower for 1925... It should reflect Indian motives (India as the home of all magic) in a free style and glitter in strong malevolent colouring." Söhnlein's design was subsequently accepted by Siegfried with some modifications.

At the same time Söhnlein was working with Kranich on a new model for the *Ring*. "Basic idea: three large iron conveyances, each built over with plastic rock forms, which could be put together in many different ways to form the basis for all the rocky scenes in the *Ring*."

During the festival of 1925 plans for *Tannhäuser* were discussed—to be produced in 1927. In the following winter, discussions continued in Hanover, where Kranich and Söhnlein were both now working. "Discussions also about Bayreuth's greatest problem: retention of the hallowed *Parsifal* decorations or renewal? A large part of the daily press was demanding the latter with marked vigour (whereas so modern a painter and so devoted a Bayreuth visitor as Max Slevogt was vigorously on the side of retention). Siegfried Wagner and I together made preliminary sketches, but gave it up with the feeling that we were committing a sacrilege."

In 1926 the reluctant decision was made to drop the plan for *Tannhäuser* in the following year on account of the cost. The less expensive *Tristan und Isolde* was substituted. Siegfried Wagner made repeated visits to Hanover to inspect and discuss the sketches and models.

In 1927, while the *Tristan und Isolde* sets were being built in Bayreuth, Siegfried Wagner suddenly decided to renew the second act of *Parsifal*. "Speedy preparation of white gauze drapes with sewn-on transparent flower petals in changing light... In the same way transformation of the garden to a wasteland as drapes with withered branches. Lastly yet another new *Klingsorturm* in place of that of 1925 which was out of keeping with the new style—more stylized: half rock, half building. Best example of mutual inspiration between Siegfried Wagner and myself (like the old folk song, 'We did not know who wrote the words and who the tune')."

In the 1927 festival the destruction of Valhalla was carried out for the first time as an optical projection, and in 1928 the projection method was used to suggest waves in the first scene of *Rheingold*. Other alterations to the *Ring* scenery were made in these years, including a separate scenic background for the Norns.

In the rest year, plans for *Tannhäuser* were taken up again—to be staged in 1930. "Working out of *Tannhäuser* sketches and models with many improvements on those of 1926 . . . happy to recognize growing maturity as reward for the unavoidable postponement."

In 1929 Söhnlein and Kranich were in Bayreuth to begin construction of the *Tannhäuser* sets. "Frequent meetings with Siegfried Wagner, thereby further planning: 1930 and 1931 *Tannhäuser*, 1932 no festival, 1933 *Lohengrin*. First discussion of ideas for this; in addition frequent mention of the *Parsifal* decoration problem."

On 22 July 1930 *Tannhäuser* was performed for the first time as Siegfried Wagner lay ill in hospital. "Tense and anxious atmosphere. Toscanini in tears at the conductor's desk. On 4 August death of Siegfried Wagner. Three weeks previously he had given me a rough crayon sketch for a very unusual cave for Mime. I immediately turned this into a complete design, which he approved: a legacy for 1931." This design was accepted by Winifred Wagner and Heinz Tietjen and staged in 1931. It was Söhnlein's as well as Siegfried Wagner's last work for Bayreuth.

Söhnlein concludes his report, "The collaboration with Siegfried Wagner—based on unclouded mutual understanding and lit by his warm, constant and friendly personality—gave me the opportunity of helping to cultivate in Bayreuth the technical and stylistic means of a new approach—step by step, in conscientious deliberation and selection, avoiding the fashionable and ephemeral (and in constant awareness of slender means). *Tristan* 1927 and *Tannhäuser* 1930 were cast in a single mould and were highly praised by old Bayreuthers and almost the entire world press. The partial renovations of the *Ring* and *Parsifal*, which were of service to the works in many points of detail, were on the other hand obliged through the mixture of old and new to remain in the tragic shadow of undeniable stylistic inconsistency. This was a temporary necessity due to lack of funds. As such it was ever present in the thoughts and discussions of Siegfried Wagner and myself and kept in view as our most urgent task for the future."

In 1912 Müller had been succeeded as chief musical coach by Karl Kittel, a position he held until 1932. Having begun his Bayreuth career in 1904 as a musical assistant, he spanned in key positions the periods of Cosima, Siegfried and Winifred Wagner, a striking example of the sort of continuity that holds the festival together through all changes of regime.

Kittel, whose descriptions of Cosima Wagner's "Bayreuth style" have been quoted in an earlier chapter, provided in the *Bayreuther Festspielführer* of 1927 an interesting statistical breakdown of the rehearsal schedule at Bayreuth which shows the magnitude of the whole operation. His picture errs in fact on the side of modesty, since in the festival of 1925, with which Kittel deals, there was no new production on hand, and the repertory consisted of only three works, *Parsifal*, the *Ring* and *Die Meistersinger*.

In the period of ten weeks from the middle of June until the end of the festival (Kittel writes) there were 24 stage rehearsals with orchestra, 23 scenery and lighting rehearsals, 47 positioning and acting rehearsals on stage, 79 acting rehearsals with individual artists in rehearsal rooms, 76 piano rehearsals with groups (Mastersingers, Flower Maidens, Valkyries, Rhinemaidens, Norns), 439 musical coachings of soloists (of whom there were 96 to sing the 84 solo parts), 159 coachings of soloists in style and presentation, 23 separate orchestra rehearsals, 16 rehearsals of stage music, 26 rehearsals of the *Parsifal* bells and the *Rheingold* anvils, an unspecified number of chorus rehearsals and 15 rehearsals of the children's chorus.

The full stage rehearsals, the orchestra rehearsals and some of the piano rehearsals with groups were taken by the three principal conductors, Muck, Balling and Kaehler. Siegfried Wagner took the scenery and lighting rehearsals, the positioning and acting rehearsals on stage and the acting rehearsals with individual artists (assisted in these last by Luise Reuss-Belce). Rüdel took the chorus rehearsals and Kittel the coachings in style and presentation as well as some of the piano rehearsals with groups. All remaining rehearsals were supervised by the various musical and technical assistants.

The heavy schedule of sole coachings in 1925 was certainly due in part to the fact that Siegfried Wagner was obliged, after the ten-year gap caused by the war, to find and train new singers for almost all the important roles. None of the great singers of the pre-war period—Soomer, Gulbranson, Saltzmann-Stevens, Bary—were available for the main roles. In fact only three important soloists were able to take up where they had left off in 1914: Eduard Habich (Alberich from 1911 to 1931), Heinrich Schultz (Beckmesser) and Lilli Hafgren-Waag (Eva).

Substitutes were not always found immediately. The Wotan of 1924 was Karl Braun, who had indeed sung important roles from 1906 onwards (including Hagen and Gurnemanz) and continued to sing them until 1931—an unparalleled case of long service. But it was not until the following year that the great Wotan of the Twenties emerged in Friedrich Schorr, who continued to sing the role until 1931, when his career at Bayreuth came to a premature end for political reasons. The Brünnhilde of those two first postwar seasons was the Swedish singer Olga Blomé, the Siegfried Rudolf Ritter, and both of them were highly praised by Puttkamer. But the two names most closely associated with these roles did not emerge

until 1927: Nanny Larsen-Todsen and Lauritz Melchior.
Like so many of her predecessors and successors in the
role of Brünnhilde Nanny Larsen-Todsen was a Scandinavian. Frida Leider writes of her in her reminiscences,
"In her offstage appearance Frau Larsen-Todsen fitted
exactly into the conservative framework of Bayreuth and
seemed at first sight to belong to a bygone time. And so I
was all the more surprised to experience what a great
artist she was. On the stage she was no longer recogniz-
able, her make-up was extremely skilful and in general
effect she could be described as beautiful. Her interpretation [of Isolde] was extremely feminine, but it did not
convince me completely, since I objected to her histrionic
gestures."

Frida Leider herself first sang Brünnhilde at Bayreuth
in 1928, alternating with Nanny Larsen-Todsen, and she
relates that she had a hard battle with the heavy armour
which she could hardly lift (in spite of the fact that she,
like Ellen Gulbranson and Nanny Larsen-Todsen, was
physically no weakling). Though Siegfried Wagner
allowed her complete artistic freedom in the role, she
felt after seeing Nanny Larsen-Todsen that she would
have a difficult time to maintain herself against this
heavy background of stylistic tradition. Yet she describes
the 1928 *Parsifal* in which she sang the role of Kundry as
one of the greatest artistic experiences of her life. "Siegfried Wagner demanded in the interpretation of *Parsifal*
absolute obedience to the master's own tradition. He
explained the character of Kundry to me as it had been
passed on to him from his father and his mother and
succeeded in making the complicated figure of Kundry
and her transformation clear without forgetting the practical demands of her realization on the stage. I was very
happy about our work together, for now Kundry began
for the first time to take shape inside me as a unified
character."

Though one might have thought that by now the understanding of Wagnerian interpretation would be widespread, Frida Leider makes it clear in her autobiography

that standards outside Bayreuth were casual, to say the least—little if at all better than in the days of the composer himself. Her first appearance on the operatic stage was in 1915 at Halle, where she was engaged to sing Venus in *Tannhäuser* without having had any dramatic training whatsoever. This was followed by a guest appearance at Nuremberg as Brünnhilde in *Die Walküre*, for which no full rehearsal was provided. And at a performance of *Siegfried* in Rostock she saw her Siegfried literally for the first time when she opened her eyes on the stage in the third act.

Obviously productions thrown together in this way could not be more than purely routine affairs, and it is not surprising that most singers made do with a few perfunctory gestures learned at first or second hand from Bayreuth to carry them through. It has been often claimed that Cosima Wagner's "Bayreuth style" had an inhibiting effect on Wagner performances outside as well as inside the Festspielhaus. But on Frida Leider's evidence one hesitates to think what performances outside Bayreuth would have been like without some stylistic guidance from the centre.

A singer who really cared about interpretation could of course find valuable help in opera houses elsewhere, as Frida Leider herself did, sacrificing immediate fame to conscientious study. In Rostock and in Königsberg, where she spent several years, she found such guides as the musicologist Professor Golther and Luise Reuss-Belce's son. Moving eventually to Hamburg, she found to her dismay an old-fashioned histrionic Wagner style in full swing. But in the ensemble was Alphons Schützendorff-Bellwidt, who had been in Bayreuth in Siegfried Wagner's pre-war period, singing Klingsor and Telramund in the much praised *Lohengrin* of 1909. "He was a rather solitary person, but a highly intelligent actor ... His acting, which was noble in every way and almost without gesture, made a strong impression on me. One day I plucked up courage and asked him what he thought of my Isolde. He acknowledged my vocal capabilities, but felt that I did not yet realize fully Wagner's dramatic intentions.

"At my request he promised to work with me. First of all he explained his own ideas on Wagnerian acting, the first principles of which lay in the harmony and aesthetics of the movements. The final expression—if the gesture were not to remain meaningless—would be conveyed through the music, which must suffuse body and soul like a warm stream. He also taught me to listen closely while my partner was singing, and how to stand with my back to the public—a position which must never suggest disassociation."

Here one sees the true influence of Bayreuth at work, an influence less concerned with outward style than with inward understanding. Even without Bayreuth there would have been—indeed there have been—intelligent people working independently on the realization of Wagner's works, and it is possible that Bayreuth has sometimes stood in their way. But on the other hand intelligent singers, as for example Frida Leider and Alphons Schützendorff-Bellwidt, have found in Bayreuth both inspiration and the freedom to express it.

The Danish singer Lauritz Melchior, described by Frida Leider as the ideal impersonator of Wagnerian heroes and the greatest dramatic tenor of his time, began his Bayreuth career with Siegmund and Parsifal in 1924 and took over the role of Siegfried in 1927. He also sang Tristan in 1930 and 1931. Alternating with him in all these roles were two other accomplished singers, the Norwegian Gunnar Graarud and the German Gotthelf Pistor. In a time unusually rich in good tenors Fritz Wolff, the sole Bayreuth Loge from 1925 to 1941, also sang Parsifal and many smaller roles, and Carl Clewing (a pupil of an early Bayreuth Siegfried and Parsifal, Wilhelm Grüning) sang Parsifal and Stolzing.

Of his pre-war conductors, Siegfried Wagner still had Karl Muck and Michael Balling at his side in 1924. He himself confined his energies to production from then on and appointed as third conductor Willibald Kaehler, who

—like Michael Balling—had worked as a musical assistant in several festivals since 1896. Another newcomer in 1924 was Fritz Busch, then at Dresden, who conducted *Die Meistersinger* and confirmed his reputation, according to Puttkamer, as one of Germany's leading conductors. "I found him best in the second act, in which the orchestra under his direction achieved the subtlety of chamber music." It was Busch's only appearance at Bayreuth: although engaged for the following year, he (to use Puttkamer's words) "left Bayreuth in the lurch a few weeks before rehearsals on grounds of ill-health—something that had never happened before." (One might observe that it has often happened since.) It is clear from Busch's own reminiscences that his illness was a diplomatic one. Fond as he had become of Siegfried Wagner as a man, Busch found the atmosphere of Bayreuth too self-satisfied for his taste.

Balling's death in 1925 at the age of fifty-nine shortly after the festival of that year set Siegfried on the search again for new conductors. He found them in Karl Elmendorff and Franz von Hoesslin, both of whom remained at Bayreuth throughout the period of Winifred Wagner and will therefore come into the story again. So too will Arturo Toscanini, whom Siegfried Wagner engaged to conduct his new *Tannhäuser* production of 1930. It was the first time in the history of Bayreuth that a non-German conductor had been invited to conduct in the Festspielhaus—and the first time that a "star" conductor with a ready-made international reputation appeared there. The other great international names—Richter, Mottl, Muck—built up their reputations on their Bayreuth beginnings.

In his book *My Life of Music*, published in 1938, Sir Henry Wood wrote, "In the old days Bayreuth was the Mecca of all true Wagnerians. To go there was regarded almost as a pilgrimage, for Wagner's traditions held good through the influence of both Cosima and Siegfried Wagner. All that is now gradually disappearing. Everything is commercialized. There must always be a 'star' conductor—Toscanini or Furtwängler—and this famous soprano or that famous tenor. In the old days we never knew who was singing and certainly we never knew who was conducting. The names were not advertised and we had to find out as best we could."

Certainly times had changed, and it could perhaps be said uncharitably that the introduction of "star" conductors (by Siegfried Wagner incidentally, a point that Sir Henry Wood overlooks) showed how far Bayreuth had by now slipped from its original position of self-contained splendour. On the other hand it can equally be claimed that, by abandoning the old incestuous tradition and introducing some fresh blood, Siegfried had done the festival a valuable service. At any rate all who experienced Toscanini's conducting of *Tannhäuser, Tristan und Isolde* and *Parsifal* seem to have felt that the artistic result outweighed the possible damage to the Bayreuth image.

Tannhäuser, 1930: Wartburgtal
(model of design by Kurt Söhnlein)
Original: Richard Wagner-Gedenkstätte, Bayreuth

Ten

Adolphe Appia and Other Experimenters

"WHAT the Swiss scenic artist Adolphe Appia called for in his book *Musik und Inszenierung* and created with his Wagner designs in the first quarter of our present century—the stage of stylized space arising out of the music and out of three-dimensional feeling, his conception of the symbolic power of colour and light in rhythmically controlled space—these are the first steps towards a reform of operatic production which has led logically to the 'new Bayreuth style'."

With these words, printed in a Bayreuth festival publication of 1955, Wagner's grandsons Wieland and Wolfgang proclaimed their indebtedness to a man whom Cosima Wagner had considered wrong-headed and Siegfried Wagner had publicly disowned.

Adolphe Appia first visited Bayreuth as a young man of twenty in 1882. What he saw of Richard Wagner's own production of *Parsifal* disappointed him and Cosima Wagner's production of *Die Meistersinger* in 1888 did nothing to reconcile him. "A living thing is being presented in an atmosphere without life," he wrote, "because on the one hand a means of expression (acting) is exploited exhaustively, while on the other hand the most effective means of expression—light, without which there can be no depth—is ignored. The drama, which is all shadow and light, violent contrasts and infinite shades of meaning, is projected against a monotonous background.

It is not surprising that this horrible discrepancy offends our receptive apparatus, but unfortunately it affects the drama as well, in particular the music, the impact of which is either distorted or weakened by the absence of the corresponding effects of light."

During the years 1891–6 Appia worked out scenic designs for the music dramas and published them with detailed comment in his book *La mise en scène du drame wagnerien*. It is much to the credit of Stewart Houston Chamberlain that he saw the value of Appia's ideas and attempted to interest Cosima Wagner in them. In vain: "Appia does not seem to know", she wrote to Chamberlain, "that the *Ring* was produced here in 1876, and therefore there is nothing more to be discovered in the field of scenery and production. Consequently all that is right in his book is superfluous, since it is in accordance with the directions in the score, and all the rest is wrong to the point of childishness."

Cosima went on in her letter to answer Appia's ideas one by one and in doing so appears much less bigoted than the above quotation might suggest, but nevertheless she made it clear that she would have none of Appia. The most she would allow is that he had some pretensions to being a useful lighting technician. "There is a lot of room for improvement here if intentions are really to be fulfilled, for we now have electric light, though it is still very garish. To carry through transitions, to bring out subtle modifications, for that there is need for a resourceful technician. But Appia must not ask for darkness where the text calls for brightness and vice versa . . ."

Evidence of the immense power that Bayreuth wielded outside its own walls is seen (though in this case in a negative sense) in the fact that Appia, rejected by Bayreuth, was unable to translate his ideas on Wagner into practice until more than a quarter of a century after he had evolved them. By that time, however, he had moved much further—in association with Emile Jaques-Dalcroze—in the direction of abstract art, so that the failure of his production of *Tristan und Isolde* at the Scala Milan (with

Toscanini conducting) in 1923 and the abrupt withdrawal of his *Ring* at Basel in 1924–5 halfway through the cycle owing to a hostile reception cannot be taken as quite such solid evidence of his ineffectualness as the Wagner traditionalists like to claim. In any case Appia's value lies in the books published in the Nineties rather than in his own efforts as a producer. And these books began very early to exercise an influence on producers outside Bayreuth, notably on Alfred Roller in Vienna and Hans Wildermann in Cologne. Growing experimentalism with Wagner's works, all traceable in a greater or lesser degree to Appia, reached its height in the Twenties and even affected Siegfried Wagner in his three-dimensional productions of *Tristan und Isolde* and *Tannhäuser,* though he did not acknowledge his debt to Appia.

The creation of a "living background" such as Appia considered necessary was however more than a matter of three-dimensional stage sets and of the proper application of light and shadow and colour. Appia also dealt at length in his writings with the question of costumes, of positioning and of movement. No detail, however small, escaped his notice. He wrote for instance, "The use of heels in 'primitive' footwear forces our way of walking on persons whom we wish to see as far as possible removed from present-day life ... The heel must be abandoned and sandals given back their simplicity by reducing or even omitting entirely the leg straps."

There is not room here to reproduce all Appia's ideas in detail. One typical example of his approach must be taken to stand for all. Dealing with the third act of *Tristan und Isolde* Appia wrote in 1896:

> Wagner tells us that the action takes place in the garden of a castle in Brittany, neglected through its owner's absence, and he carefully describes this garden as it must have appeared, so to speak, in the eyes of Kurwenal. But, [Appia goes on] the complete drama is contained in the words and in the music, and if we want to reproduce this drama, that is to say to make it

comprehensible through the eye, we must give it a visual shape that conforms to the music as closely as possible.

If we do that, we are forced to admit that there is a huge discrepancy between Wagner's wholly realistic stage picture and the poetic and musical shape of his drama as contained in the score itself. On the one hand Wagner *sees* the third act, this immortal wonder, with the *physical eyes of Kurwenal,* on the other he feels and *experiences* it with the *soul of Tristan.* What of ourselves? Which of these two conceptions have we to follow? Are we to leave this music drama, the poetry and music of this work to make its own effect and present it in a form with which it essentially has nothing to do—in the form which only Kurwenal and the Wagner who wrote the stage directions see it? This is the way it is done on our stages, and we suffer the painful discrepancy of orchestra and singers imparting the real drama truthfully against a background which contradicts and vulgarly denies the words and music we are hearing.

This is completely wrong. What we are here experiencing is the drama of Tristan and, since that is what it is, we want at all costs to see it with Tristan's own eyes. And for this we can regard only the words and music set down in the score as binding.

Words and music tell us this: Tristan on waking does not know where he is. When he is told, he does not understand. The name of the castle, his own property, leaves him completely indifferent. The forlorn melody that woke him gives no means of orientation. When he tries to express what he is feeling he is aware only of a sense of light that disturbs him and causes him pain and a sense of darkness that eludes him and for which he longs. He connects Isolde with both senses, because with his waking Isolde has been brought back to the light of day. In this blinding daylight he must "seek, see and find" her, and yet it is this daylight that—like the menacing torch in the second act—keeps her from him.

When he learns that she is coming, that she is near,

the castle all at once assumes significance for him: it towers above the sea, therefore one can see from it a wide horizon over which the ship bearing Isolde is approaching. In the fever of his desire this idea takes shape in his mind: Tristan, who from his bed of suffering cannot even see the sea, perceives the ship.

Now the melody that woke him speaks to him more clearly than all faces. But the longing remains alive: his fever makes it even sharper, the sunlight keeps it inexorably from going out. There is no possible relief, no possible cure. In a paroxysm of despair Tristan is swept again into incoherence. He loses consciousness. But this time it is not the forlorn melody that wakes him, not the impudent enmity of daylight. From the depth of night a wonderful ray strikes through to him: Isolde is near, Isolde is there.

After the heavenly vision, reality returns. The burning sun, the bleeding wound are now only manifestations of joy: they should flood the castle. She "who shall close his wound for ever" approaches ... her voice is heard ... radiant. Yet to reach her the torch must be extinguished. Tristan sways and falls lifeless into Isolde's arms. The lovely light of day, which had been its greatest illusion, sinks slowly into the sea and casts its last blood-red glimmer like a wreath about the united lovers.

The role of the lighting in this act is thus clearly defined. So long as light is nothing but a symbol of Tristan's suffering, it should not strike him directly. As soon as he grasps the reality of it, however, and is caught up in beatific visions, it should illuminate his countenance. Herein lies the whole purpose of the stage presentation, and this alone should determine the sort of scenery to be used. It is easy enough to see the utter minimum to which a production evolved in this way out of the music drama can confine itself.

One is immediately reminded, in reading this penetrating analysis, of those words of Cosima Wagner to Hermann

Levi about the difficulties of staging *Tristan und Isolde,* "in which the most intricate drama of the soul revealed in the music scarcely allows of a corresponding gesture without absurdity, and scarcely any facial expression can match the power of the music". Her solution was on her own admission a negative one. Yet, though she clearly felt as strongly as Appia the introspection of the Tristan drama, she was not, like him, prepared to make a virtue of necessity and produce it introspectively. Let the actor stand still, she said: at any rate it can do no harm.

Alfred Roller, working with Gustav Mahler at the Vienna State Opera, did not go quite as far as Appia in his production of *Tristan und Isolde* in 1903, and perhaps for that very reason the third act did not live up to the promise of the first and second. Joseph Gregor in his book *Kulturgeschichte der Oper* describes Roller's second act as the most effective—a scene "in which the play of light of the torch and the deep blue night was as unforgettable as the pale sulphurous rays which suffused the horizon after Melot's betrayal." Roller's colleague Oskar Strnad later created a third act which, according to Gregor, "with its huge tree, its view over the wide empty sea and its omission of all architectural details was completely at one with the music."

This insistence on finding the visual form for the music drama within the words and the music rather than in the written stage directions is a feature of all the experimentalists, whether it is Wildermann at Cologne, Ludwig Sievert at Freiburg, Leo Pasetti in Munich or Roller and Strnad in Vienna. One can perhaps say that they saw Wagner's stage directions simply as blueprints of his vision, standing in as much need of interpretation as the written score of the music, which cannot be said to live until it is translated, either in fact or in imagination, into sound. Just as the music is interpreted for the audience by conductor, orchestra and singers, so must the scenic directions be interpreted by the designer.

Obviously scenery in Wagner's works can be presented in a naturalistic or an impressionistic way—possibly even (though this is more doubtful) in an abstract way. Whichever way is chosen, the movements and gestures of the actors must clearly be consistent with it. Mahler, for instance, discouraged his singers from "acting" the music in Cosima Wagner's way and exhorted them to find their inspiration in the broad sweep rather than in the detail of the music—while however insisting on absolute fidelity to the written vocal line. Wagner's own dream was of "dramatic naturalness", of which he must have been thinking when he wrote to his first Siegfried (Georg Unger), "Do not on any account imagine that normal behaviour and stage acting are two separate things which have nothing to do with one another. In my opinion they must be brought together to the greatest possible extent." But he himself found, when it came to the practical point, that this could not be so easily achieved with any but the most talented actors. The aids which he evolved, and Cosima perfected to help the less talented, obviously had to defeat their own purpose by destroying spontaneity.

The methods of Appia were no more conducive to spontaneity. He saw what he called the choreography of a scene as the most difficult part to control, since it was dependent not on machines but on human beings. His advice to the producer was to limit the freedom of the individual actor to the greatest extent compatible with allowing him to express himself, which means in other words to tell him exactly what to do and where to go—a method indistinguishable in effect from that of Cosima Wagner. There seems to be a definite discrepancy here between Wagner's own conception of human character as the mainspring of his drama, with all artistic means used to bring it to expression, and a method which seeks to use character as only one of the means—together with music and scenery—of expressing an undefinable idea: enough of a discrepancy, at any rate, to suggest that whatever Appia and the other experimenters might have done to integrate the background, both visual and aural, of the music dramas they had not achieved the perfect balance of Wagner's imagination.

Human psychology, the art of getting the singer to understand exactly what he is trying to express, was applied to their singers by both Richard and Cosima Wagner—sometimes successfully, sometimes not. But in all cases the effect was minimized by an insistence on tying the actor's expression of a reaction to the music accompanying it. A similar sort of limitation, in accordance with either the music or the scenery, appears to have been applied by all producers—as far as they cared at all about acting as distinct from singing—up to the time of the grandsons Wieland and Wolfgang Wagner, who took the deliberate step of freeing the singer from the need to react in line with anything but his own impulses.

This simple and practical modification of Appia's ideas was a long time in the making. But the delay was not due only to the strength of Bayreuth's example, working, as it was up to the time of Appia's death, in the opposite direction. The stultifying effect of dictatorship relegated all experimentalism within Germany to the realm of degenerate art. What Hitler wanted in his Wagner was the maximum of realistic visual splendour. So Appia and the questions he raised were temporarily forgotten, and at Bayreuth Heinz Tietjen and Emil Preetorius sought their solutions in a completely different way.

Eleven

Winifred Wagner

IT is one of the constant surprises of Bayreuth today
to find the living links with the composer so much
younger than one would really expect. There cannot
be many people able, as Wieland and Wolfgang Wagner
are, to boast a grandfather more than a century older
than themselves. And it is equally surprising to see
Wagner's daughter-in-law Winifred, a large commanding
figure, still very much in evidence at her house in the
grounds of Wahnfried, though she no longer takes any
active part in the productions at the Festspielhaus.

Winifred Wagner was born in Hastings in 1897, the
daughter of a Welsh journalist and his half-English, half-
Danish actress wife, and she was christened Winifred
Marjorie Williams. Both father and mother died before she
was two years old. In an article published in a Berlin
periodical in 1933 Winifred Wagner tells the story of her
early years. "Kindergarten and boarding school were the
first stations of my life. Then I was adopted by the
musician Karl Klindworth, with whom Richard Wagner
had been friends since his London stay of 1854. Klindworth, to whose wife I was related [through the Danish
connections of Winifred's mother], brought me to Germany.

"So began—unknown to me—my journey towards
Bayreuth. Klindworth, the pupil of Franz Liszt and 'piano
arranger' of Richard Wagner, was working at the time on

a simplified edition of his piano versions. Daily I was hearing the sounds of Wagner's music and, once I had mastered the German language sufficiently, he began to introduce me methodically to the musical works. This progressed side by side with a thorough school education. . . .

"Karl Klindworth never allowed me during these years to visit an opera house. And so effective was his veto that my first impressions in this field were gained exclusively at Bayreuth. I was seventeen years old before he considered me mature enough to be taken to the dress rehearsals of *Der Fliegende Holländer,* the *Ring* and *Parsifal.* That was in 1914. He introduced me to Wahnfried as his adopted daughter. Every morning I joined in the walks which Cosima Wagner and Klindworth took together. Every day during the first interval I sat at the Wagner's tea table, and it was Siegfried Wagner who with his cheerfulness and kindness helped me to overcome my shyness and awkwardness. At that time the first threads were spun between us: a year later I was Siegfried Wagner's wife."

One cannot help wondering whether Klindworth's careful training and the daily walks and tea parties at Bayreuth had any other purpose than the one to which they did in fact lead: to provide a suitable wife for Siegfried, who was already past forty. The only snag—that Winifred was in fact still a British subject and by this time Britain was at war with Germany—was easily circumvented when Winifred assumed German nationality shortly before her marriage. At this period of her life she bore the Christian name of Senta (one sees how thoroughly Klindworth had done his work), but on marriage she reassumed her English Christian name at Siegfried's own request—a slight indication that Siegfried had not allowed the dynastic Bayreuth atmosphere in which he was brought up to kill his commonsense.

In spite of the great difference in their ages—Siegfried was forty-six at the time of his wedding, his bride eighteen —the marriage proved a happy one. Four children followed in quick succession, and one can assume that Winifred's maternal preoccupations, together with the fact that in the first nine years of her marriage no festival took place at Bayreuth, made her position in Wahnfried tolerable enough. Klindworth's training certainly also played its part in equipping Siegfried's young wife to accept the facts of Siegfried's predominantly female world, in which not only Cosima but also his sisters Daniela and Eva had their say.

Family jealousies were kept at bay as long as Siegfried was alive. But though Winifred took no active part in the running of the festival during her husband's lifetime she was far more than just an anonymous and obedient housewife. Even as a young wife she had a considerable will of her own, which was shown among other things by her warm championship of a young man with radical political ideas named Adolf Hitler, who became a frequent visitor at Wahnfried during the Twenties.

It is not really surprising that the young Hitler should have found acceptance at Bayreuth during the time of his early struggles. From Richard Wagner's own day, ideas of Germanic supremacy had always been in the air there. Curiously they had been fostered by a succession of foreigners, beginning with the Frenchman Gobineau and continuing with the Englishman Stewart Houston Chamberlain. When therefore Siegfried's young English wife introduced an Austrian radical into the circle, there could have been no reason for protest, particularly since the young Hitler possessed not only great personality but also a passionate love for and an expert knowledge of the master's works.

True, the Germanic ideas of Bayreuth moved on a high philosophical plane rather than on the more realistic one of politics, but so also did Adolf Hitler's at that time—or seemed to do so. Certainly he had been involved in a bloody fight in Munich and had been sent to prison for his pains, but there was no sign then that he would ever assume the tremendous power at which he aimed. Thus Siegfried, the most liberal of the Bayreuth group, the man who had firmly refused to allow any racial theories to interfere with his management of the Bayreuth festival,

saw no great danger in his wife's young friend. According
to Winifred Wagner his attitude to Hitler was that of a
benevolent uncle: the young man had some bright ideas
—good luck to him if he could bring them off.

It was perhaps fortunate for Siegfried that he died
before Hitler came to power. It was certainly—but only on
a short and superficial view—fortunate for Bayreuth that
his successor enjoyed Hitler's personal friendship to the
extent that she did. The Hitler of Bayreuth, Winifred
Wagner has since said, was an entirely different person
from the dictator of Germany that the rest of the world
knew. In Wahnfried he could be relaxed and human.

It is very possible that this was so: the family of his
revered Wagner had accepted him for himself in the days
of his obscurity; he saw no reason to be suspicious of their
motives, which could not have been selfish ones in those
difficult early days. And Bayreuth was Germany's greatest
international asset in the cultural field. Under these
circumstances it was obvious that Hitler should regard it
as his own particular care, and not really surprising that
Winifred Wagner should utilize her advantageous position
to the full to keep Bayreuth's special place intact.

However in 1930, when Siegfried Wagner, died, Hitler
had not yet attained to power, and Winifred found herself very much alone. She was the first director of the
festival who had had no direct contact with the composer
and, though possibly as the adopted daughter of Wagner's
valued associate Klindworth she was the next best thing,
Siegfried's surviving sisters did not consider her sufficiently
well equipped to assume the directorship of Bayreuth.
The jealousies which had been kept under during Siegfried's time now came out into the open, and it soon came
to a break between Winifred and her sisters-in-law.

There was of course something to be said for the attitude of Daniela and Eva. Winifred Wagner was only
thirty-three years old; she had taken no direct part in
productions at the Festspielhaus; and she was not a
trained musician. Nor of course was Cosima, but Cosima
had been sustained not only by her direct relationship

with the composer but also by that divine sense of mission which enabled her in the absence of any real contestants simply to take the festival to herself with complete authority.

Winifred Wagner's position was further weakened by jealousies among the artists to whom she had to look for help. The senior conductor, Karl Muck, who had taken part in every single festival since 1901, chose the occasion of Siegfried's death to sever his connection with Bayreuth entirely: it has been said because he disapproved of Winifred Wagner's intention to re-engage Toscanini as a conductor in the following year. It is not an explanation that Winifred Wagner herself accepts. The reason Muck gave her for his withdrawal was that he had begun to feel the weight of his years (he was seventy-one at the time) and, having now fulfilled his pledge to Cosima that he would "see Siegfried through", he felt that he could retire with a clear conscience. It can hardly be considered a very convincing explanation in view of the fact that the sixty-year-old Siegfried had clearly stood in less need of Muck's aid than his inexperienced young widow.

Whatever the real reason Winifred Wagner was faced with the need to replace him, since obviously she needed a strong musical director. Her choice fell on Wilhelm Furtwängler who, though already famous as a Wagnerian conductor, had never before appeared at Bayreuth.

Berta Geissmar, Furtwängler's and later Sir Thomas Beecham's secretary, describes in her book *The Baton and the Jackboot* Furtwängler's first meeting with Winifred Wagner at Wahnfried in the presence of Daniela and Eva. "It was this deep chasm between the two generations in the Wagner family that I felt acutely on that strange evening; and a strange evening it was, spent in the unique atmosphere of Wahnfried, with the two old ladies, symbols of past splendour and greatness: Winifred, the young, energetic trustee and heir to it all, the mother of the coming generation: and Furtwängler, the fervent Wagner adherent, filled with holy determination to do his best and live up to his new task."

Furtwängler's holy determination did not last long. Though in 1931, the first year of Winifred Wagner's sole directorship, both he and Toscanini conducted, trouble arose between them over a memorial concert for Siegfried Wagner, and Toscanini left Bayreuth never to return. And before the next season Furtwängler had himself resigned, giving as his reason in a newspaper article that he was not prepared to take orders in musical matters from a non-musician such as he held Winifred to be.

The following year was the traditional rest year, which gave Winifred a breathing space to reorganize her forces. Not even a personal letter from Hitler, now come to power as Germany's chancellor, could persuade Toscanini to return to Bayreuth and, with Furtwängler also lost to her, Winifred found herself in a dangerously weak position. So, disregarding the fact that Richard Strauss had not been on the best of terms with her husband, she made a personal pilgrimage to Garmisch to invite his participation. To her relief he accepted and thus in 1933 stood again at the conductor's desk in Bayreuth, which he had not occupied since he had conducted Cosima Wagner's production of *Tannhäuser* in 1894.

Of far greater significance than this, however, was Winifred Wagner's decision to appoint Heinz Tietjen, the *Intendant* of the Prussian State theatres, as artistic director of the festival. Siegfried Wagner had much admired his production of *Lohengrin* in Berlin and it was mainly for this reason that his widow invited Tietjen to take over production at Bayreuth—the first non-member of the Wagner family to do so. It was a wise decision on tactical as well as artistic grounds. Not only did Bayreuth gain a producer of the first rank and a capable conductor (Tietjen had been a pupil of Nikisch), but also through him direct access to many leading Wagnerian singers of the day who were members of the Berlin ensemble. It was an important advantage. In the days of Richard and Cosima Wagner the operatic season in the main cities had usually ended in April, so that singers had been able to come to Bayreuth in good time for rehearsals. But in later years the operatic season had tended to go on well into June, so that rehearsal time at Bayreuth became increasingly short. By means of this close association with the Prussian theatres—notably Berlin and Dresden—Bayreuth got the best of both worlds.

The reproach that at this period the Festspielhaus became nothing more than Berlin's summer theatre leaves Winifred Wagner now, as before, unmoved. The productions of the music dramas at Berlin, she maintains, could rather be regarded as preliminary studies, eventually brought to completion in the proper surroundings of Bayreuth. Certainly there can be no doubt that Tietjen with the help of his scenic designer Emil Preetorius brought to the Bayreuth stage of the Thirties productions of surpassing excellence. And Winifred Wagner showed her personal confidence in Tietjen by appointing him legal guardian of her children.

With Tietjen now in full artistic control, Winifred was able to devote herself to administration, acting in addition as a powerful intermediary between the Nazi government and the festival. In the Thirties Bayreuth became a show place of Nazi glory, with Hitler temporarily in residence at Wahnfried during the festivals, with *Führer* receptions in the grounds and swastika flags everywhere. It was this, and Winifred Wagner's unconcealed relish in it, rather than happenings in the Festspielhaus itself, that eventually put the festival under a cloud and made its resumption after the war a matter of such difficulty. If we accept as we certainly can that it was always Winifred Wagner's concern to keep the artistic standards of Bayreuth at the highest possible level, we can still question the wisdom of her method. She chose to use Hitler as an ally against his own party in an effort to keep Bayreuth free from the most flagrant Nazi excesses. If she had had larger vision she would have seen Hitler as ultimately responsible for these excesses and held him and his whole party at arm's length, relying on their sensitivity to world opinion to protect the festival. Whether such a policy would have been effective we cannot of course know and since it did not happen, there is no point in speculating about it. It could not happen because Winifred Wagner genuinely believed in Hitler and his ideas.

The intoxicated atmosphere of those nationalistic times may best be illustrated by quoting two extracts from articles which appeared in the official festival handbook.

"What better examples," we read of *Die Meistersinger* in 1933, "can we find than Walther von Stolzing, the young hero who ardently loves and is ready to use his sword against outward enemies, and Hans Sachs, the warm-hearted sage who also lives and fights—against the enemy inside him, thus carrying off the noblest victory that we know: the victory over himself. The man who conceived these figures once said, 'When I entered with full knowledge on the course I had chosen for myself I wrote on my flag: with Germany to stand or fall!' Germans, hear the voice of our master: love and—fight! Then—with him—you will not fall, but stand!"

Even the conductor had his part to play in the great bid for German supremacy. "The conductor," we are told in 1938 in a portentous article entitled 'Richard Wagner and the German Conductor of Today', "who does not feel that the art of our master is the art of the present in its noblest sense, because it points to the future; because it teaches us hardness in the figure of Lohengrin, who scorns to cultivate sweet repose and proclaims the blessing of an exalted calling; because with Hans Sachs it teaches us to plant the roots of art in the German people and to honour all things German; because it teaches us like Siegfried to perform the liberating act without thought of the reward; because it brings to our consciousness with unexampled clarity in the *Ring* the terrible seriousness of the racial problem; because from the start to the finish it sings the praises of Woman; because finally it shows us in *Parsifal* the only religion that a German can embrace, namely, that of struggle towards a life made divine; whatever conductor, I say, does not feel all this within his heart would do better not to raise his baton in German lands."

One may wonder how it is possible for a conductor to

suggest the terrible seriousness of the racial problem through the medium of his baton, whatever the state of his feelings. However, though it may not be possible to put such inspired idiocy into practice, it is also not possible to stop people thinking in such terms and imagining that this is what they are experiencing. Perhaps this was a part of the price that Bayreuth felt it was tactful to pay to keep the Nazi party officials sweet. If so, it certainly did Wagner no service.

On a purely material plane Hitler's support meant much to Bayreuth. He was in fact the first head of the German state ever to take an active interest in the festival. After the death of Ludwig II Bayreuth had enjoyed no royal or state patronage and had been obliged to look to private people for financial support. Hitler not only granted the festival a yearly sum of fifty thousand marks from his own private funds but also granted it tax exemption. His personal deference to Winifred Wagner's wishes was also responsible for the fact that a number of singers of Jewish extraction or with Jewish connections continued to sing in Bayreuth for a few years after Jewish artists had been banned elsewhere.

Neither Hitler nor Winifred Wagner could however influence the feelings of the singers themselves, who found as little pleasure in being allowed to sing at Bayreuth as in seeing many of their so-called Aryan colleagues making use of their political connections to further their own ends. Gradually eminent singers began to drop out—not only the Jewish or the Jewish-connected ones, but also others who disapproved of racial discrimination in any shape or form.

This is not to say that those who remained were all supporters of Hitler or that the audiences that came to hear them were all imbued with the spirit of Nazism. But certainly in these years the audience became for the first time a predominantly German one.

There is deep irony in the fact that it was in Nazi times that Bayreuth came closest to Richard Wagner's original conception of a theatre for the German people, though one likes to feel that he would have noted and deplored the hollowness that lay beneath the outward show. Hitler was of course genuinely devoted to Wagner's music, drunk on it, in the same way that the young King Ludwig had been, but with none of Ludwig's sense of humility. In the intimate make-believe world that he created with the composer, Ludwig identified himself with Parsifal, the humblest of all Wagner's heroes. Hitler, one feels, saw himself unquestionably as Wotan—and was Wotan in the sense that he sowed with his own hand the seeds of his undoing. If he had understood his Wagner as well as he knew it he would have foreseen to what inevitable twilight his acts were leading him.

The outbreak of the Second World War did not put an end to the festival as the First World War had done, but it continued in a reduced form with no new productions and with audiences comprised of workers and members of the forces who were given tickets and a period of leave to attend the performances. After 1939 *Parsifal* was dropped: one suspects because its Christian message was felt to be out of keeping with the times. The *Ring* was rather more suitable if one did not look too deeply into it, and *Die Meistersinger* even better as a manifestation of the true Germanic spirit. Does not Hans Sachs himself proclaim it with his words *Was deutsch und echt, wüsst' keiner mehr, lebt's nicht in deutscher Meister Ehr'* ("What is German and true none would know, were it not embedded in the honour of German masters")?

Whether Sachs meant it in quite the same way that his wartime audiences were expected to take it is a question to which we shall return in a later chapter. But, however that may be, *Die Meistersinger* held the stage alone in the last two festivals of 1943 and 1944, and it was with those defiant words of Sachs that the Festspielhaus fell silent until Winifred Wagner's sons opened it again in a very different political context seven years later.

Twelve

The Productions of Tietjen and Preetorius

OR most people under the age of sixty the old Bayreuth with which they compare the new is the Bayreuth of Winifred Wagner and the productions are those of Heinz Tietjen, who between the years 1933 and 1939 staged anew all the works with the exception of *Tannhäuser.* The sets and costumes for all but *Parsifal* were done by Emil Preetorius. *Parsifal* in 1934 was designed by the great Alfred Roller, who together with Gustav Mahler had evolved those productions of the music dramas in Vienna which might be regarded as the most formidable rivals to the Bayreuth productions of Cosima and Siegfried Wagner. Roller's sets for *Parsifal* at Bayreuth are generally spoken of as unsuccessful, the excuse being made that Roller was already an old and sick man at the time. Whether the criticism was justified or not there is now no means of telling, since sets and costumes were used in only two seasons before being superseded by the first designs of Wieland Wagner, and no pictorial record of them was made. In the opinion of Emil Preetorius, Roller's sets, though not his strongest achievement, were certainly not unworthy of him: the *Gralstempel* in particular was very striking for all its simplicity.

The style of production evolved by Tietjen and Preetorius was not the culmination of the traditional Bayreuth style of Cosima and Siegfried but rather a new style in its own right. The traditional style—already challenged by Siegfried Wagner himself in his *Tannhäuser* of 1930—

lingered on a further year after Siegfried's death and then faded out: the year 1931 was notable for its number of farewell appearances. Of the great Wagnerian singers of Siegfried Wagner's era, Friedrich Schorr (Wotan), Nanny Larsen-Todsen (Brünnhilde and Isolde), Gotthelf Pistor (Siegfried and Tristan) and Eduard Habich (the Alberich since 1911) appeared for the last time.

From 1933 the Bayreuth stage was dominated by a new generation of singers, almost all of them members of the Berlin State Opera of Tietjin, among them Rudolf Bockelmann, Jaro Prohaska, Frida Leider, Margarete Klose, Maria Müller, Marta Fuchs, Max Lorenz, Franz Völker, Ludwig Hofmann, Josef von Manowarda and Herbert Janssen. Neither before nor since in the history of Bayreuth was such continuity over the whole range of leading roles maintained as in the period 1933-9. Certainly there were some notable omissions, due in the main to political causes. Lauritz Melchior, like Toscanini, left Bayreuth in 1931 never to return; Emanuel List played Hagen and Alexander Kipnis played Gurnemanz for the last time in 1933. Frida Leider, the leading Brünnhilde of her day, severed her connection with Bayreuth in 1938 after things had become too difficult for her Jewish husband Rudolf Deman, hitherto protected by an Austrian passport. Herbert Janssen was another whose association with Bayreuth ended when he was in full career in 1937.

Some of the leading singers may have been supporters of the Nazi party, but certainly not all. The main attraction of Bayreuth for them was still its position as the Wagnerian mecca and not as the cultural showpiece of Nazi Germany. It is however notable that in no other period except that of Richard Wagner himself did German singers or at any rate singers permanently resident in Germany so overwhelmingly dominate the Bayreuth stage. The reason was largely political. Appearance at Bayreuth could not carry any political implications for singers who earned their main living in Germany, but it could have repercussions for a foreign singer. Kirsten Flagstad for instance, who accepted Winifred Wagner's invitation to sing a Valkyrie and a Norn in 1933 and Sieglinde and Gutrune in 1934, relates in her memoirs that these appearances led to some ill-feeling against her outside Germany, particularly in the United States, and in consequence she accepted no further engagements in Bayreuth.

It was certainly easier for Toscanini as a foreigner to proclaim his disapproval of the Nazi exploitation of Bayreuth by complete abstention than it was for the German Furtwängler, whose attitude towards the Nazi regime was and still is somewhat unclear, possibly because it was unclear to himself. Anxious as he undoubtedly was to demonstrate the independence of art from politics, he lacked the diplomatic skill of Tietjen in getting his own way without seeming to do so. His incurable German insistence on defining his attitude kept him at constant loggerheads with the Nazi bosses, though for propaganda reasons they were as anxious to retain their leading conductor in Germany as he for artistic reasons was anxious to remain. But Furtwängler made artistic as well as political difficulties for himself through his insistence on being a law unto himself. As we have seen, he fell out with Winifred Wagner at the start through questioning her right to use the powers which she had legitimately inherited in Bayreuth, and he even set his cap at Richard Wagner himself by trying to get the hood over the orchestra pit in the Festspielhaus removed—an attempt that was of course strenuously and successfully resisted. Yet, in spite of all these difficulties, he remained Bayreuth's most eminent conductor in the Thirties, particularly in the years 1936 and 1937, when he conducted the *Ring*, *Parsifal* and *Lohengrin*.

The other conductors during this period were Franz von Hoesslin (who eventually left Germany with his wife, the singer Erna Lilienthal, when she was banned from singing in Germany), Karl Elmendorff and Tietjen himself, with the Italian Victor de Sabata making an isolated appearance as conductor of *Tristan und Isolde* in 1939. Both Hoesslin and Elmendorff were survivors from the period of Siegfried Wagner, having begun their Bayreuth careers in 1927, Hoesslin conducting the *Ring* and Elmendorff *Tristan und Isolde*. Hoesslin, conductor at Mannheim and Berlin, could claim a direct link with Richard Wagner's own day through having been a pupil of Felix Mottl, while Elmendorff was at the time of his call to Bayreuth principal conductor at Munich. He later became musical director at Mannheim and in 1942 in Dresden. Tietjen would undoubtedly have made a more distinguished name for himself as a conductor if he had not overshadowed this side of his talent through his ability as a producer.

In two other important fields continuity with the past was maintained. The chorus master Hugo Rüdel, who had held this post without a break since 1906, remained for three festivals under Winifred Wagner's direction and was succeeded in 1936 by Friedrich Jung. The chief musical coach, Karl Kittel, who had been at Bayreuth since 1912, continued in his post until 1939.

In spite of family jealousies Siegfried Wagner's sisters continued their association with Bayreuth for a short while. Daniela was even invited to produce *Parsifal* in 1933. So on this single occasion Daniela followed in her mother's footsteps, exercising complete authority on the stage under the friendly eye of Tietjen. Her gratification at this tribute to her generation was none the less tinged with a general bitterness, and the Wagner villa Tribschen in Switzerland, to which she and her sister Eva now withdrew, soon became the meeting-ground of all who disapproved of or felt themselves aggrieved by Winifred Wagner's activities in Bayreuth.

Disapproval of Winifred and of Tietjen was concentrated in the main on their political rather than their artistic behaviour. Of Tietjen's first season in 1933 Frida Leider writes, "The *Ring* performances had already been remarkable in Berlin. But the ideal stage and the atmosphere of the Festspielhaus together with the *élite* of Wagner singers, the highly efficient orchestra and the Bayreuth choruses contributed now to performances of the highest quality. At this time the public still streamed to Bayreuth from all corners of the earth: art had not yet become the servant of politics . . . The production of the *Ring* was hailed as an artistic event, and competent judges proclaimed that the music drama had here reached its consummation."

More qualified in her recognition of Tietjen is Friedelind Wagner, Winifred's elder daughter, who writes, "As a stage director I considered him great, although I was sorry when he fell a victim to the lavishness of the Reinhardt school. He was no longer satisfied unless he had at least eight hundred people and a dozen horses milling around on the stage. Comparing his manner with Father's I was finally convinced that many of his productions were too elaborate and a departure from the inner meaning of the music dramas."

Allowing here for a certain prejudice due to personal differences between Friedelind Wagner and Tietjen, we can nevertheless accept the picture of a lavishness in production which is not immediately apparent in the Bayreuth productions of today, although these, in their use of space and light, are lavish too in their own way. It can in fact be shown statistically that in Tietjen's time there was a large increase in the size of the chorus. In 1876 Richard Wagner had twenty-six male singers as Gibichungs in Act Two of *Götterdämmerung*. In Siegfried Wagner's time the number rose to sixty-four. In 1933 Tietjen had a male chorus of one hundred and one. In the period of the grandsons the number has reverted to between seventy and eighty.

This should not of course be taken as a proof that Tietjen suffered from artistic elephantiasis. We can be fairly certain that both Richard and Siegfried Wagner would have employed a larger chorus if they had been able to afford it, though whether it would have been as large as Tietjen's we cannot know. However, it is undeniable that the period of Winifred Wagner was the only one in the history of Bayreuth before or since in which lack of funds did not play too inhibiting a role. Nazi Germany shared the common feature of all dictatorships: a love of ostentation and display. And since Hitler enjoyed his Wagner in splendid array and was prepared to pay for it, Tietjen obviously made full use of his opportunity. There were, of course, limits beyond which one could not go. The suggestion, made in certain Nazi quarters, that swastikas should be painted on the shields of the Gibichungs in *Götterdämmerung* on the grounds that it was an old Germanic sign was rejected out of hand.

In his production of *Die Meistersinger* in 1933 Tietjen began to reveal his divergence from former Bayreuth precepts. The conception of the chorus as a group of individuals was abandoned in favour of a more stylized mass approach with a certain uniformity of costume applied not to the chorus as a whole so much as to different groups within it. Less attention was paid to historical accuracy, more to providing by means of balanced variety a harmonious picture. Realistic detail was subordinated both in scenery and costume to an overall effect that sought its inspiration in the music itself.

The essay *Wagner: Bild und Vision* which Preetorius published in 1949 throws interesting light on the problems involved in producing the music dramas effectively from Tietjen's point of view. Preetorius puts the elements of the music drama in this order of importance: music, vision, text. The designer, in seeking ways of overcoming the scenic problems set in the stage directions, must not lose sight of the composer's basic vision. "For his penetratingly descriptive music Wagner needs a certain nearness to nature which should however not be naturalistic in the literal sense. Thunder and lightning, rainbow, river and moonlight, the flickering of flames, cloud formations, the sound of the sea, sunshine and forest murmurs —all of this must be depicted clearly and with a certain power of illusion; the horse Grane, swan, dove and dragon cannot simply be ignored. Even the reed from which Siegfried fashions his flute is still necessary. Wagner's music needs these natural elements and processes in the same way that it needs words as co-ordinating frame-

Die Walküre, 1933: Act III
(painting by Emil Preetorius)
Original: Richard Wagner-Gedenkstätte, Bayreuth

work to prevent it from losing itself in formlessness."

Preetorius shows in his essay that he is fully alive to the symbolic nature of the music dramas, an aspect which plays an important part in the designer's thinking. "All Wagner's works, not just the late ones such as the *Ring* and *Parsifal*, are conceived as allegories in the widest sense, as depictions of the eternal forces of life. The designer must give full effect to this symbolic character by means of definite, clearly differentiating accents, by means of an overall harmony and contrast of colour, form and mass both in parts and in the whole, in scenery, figures and stage properties. He must exclude all that is of only secondary importance and place his emphasis on the things that carry symbolic weight ... And all the necessary elements must be co-ordinated, must be made subservient to a rhythmically compact overall shape. The essential thing is to create the visual foundations on which another and larger world of supra-realism can unfold itself in effective symbolism. But on no account may one simplify or stylize at will or be diverted into mere suggestiveness or get involved in the abstract. One must always remain fixed on the firm ground of natural truth and concrete image."

No other composer, Preetorius says, has received his creative impulse from the pictorial element to the same extent as Wagner, but, essential as the other elements of the music drama are, it is always the music and particularly the orchestra which carries the main weight of the drama. Thus it is the scenic designer's main consideration to do nothing that will distract attention from the music. "Restraint in execution, simplicity and largeness of form, breadth and clarity of overall construction, avoidance of strong colour contrasts but all the more awareness of differentiating values to create subtle and intermerging mood changes, above all through the medium of light, the element which in its subtle power to change and to create change is of all elements the one most nearly related to sound: these remain at all times the main requirements."

With costumes, too, a balance must be kept between

realism and symbolism. Strong accents must be sparingly used, even in those scenes (for example in *Tannhäuser* and *Lohengrin*) where scenic display and historical detail are demanded.

Preetorius comes to the conclusion that there are particular difficulties in meeting Wagner's scenic demands which are not encountered with Mozart, Gluck or Shakespeare for instance. "The stage setting is an indivisible part of the Wagnerian *Gesamtkunstwerk* and has within this framework to fulfil certain clearly defined functions in relation to the language of music. And in consequence of that, certain scenic demands remain inescapable, the possibility of a fully free embodiment of the visual, of a basically new approach in the direction of simplification, of bare symbolism is only applicable to Wagner to a very limited extent if one is not to obscure the basic idea of his work."

In a volume of essays published in 1953 to mark Preetorius's seventieth birthday Tietjen gives his view of the work they did together. "What we had been tirelessly striving to achieve with the music dramas at both Berlin opera houses since 1925—a scenic renewal that nevertheless remained faithful to the spirit of the works—stood us in good stead when on the death of Siegfried Wagner we were honoured with the task of continuing and building up the work at Bayreuth. We set ourselves in the face of obstinate and often actively hostile resistance, rooted in a narrow and rigid view of a misunderstood 'old tradition', to create a new tradition—one, however, which did not simply throw the old tradition overboard but sought to draw it fruitfully into our efforts of renewal. Both of us, scenic designer and producer, saw light as the basic element in the visual realization of all Wagner's works, and we sought to evolve a stage setting which restricted the use of objects to essentials and gave the main role to the adaptable and highly effective visual instrument of lighting. We did all in our power to improve the technical facilities on this side in particular."

Preetorius's ideas were based, as he has later said, on his own interpretation of Wagner's requirements. When in 1931 he made his first designs for a Wagner work at Bayreuth he had seen neither Siegfried Wagner's *Tannhäuser* production of 1930 nor anything of Roller or Appia. Appia's work, which he came subsequently to know, seemed to him theoretically significant but insufficiently thought out in practical terms of the stage. Preetorius himself, as we have seen, is no enemy of theory, but he is always thoroughly aware of practical considerations. Unawed by the weight of Bayreuth tradition, as Söhnlein had been, he was nevertheless sensitive to the peculiarities of the Bayreuth Festspielhaus—not only to the physical facts of it but also to its unique atmosphere. "Every theatre is a living organism with its own character," he says, "and thus my *Ring* or my *Tristan* looked different according to whether they were designed for Bayreuth, Berlin, Vienna, Milan or Paris, though of course my basic ideas on Wagner production remained throughout the same."

In his essay he sums up these ideas in the following way: "To combine two demands which are a contradiction in terms: symbol and illusion, dream and reality, inner vision and outward nature—to make these things intermingle, to weld them together in one comprehensive scenic whole."

It was a conception which, combined with Tietjen's musicality and love of display and a group of fine voices, produced performances of more sensuous beauty than have probably been seen at Bayreuth either before or since. The philosophical and psychological ideas behind the music dramas, with which Cosima Wagner had once been so deeply concerned, gave way to a more conventionally operatic interpretation, though one of true artistry. Fine and exciting as it was, it cannot be regarded as a full realization of Wagner's intentions, mainly because it allowed the philosophical side insufficient weight.

The Wagner grandsons Wieland and Wolfgang, when they came in 1951 to apply their ideas, restored this aspect to the forefront, thus showing in this matter at least more affinity with their grandmother than with their immediate predecessors.

Thirteen

Wieland and Wolfgang Wagner

WITH the onset of "total war" in 1944 the
Festspielhaus, in common with all German
opera houses, was closed, and it did not reopen
with Wagner performances until 1951. The building itself
was used after the war for performances of another kind,
most strikingly for variety shows for the occupying
American forces—a use of it which is looked on by fervent
Wagnerians as tantamount to desecration, though that is
surely to make no allowance for the blunting of suscepti-
bilities which is an inevitable result of war.

Even after more normal human relations had been
restored the Festspielhaus remained an object of considerable embarrassment. By the terms of Siegfried
Wagner's will it was the sole property of his widow
Winifred, whom a Denazification Court placed in 1947 in
the group of major collaborators with the Nazi regime,
and among other penalties she was forbidden to continue
her work at the Festspielhaus. The penalties were subsequently reduced on appeal, but still there was no
question of allowing Winifred Wagner to reopen the
festival. Various other schemes were considered: to turn
the Festspielhaus into an ordinary opera house for the
town of Bayreuth; to entrust a committee of outside experts (including Ernest Newman and Albert Schweitzer)
with the reopening of the festival; to invite Winifred
Wagner's daughter Friedelind, who had emigrated to
America during the Hitler period, to return. All such

schemes foundered, however, on the incontrovertible legal fact that the Festspielhaus was Winifred Wagner's personal property. The impasse was eventually overcome by Winifred Wagner herself, who relinquished control in favour of her sons Wieland and Wolfgang and withdrew from all personal participation.

The situation at the reopening of the festival in 1951 differed entirely from that at the reopening in 1924. It is true that after the First World War there had been a reaction on political grounds against Wagner. Anti-nationalistic feeling at that time may have given the experimenters their chance to thrive, but in the public mind Bayreuth's position of authority was not seriously endangered. Siegfried Wagner—once he had mastered his financial difficulties—could permit himself to reopen the festival with a production of *Die Meistersiger* dating back to 1912. After the Second World War the reaction against Wagner was far more savage, and it extended—through Hitler's direct association with it—to Bayreuth itself. This time the festival's position of authority *was* disputed—and dangerously. It was unthinkable that the grandsons could, like their father, simply resume the festival where it had left off. The need to dissociate themselves from their immediate predecessors was paramount. But that very fact posed a dangerous problem: if what they did appeared only to be an expedient political gesture, the grandsons would have failed in their bid to restore Bayreuth's artistic authority. In order to re-establish the festival they had to show at the very start that the line they proposed to take was—from an artistic and not just a political point of view—legitimate.

They could of course have chosen to return to the old "Bayreuth style", which they were in a unique position to propagate. Certainly they could have found in the work of their mother and Heinz Tietjen enough divergence from the composer's commands to justify such a step, and they would have won the approval of the purists, of whom there were still a great many about. Instead, they decided to go right back to the works themselves and to Richard

Wagner's writings and to interpret these in their own way for themselves.

With his production of *Parsifal* in 1951 Wieland Wagner proclaimed the direction in which Bayreuth was now to go. No leafy wood and lake for the first scene, but the bare shadow of great tree trunks in a cool grey morning light; no richly decorated temple interior with pillars and cupola, only four plain columns and a bare round table and bench dimly discernible in a vast gloom; no battlements for Klingsor, but a projection of light, white on black, which seemed at first to be a spider's web with Klingsor's head and shoulders brilliantly lit at the centre, but could be rationalized as a round tower up which one looks from the base; no flower garden of bright colours, but a mauve-lit vagueness peopled with graceful fluttering wraiths; no Good Friday meadow-carpet, but a bare desert landscape in which hope seemed lost and only endurance remained; and then back to the sombreness of the great temple, where at the end fulfilment was reached and the darkness yielded to a rich red glowing.

Such a *Parsifal*, or something resembling it in many respects, may have been seen in other places before, but never on a stage as vast or as immediate in impact as Bayreuth, and Wieland Wagner's production made a deep impression. "This was not only the best *Parsifal* that I have ever seen or heard," wrote Ernest Newman in the *Sunday Times*, "but one of the three or four most moving spiritual experiences of my life", and he hailed Wieland Wagner as a young genius who had given Bayreuth a new line of extraordinary potentiality.

There were of course plenty of hostile notices. "What the master's grandson has conjured up for us", one critic wrote, "is a symphony in gloom, a formless play of patterns and shadows which dispenses with individual dramatic relationships, confines itself exclusively to symbols and thereby becomes wearisome. There are unquestionably some moments of beauty and power: the *Gralstempel* for example, which exudes an atmosphere of ghostly mysticism. But with that the scenic beauty is all but done. The vast remainder is a grey monotone. The true scenic designer of *Parsifal* and the *Ring* is the spotlight. It follows the actor anxiously with its thin beam, weaves a weak halo of light around the heads of people whose task it is to present a musical drama and whose movement and acting were formerly considered to be— beside the words they sing—essential means of expression."

In general however Wieland Wagner's *Parsifal* production was received far more calmly than his *Ring*, which he also launched in the opening season. The *Ring* is of course the most politically explosive of all Wagner's works, and apart from that the producer had not succeeded in solving its many scenic problems as effectively as he had solved them in *Parsifal*—not surprisingly in view of the vastness of the work and the many differing levels of experience on which it plays. Probably no one, either in Bayreuth or outside, has ever achieved a completely satisfactory production of the *Ring*, and it was consequently somewhat unfair to attack Wieland Wagner so savagely for having failed at his first attempt to master all its difficulties. His fault lay in the fact that he dealt less radically with the *Ring* than with *Parsifal* and in doing so fell between two stools, earning the disapproval of the traditionalists for his lack of realism and the criticism of his supporters for retaining some realistic details, which seemed all the more out of place in view of the prevailing lack of realism elsewhere in the production.

However, for all its occasional lapses, Wieland Wagner's first *Ring* clearly proclaimed the contemporary Bayreuth style. By freeing himself from naturalism with its inevitable condition of chronological progression, the producer was able to give a unifying shape to the work as a whole. The end of this *Ring* was already apparent in its beginning, where in the second scene of *Rheingold* one became conscious of the circular platform, symbolic of the ring itself, on which the whole action of the cycle was to be played out. Here we saw it in its plain first form and behind it the cinematic projection of a vast Valhalla with

all the ecstatic allure of an impossible dream. It was a
mirage, and mirages are apt to lead to disaster. In the
course of the cycle the symbolic circular platform became
increasingly obscured, as Wotan's own ambition became
increasingly obscured by the unforeseen complications that
beset his way to it. Only at the very end, after all had
perished and the dreamlike projection of Valhalla had
dissolved in flames, did the circle appear once more in its
complete state, alone and empty and bathed in a dim
blue-green light like a ring lying submerged in deep
water. It was a symbol not only of the fatal ring but of the
drama of greedy power come full circle.

One may protest that this is not the drama that Wagner
had in mind—or at any rate not the whole of it. It was a
drama purely of retribution, Wotan the helpless victim of
his own initial unscrupulousness and not the conscious
and willing instrument of his own destruction in favour of
something superior, which we are taught to regard as
Wagner's own conception. Here was no message of hope
but a complete destruction, a world ending. But none the
less it was a valid interpretation and a moral tale which
fitted the mood of its time. One feels that if Hitler had
seen this *Ring* he would perhaps have been unenthusi-
astic but enlightened.

Wieland Wagner's most significant achievement was to
have demonstrated clearly that the *Ring* is as much as
Parsifal a spiritual drama and can achieve only on this
level the unity which makes it a single work and not four
separate ones. Played thus, it becomes simply irrelevant
whether Wotan wears a hat or an eye-shade, whether the
Valkyries are armed or whether Brünnhilde rides a horse
into the flames of Siegfried's funeral pyre. However, all
production problems are not to be solved as simply as
this statement may seem to suggest. There are many
moments in the *Ring* which defy such spiritual treatment,
such as the Nibelheim scene in *Rheingold* with all its
fairy-tale magic of a dwarf turning into a serpent and so
on; Hunding's domestic hearth in *Die Walküre*; and the
forging of the sword and the fight with the dragon in

Wieland Wagner

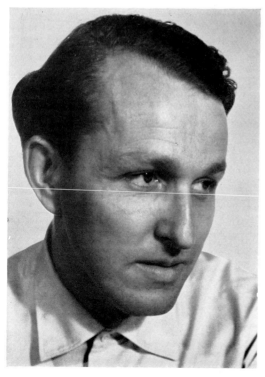

Wolfgang Wagner

Wieland Wagner's production of *Parsifal*: *Klingsorturm*, 1955 (Martha Mödl as Kundry): *Gralstempel*, 1958

Siegfried. There is no way of spiritualizing these or, if there is, the way has not yet been demonstrated. If one demands uniformity of presentation, one must either present the gods in the same framework of realism as the dwarfs, the giants and the humans, as Richard Wagner and all his previous Bayreuth successors did; or one must intellectualize the realistic scenes as best one can. In his 1951 production Wieland Wagner stopped short of this attempt and allowed the realistic scenes to be revealed in all their basic absurdity. He chose in other words the method of contrast, which may possibly be the best way, but is also the most difficult if the unity of the whole is to be preserved intact.

If he failed at this first attempt to achieve complete conviction he accomplished much: the grandeur of Wotan's farewell to Brünnhilde on an all but bare stage; Siegfried's first kiss, delivered seemingly on the bare top of a world inhabited by him and Brünnhilde alone; the gaunt hall of the Gibichungs and Hagen brooding alone in the fading light until nothing could be seen but his white face and a last gleam on the rough wall. These moments, in themselves unforgettable, hinted at a rich field for future exploration.

"The general handling of the action", Ernest Newman wrote in the *Sunday Times* of this *Ring* production, "in combination with the impression of timelessness and space-lessness created by the dim lighting at Bayreuth, did away with the necessity of much of the woeful stuff that currently passes for acting in the Wagner operas. Most of what is required in the way of tracking out subtle psychological nuances is done by the music." Describing the handling of the scene in Act Two of *Götterdämmerung* in which Brünnhilde and Gunther, watched by Hagen, realize that Siegfried has practised a fraud on them, Newman goes on, "There the three remained for some minutes, without movement, without gesture, each of them obviously sunk in silent brooding upon the individual problem now confronting him, while the orchestra poured out its flood of tragic comment upon it all. Here, as in

countless other places, the production showed that the
greatest actor in these Wagnerian dramas is the orchestra;
and for that demonstration, and for all it spared us in the
way of puny human acting, how grateful we were!"

This fine tribute from England's greatest Wagner
specialist, a man whose age might have put him understandably among the old guard, must have given Wieland
Wagner deep satisfaction, not only because it approved,
but also because it showed that Newman had grasped
what the producer was trying to do, namely to allow the
acting role of the orchestra to emerge in its full force.

For the third production of the 1951 festival the grandsons chose *Die Meistersinger*, which shares with the *Ring*
the reputation of being the most politically suspect of
Wagner's works. It was therefore an astute move on their
part—whether deliberate or not—to entrust the production of it to an outsider: to Rudolf Hartmann of Munich,
who staged it in the traditional realistic way. The astute-
ness lay in the fact that, if exception was going to be taken
to the supposedly nationalistic flavour of this favourite
work, the blame could not be laid directly at the grandsons'
door. Furthermore, the traditionalists received a production in which they could delight while the supporters of the
new approach could find evidence of Wieland Wagner's
sober lack of fanaticism in his explicit statement that *Die
Meistersinger*, as Wagner's only historical comedy, could
not be treated in a symbolic way. As we were later to find
out, Wieland Wagner subsequently reversed his opinion,
but in 1951 that was not yet known.

There was yet another advantage in putting on a
traditional production by another hand. "How much
Bayreuth stands in need of a new approach and of experiment", wrote a German critic, "in order to remain
significant and effective was shown by the production of
Die Meistersinger. Excellent as the performance was in
its individual parts, balanced as it was as a whole, there
was nothing exceptional about it and certainly nothing
unique. It was not itself of the stuff of which festivals are
made. This evening of uninhibited playing showed clearly

that only the penetrating, questioning approach and not easy habit can preserve Wagner with all his unanswered questions as an essential living reality."

How large a role political considerations played in the reopening of 1951 and how much was dictated by practical necessity it would be difficult to decide. But undoubtedly the grandsons succeeded in getting the best of both worlds. Whatever they did they were bound to be attacked. Yet with an undoubtedly successful new production of *Parsifal*, with an unripe yet interesting *Ring* and with a fine traditional *Meistersinger*, with which they however were not personally identified, they had managed to show that whatever criticisms could be levelled at them they could not be accused of either irresponsibility or incompetence. And their determination to work in the spirit of their grandfather, if not always in the deed, was emphasized by their decision to include Beethoven's Ninth Symphony in the yearly festival offering—thus reminding us that Wagner chose this work to launch his great enterprise in 1872.

Albert Schweitzer, in an encouraging letter written from Lambarene in Africa, gave the grandsons some advice based on his long acquaintance with Bayreuth. He wrote, "I can still vividly remember the so splendidly simple production of the *Ring* in 1896, which went back to the very first production, and also the *Parsifal* of the Eighties. But one cannot simply reproduce them. A modern audience has other standards through its experience of stage and film. The essential task is to reconcile old and new in the right way. The audience does not see the problem clearly: it makes irreconcilable demands. Even your father, if he were to be directing Bayreuth under the circumstances of today, would be the subject of much controversy.

"If as his friend, and in his spirit, I may be permitted to advise you in the position in which you find yourselves, I would say this: Let people discuss you in speech and in writing. Keep your own counsels. Do not attempt to join in the discussion and to influence them or to justify your-

selves. Go quietly on your way—towards the festivals of
the coming years, endeavouring to be true to the spirit of
Bayreuth and to conserve it as your father did, to give the
Bayreuth tradition a modern profile, making use of the
experience of experts who support Bayreuth. For this last
was something that helped your father to his great
achievements. Go your way in everything in the same
spirit as your father with his quiet and tranquil nature
would do. Then you will be on the right path.

"Answer criticism with achievement. And do not take
notice only of the criticisms but also of that which is
stronger than they are, that is, the feeling of satisfaction
in so many hearts that Bayreuth still goes on under the
direction of the great master's own descendants . . . Bayreuth is not music, but the experience of emotion and
exaltation through ideas above earthly existence, ideas
which have been given form in the dramas of Richard
Wagner. To preserve this heritage in its pure state for the
world, to keep Bayreuth alive as the Bayreuth which it
became—that is the great and difficult task that has been
allotted to you."

At the time of the reopening Wieland Wagner was
thirty-four, Wolfgang thirty-two. They were both married
and the fathers of growing families. In 1941 Wieland had
married Gertrud Reisinger, a friend from the school in
Bayreuth which both attended. Their four children—
Wolf-Siegfried and the three daughters Iris, Nike and
Daphne—were born between the years 1942 and 1946.
Wolfgang married Ellen Drexel in 1943 and their two
children, Eva and Gottfried, were born in 1945 and 1947.
These, together with the five children of Siegfried
Wagner's younger daughter Verena, who herself takes
no part in the running of the festival, make up the strong
contingent of fourth-generation descendants.

In contrast to their grandmother and their father both
Wieland and Wolfgang Wagner had gathered experience
of opera production outside Bayreuth before they assumed
control of the festival. Wieland spent the war years at
Altenburg in the neighbourhood of Leipzig, one of those

former court theatres which in Germany still continue to exist even though the court is gone and the public to be served is small. The advantage of such a small theatre is that the staff has to cope with everything: there is no room for specialization. Wieland Wagner produced a great many works of the general operatic repertoire in Altenburg and he also produced the *Ring*. Here one can see the seed from which his Bayreuth production style was to grow. The existing *Ring* sets at Altenburg had remained unchanged since the beginning of the century. Finding them no longer usable, but being unable during wartime to have new sets made, Wieland Wagner produced the *Ring* on a bare stage—and nobody complained.

His brother Wolfgang, discharged from the German armed forces early in the war after he had been seriously wounded, was taken on by Tietjen at the Berlin State Opera. In this large organization he did not have the opportunities of Wieland at Altenburg to work his way through all aspects of operatic production, but in 1944 he was entrusted with the production of his father's opera *Schwarzschwanenreich*, brought out to mark the seventy-fifth anniversary of Siegfried Wagner's birth. Wieland had also produced another opera by Siegfried Wagner with the Altenburg ensemble to celebrate the same occasion, and his production was played at Bayreuth (though not in the Festspielhaus) while Wolfgang's production was being performed in Berlin.

The division of labour between the grandsons when they took over the control of the festival was based on the recognition that, of the two, Wolfgang was the more practical, and thus from the very first he assumed responsibility for the administrative side of the festival, allowing his elder brother to concentrate on production. It was not until 1953 that Wolfgang found time to produce on the Bayreuth stage. Beginning with *Lohengrin*, he has so far directed *Der Fliegende Holländer*, *Tristan und Isolde* and the *Ring*, the last of which was presented yearly from 1960 to 1964.

Inevitably in these circumstances Wolfgang Wagner

has been overshadowed as a producer by his brother
Wieland, who was able to give all his thoughts to production—not only in Bayreuth but in the months between
festivals in opera houses outside. In Stuttgart, Hamburg
and Cologne, in Brussels, in Copenhagen and elsewhere
he has produced in addition to his grandfather's works
Der Freischütz, Fidelio, Aida, Salome, Wozzeck and *Don
Giovanni.* Wolfgang Wagner's administrative duties on the
other hand keep him tied to Bayreuth all the year round.

As producers, the grandsons have a common approach,
but the results differ to the extent that it would be impossible to mistake the work of one for the work of the other.
Where Wolfgang tends to be functional, Wieland tends
to be visionary. Wieland is a master of movement, in
which his singers and chorus are drilled down to the
smallest detail. Wolfgang's method is less rigorous, with
the result that his productions lack the formal tension of
Wieland's. They are altogether in appearance more austere,
more logical. One feels that, though as sparing in his
visual methods as Wieland and equally addicted to
symbolism, Wolfgang's thinking is still basically realistic.
In his *Ring* production he made use for example of a large
sloping circular platform which could be broken up into
various segments and used to construct each of the scenes
of the cycle in turn. The symbolic significance of the disc
was as clear here as in Wieland Wagner's *Ring* production
of 1951. The perfect circle broken up and distorted and
at the end restored to perfection matched the shape of the
drama exactly, yet the use of its segments to form such
scenes as Hunding's hut, Mime's cave and Gunther's
palace was not always convincing, since they were unrealistic shapes with which to build fundamentally realistic
sets. One could admire the idea and the ingenuity of it
without feeling particularly moved. In Wieland Wagner's
productions a much stronger emotional element helps to
carry one past such doubts. But before examining Wieland
Wagner's production methods in detail it would be as
well to consider the aims of the grandsons in relation to
those of their predecessors at Bayreuth.

Fourteen

The New Bayreuth Style

IT is a strange fact that even at this distance of time
the work of Richard Wagner still arouses the same
spirit of passionate partisanship that it aroused in his
own lifetime. There is little chance of forming a really
objective judgment about the grandsons' production
approach. One is either for it or against it and even today,
after it has held the Bayreuth stage for fourteen years,
there is no lessening of the emotional atmosphere in which
the debate between supporters and opponents is carried
out. We find an opponent, for instance, pouncing on a
sarcastic remark by Wieland Wagner that he had produced *Die Meistersinger* in a particular way in order to
give the critics something to write about and drawing the
conclusion that "the young generation of the Wagner
dynasty seems to think that nothing matters except that
they should remain in the centre of discussion."

All the absurdity is not only on the one side: the
grandsons also have their idolaters, for whom everything
they do is beyond criticism. And since Wieland Wagner
in particular, with the restlessness of his experimental
nature, is constantly trying new approaches in existing as
well as in fresh productions, we get a third group to add
to his outright detractors and his outright supporters:
those who proclaim that he "has gone too far this time"
and hold up as an instance of perfection his previous
production, forgetting that when this was new they had
condemned it also for going too far.

167

It is obviously absurd to suggest (as has been done, apparently in all seriousness) that the logical extension of the grandsons' production method would be a concert performance of the music dramas. If it is, as we shall see, their object to avoid too much visual distraction from the music, they would clearly find no solution in the concert hall, where the sight of a Siegfried in tails and a Brünnhilde in an evening gown would be the most distracting sight of all. In fact it is obvious that the grandsons work with all possible theatrical means—with movement, costume, scenery and lighting, however austerely and nonrealistically they may do it.

Is there anything in the composer's ideas—apart from the fact that he himself chose to work that way—which makes naturalism inevitable? Long before Wieland and Wolfgang Wagner asked this question Appia, Wildermann, Sievert and others had asked it too. However, it is a question that can be authoritatively answered only in Bayreuth, where alone the conditions exist for presenting Wagner's works in the surroundings and atmosphere created especially for them and where any tamperings with the original to fit experimental conceptions are bound to be instantly detected.

Wieland Wagner says that the conviction that naturalism was not the right way came to him when he was seated one day with the orchestra in the mystical chasm and felt the action on the stage before his eyes working against the music with which he was so directly in contact. Wolfgang Wagner puts his feelings in a more reasoning way: he says that people today tend to make far greater use of their eyes than their ears and are therefore more susceptible than formerly to visual distraction; therefore it is important to encourage the ear at the expense of the eye in order to maintain the right balance for Richard Wagner's works.

In seeing Richard Wagner's works as mystery plays—that is to say, works with a definite moral purpose—the grandsons are in no way at odds with the composer. Nobody can seriously maintain that Wagner wanted

Parsifal, 1951: Act III, Scene 1
(photograph of setting by Wieland Wagner)
Photo Antal Kövesdi

simply to supply a lavish entertainment, though as a true man of the theatre he was alive to the need of keeping the attention of the audience and of supplying material for the eye. However, the power of beguiling the eye is not confined to naturalism alone: it can be achieved equally well by more formalized, more stylized, even indeed by abstract methods, though this is a method which, as far as Wagner's works are concerned, the grandsons reject. The composer himself, in choosing the naturalistic approach, was not necessarily guided by the feeling that this was the only possible way. Here, as again today, the existing conditions of the time played their part.

Richard Wagner's own reactions were, as has already been pointed out, against a type of formalism which placed the singer at the centre of attention: he objected to opera being used simply as a vehicle to show off a singer's talents. It was natural therefore that he should turn for ideas to the theatre in Meiningen, which placed the historical accuracy of scenery and costume in the forefront—in other words put the play before the actor. Now that naturalistic methods have fallen out of fashion in the theatre generally, it is much easier than it was in the composer's own time to see where they fall short of Wagner's basic dramatic needs. As Wieland Wagner points out, the important influences in Wagner's work were the classical Greek theatre, Shakespeare and Calderon, and none of these can be described as realistic. How, Wieland Wagner asks, does one set about presenting *The Tempest* realistically? This is perhaps to put the problem too simply, since there are other plays of Shakespeare, notably the histories, which can be presented realistically, just as among Wagner's works *Die Meistersinger* and even *Lohengrin* are historically based and are consequently capable of realistic treatment. Yet it is undeniable that Wagner took from the Greek drama the quality of high moral purpose, from Shakespeare a sense of character and from Calderon the element of religious mystery. And, having got this far, it is reasonable to doubt the relevance of a naturalistic technique to his work as a whole.

Wieland Wagner's arguments would be strong indeed if Wagner's works were purely literary. In fact, they would be almost unanswerable, for in the texts alone one would search practically in vain for any evidence of naturalism. What naturalism there is in the works as written lies in the music, which depicts physical actions in a remarkably straightforward way. And it is this naturalism within the music which argues most strongly for those who favour a naturalistic scenic approach to the music dramas. Yet even Cosima, who had rejected the ideas of Appia, equally rejected the Meiningen method as being (particularly in the matter of costumes) historically too exact for Wagner's essentially timeless dramas. She was clearly as well aware of the psychological nature of the works as are her grandsons, yet felt herself bound to the naturalistic approach (however stylized in essence) by the music. Where fire is musically depicted, fire must be seen; where dwarfs are heard hammering away in Nibelheim, dwarfs with hammers must be seen; and so on. Every gesture depicted in the music must be shown in action. Something of the same approach is also evident in the remark of Emil Preetorius that the natural elements which play such a definite part in Wagner's works must be made visible.

The decision of the grandsons to free singers and scenic designers from slavish imitation of the musical line marks their most radical departure from the methods of their predecessors. They take the view that the orchestra can safely be allowed to play its allotted part unaided and does not need the actor's ostentatious gesture to make the point. To take one obvious example where the naturalistic method must fail in effect: it is impossible, short of supplying them with stilts, to make Fasolt and Fafner real giants in stature and, with the amount they have to do, it would be cruelty to the singers to hamper them with such unwieldy devices. Thus, even in a naturalistic production the size of the giants, in height if not in width, must be taken on trust. That a convincing illusion of giant size can nevertheless be conveyed is due simply to the character of their music, which is as essentially giant's music as Mime's music is dwarf's music. If, however, the giants are made to copy in action the implications of the music, they thereby draw attention to the shortcomings of their physical appearance and defeat the music's object of making them seem larger than they really are. Obviously a producer must make some attempt to differentiate between his gods, giants and dwarfs in visual appearance, since he is working on a stage and not in a concert hall: the problem lies only in the amount of emphasis that is to be given to the ear as distinct from the eye in creating the necessary illusion. Essentially the aim of the grandsons is to apply the composer's plea for an unobtrusive practical background to the action as well as to the scenery.

How much scope for development lies within the stylistic limits of scenery and acting which the grandsons have set themselves? Here we have some guide in the differing productions of the works which have been seen since the reopening in 1951 and in particular in the productions of Wieland Wagner, which are apt to vary in detail from year to year even when the basic conception remains the same.

The most striking improvement, when one looks back on the early post-war productions, has been in the field of lighting. The heavy reliance on the spotlight, picking holes in a generally dark background, has given way to more diffuse lighting of often extraordinary subtlety, and in general the tendency has been away from the original rather wearisome obscurity towards a greater brightness, culminating in a *Tannhäuser* first-act finale, for example, which was one great blaze of scarlet, green and gold. The abandonment of gauzes equally reveals the producer's growing confidence in bringing his at first somewhat muted scenic conceptions out into the open. The early productions, being a matter mainly of shadows, required in fact less scenery than the later, more brightly lit ones. Wieland Wagner describes his scenic policy as one of putting in only what is necessary, rather than one of leaving out what is unnecessary: a very subtle distinction which however makes no difference to the need to provide more for the eye to rest on as the scene becomes brighter.

In a work such as *Tristan und Isolde,* in which the number of human figures on the stage at any one time is few, it has brought him into certain difficulties. In the first, mainly spotlit production of 1952 a remarkable intimacy was achieved on a very bare stage, from which all but the seven solo singers had been banished. The more diffusely lit new production of 1962 not only restored into sight the sailors and Marke's court attendants but had as dominant feature in each act large symbolic constructions of vaguely Celtic implications, representing in the first act the prow of the ship, in the second a monument and in the third the battlements of Tristan's castle. The result was a shift of emphasis from the personal to the philosophical plane.

Without going into the relative merits of either conception, one can see here the scope that is possible within the stylistic limits of the non-realistic approach to Wagner's works. Another instance can be found in the Venusberg scene of *Tannhäuser,* which was set in Wieland Wagner's first production in 1954 within a sort of gigantic shell, the main figures on the stage being anonymous male and female forms which danced a grave *pas de deux* while Venus and Tannhäuser reclined far away in the background. In the second production of 1961 this scene was replaced by a dark cavern, dominated throughout by a Venus clad fully in gold, who sat enthroned at the forefront of the stage and remained motionless from beginning to end. Behind her a huge net was let down from the ceiling, from which a horde of youths emerged, their apparent nakedness and that of the maidens who emerged from the shadows to meet them emphasized by the red light in which they mimed acts of sexual union.

Both versions produced, as they were intended to produce, an erotic effect, but it was in each case a completely different effect. The first was a fascinating dream vision of obsessive sensuality, the second a straightforward depiction of sexual lust. It might be mentioned in passing that this second version featured the famous "black Venus" of the coloured singer Grace Bumbry, which was cited by Wieland Wagner's critics as yet one more example of his anxiety to get himself talked about. In fact the black Venus did no more than show that, once one frees oneself from realism, such matters of outward appearance become almost irrelevant.

The reproach of the traditionalists remains—and it is of course their strongest argument—that the success or otherwise of such interpretative attempts cannot alter the fact that the composer wrote long and detailed stage directions for all of his works and therefore the most successful production will be that in which these stage directions are most nearly realized. But one has only to read for example the stage directions for the closing scene of *Götterdämmerung* with its rising river and crumbling Valhalla to feel that Wagner could not possibly have imagined that all this could be depicted on the stage, and certainly not with the technical resources of his own time. If he pinned his hopes on the technicians of the future, he would have been sorely disappointed. All sorts of devices have been employed on this scene over the years, in the most elaborate of which the machinery has been visible at the expense of the illusion and in the simplest of which actual detail has of necessity been left out. If Wieland Wagner's impressionistic attempt of 1951, described in the previous chapter, had a definite emotional appeal, Wolfgang Wagner's more literal interpretation, involving as it did the dropping of a guillotine-like curtain in the middle of the dissolution process, was one of the least successful. In fact such a scene could be literally realized only in terms of the cinema.

As the grandsons have pointed out, Wagner in his use of the dissolve technique in this and in other scenes such as the second act of *Parsifal* anticipated the cinema, yet they feel it is impossible for a producer to call the cinema to his aid since cinema (which is in essence a less realistic medium than the theatre itself) and direct stage action are demonstrably incompatible. Now that we have entered the era of cinema in the round and are no longer confined to projection on a flat screen giving the illusion of depth and not the actuality, it is perhaps not impossible to envisage a convincing literal interpretation of the *Götterdämmerung* closing scene with living actors against a cinematic background, yet obviously when Wagner wrote his stage directions he could have had no such possibility in mind. It therefore seems reasonable to assume, as the grandsons do, that Wagner wrote his stage directions rather as a help to the reader's imagination than as a practical guide to the producer.

If we admit this right of the grandsons, along with all other producers, to make what they can of the composer's stage directions, we are still confronted with the question of what they actually do. Do the music dramas need stage spectacle to make their full effect? Leaving the stage directions aside, we can still find in Wagner's writings something more explicit than his desire for an unobtrusive practical background: namely, the recognition that, though human actions are his main concern, these must be shown in a natural or characteristic setting. This argument in favour of a naturalistic treatment is somewhat mitigated by the fact that works which are not historically based (*Tristan und Isolde*, the *Ring*, *Parsifal*) cannot by the nature of things be given an authentically realistic background. And we may remember that Wagner deliberately turned away from historical subjects such as *Tannhäuser* and *Lohengrin* in order to deprive producers of the opportunity of indulging in lavish historical reconstructions. From this we can surely conclude that Wagner was as little interested in stage spectacles for their own sake as he would have been in mere abstractions.

The grandsons cannot be accused of dealing in abstractions. However bare their background, however symbolic, it nevertheless makes use of natural objects—shapes of rocks and trees and buildings or the shadows of these. Certainly when the curtain rises on the second act of *Tannhäuser* or *Lohengrin* one misses the thrill of those detailed reconstructions of the Wartburg and the palace precincts, for the functional stage of the grandsons looks drab and uninteresting when it is empty. On the other hand, when it fills up with people its advantages become apparent. Being constructed purely on a functional basis, it allows free movement and also keeps the audience's attention fixed where it belongs: on the actors.

Stylized or impressionistic scenery makes certain demands on the behaviour of the actors, and these demands undoubtedly conflict at times with Wagner's own directions, particularly in relation to the chorus, which he saw as a collection of individuals. Of the second act of *Tannhäuser* he wrote, "The entry of the guests must be so ordered as thoroughly to imitate real life in its noblest, freest forms. Away with the painful regularity of the traditional marching order! The more varied and unconstrained are the groups of incomers, divided into separate knots of friends or relatives, the more attractive will be the effect of the whole entry. Each knight and dame must be greeted with friendly dignity on arrival by the Landgrave and Elisabeth; but naturally there must be no visible pretence of conversation."

Not a trace of "real life in its noblest, freest forms" is discernible in the entry of Wieland Wagner's uniformly clad guests as they move in this scene in slow procession to their appointed places. But one has only to visualize them entering informally, greeting friends, smiling and bowing, to see how ludicrous such behaviour would appear against the given background.

Here something has certainly been abandoned which the composer thought important, but there is compensation to be found in the use to which Wieland Wagner puts his stage chorus and extras. They become in his hands a binding link between the aural and the visual scene, reinforcing the orchestral "chorus" and at the same time forming both moving and static additions to the scenery. The effect is to strengthen the unity of the elements comprising the work as a whole and at the same time to bring into higher relief the dramatic conflict of the main

characters. Since we know this dramatic conflict to have
been the composer's main aim, we might describe this as
an instance of the end justifying the means. The test of its
success or otherwise lies in the ability of the music to
shoulder the extra responsibility that is thus thrown on it,
since the music must now virtually alone convey all the
splendour and variety of mass scenes such as the *Sängerkrieg* in *Tannhäuser* and the wedding procession in *Lohengrin*. That the music at such points is well able to meet its
responsibilities appears to me undeniable. But even those
who may be less convinced will, I think, agree that in
scenes of this sort the music has never been *heard* to
better advantage than in the post-war productions at
Bayreuth.

Whatever they may have done on the scenic side, the
grandsons have fully respected both music and words in
the music dramas from *Rheingold* onwards. Wieland
Wagner has allowed himself small cuts in *Der Fliegende
Holländer* and *Lohengrin,* and his version of *Tannhäuser*
is a synthesis of all the versions which the composer left
behind. Since Wagner considered none of these final,
Wieland Wagner has also felt himself under no obligation
to regard any one of them as sacrosanct. The cut in *Lohengrin* consists of one rather nationalistically flavoured
chorus in the third act.

Of the later works Wieland Wagner regards only *Tristan
und Isolde* as artistically perfect and therefore untouch-
able. In productions of the *Ring* outside Bayreuth he has
sometimes made slight cuts—and remarks wryly that no
one appears to have noticed them. In Bayreuth itself the
grandsons are more circumspect: a sign that, though
they are not prepared to go to the length of regarding the
Festspielhaus as a museum, family tradition still exercises
its power over them.

Their respect for the text, even when it conflicts with
the visual realization, as it must when Wotan wears
neither hat nor eye-shade, when there is no visible Grane
and when Magdalene is a young and spirited girl, is due to
their consciousness that the colour and shape of the

The *Ring*, 1954: *Siegfried*, Act III (Wieland Wagner)

The *Ring*, 1960: *Götterdämmerung*, Act II (Wolfgang Wagner)

Tannhäuser, 1954: Wieland Wagner at rehearsal

words have an inherent musical function which any alteration would destroy. Wieland Wagner feels that Wagner's texts do not stand up to the test of time as his music does, but for that there is no remedy. Since the words cannot be altered, the only solution is to seek the true emotion behind their romantic excess and to use this rather than the words themselves as a practical guide. In the next chapter, based on personal observation of rehearsals, I shall describe how Wieland Wagner deals with this problem in practice.

Fifteen

Wieland Wagner as Producer

WIELAND WAGNER'S first step as a producer is to ensure that the singer has a clear idea of the character he is depicting and understands how this person would react to the situation in which he finds himself. These discussions between producer and singer on the psychological aspects, which take place before rehearsals actually begin, are acknowledged by the singers themselves to be of great value, particularly if they have sung the role in other places before and have thought of it only from the singing point of view. Wieland Wagner, though he has firm ideas of the character as he sees it, is not dogmatic about the means of expressing it. The whole process is one of mutual search for a means of fitting the character to the personality of the singer playing it.

Once producer and singer are agreed on what they want to convey they start to look together for the most effective way of presenting it on the stage. Wieland Wagner has inherited from his grandfather a remarkable acting talent. He can think himself into any part, male or female, and will demonstrate gestures and movements which he feels may convey the required illusion. The singer comments and offers suggestions of his own until at last something emerges with which both can be satisfied. It is a lengthy process of trial and error, and one hardly suited to the scant rehearsal opportunities of a normal opera house.

I watched Wieland Wagner at work throughout re-hearsals of the scene between Ortrud and Telramund at the beginning of Act Two of *Lohengrin*. It is a scene which lasts in performance for fifteen minutes, and Wie-land Wagner spent fourteen hours, spread over several days, in preparing it. The singers were Irene Dalis, who had sung Ortrud before, though not at Bayreuth, and Ramon Vinay, who was singing Telramund for the first time.

The fact that both singers are non-German—Irene Dalis comes from the United States, Ramon Vinay from Chile—gave extra point to Wieland Wagner's highly personal way of dealing with the words. Richard Wagner's poetry is the product of its own time or even earlier, for his style was often deliberately archaic. It is in any case not the German of today, and even a native German finds it sometimes difficult to understand. The non-German singer with a limited knowledge of the language is in an even more perilous position. He can of course consult translations, but as translators are restricted by the need to keep to a set musical line they are not always models of clarity—or even always of good sense. Even more dangerous to the singer than archaisms and occasional obscurities is the nineteenth-century romantic fervour of the verse. It is a style of writing that encourages emotional reactions and flamboyant gestures, all of which are apt to appear ridiculous in this ascetic age of ours.

Since Wieland Wagner's aim is to present the music dramas in a way that is effective according to modern conceptions of behaviour, he has to get into the singer's head not only the sense of what is being said but also the emotional level on which it is expressed. His method, though it may appear outwardly crude, is effective: he simply translates words and reactions into terms of every-day life. In the scene between Ortrud and Telramund he descended at times to terms of vulgar abuse such as modern husbands and wives may hurl at each other in the heat of a domestic quarrel. "You bitch!" Telramund was exhorted to think when he was in fact singing *"Du fürchterliches Weib"* (you terrible woman), and Ortrud, trying to provoke her husband to action, was encouraged to align magic with Communism—a word which in an American of the twentieth century might be expected to arouse the same sort of fury as the word magician in the breast of a God-fearing knight of the Middle Ages.

Ortrud and Telramund are of course the villains of *Lohengrin,* and Wieland Wagner did not attempt, in trying to make them humanly credible, to win sympathy for them. Ortrud is a cold woman, incapable of love (the composer, Wieland Wagner pointed out, called her a political woman); Telramund is a knight of rather limited intelligence, obsessed with the idea of honour. In the scene in the second act Ortrud is intent on regaining their lost power; Telramund cares nothing for power as long as he can regain his knightly reputation. The scene in which they plan their revenge (or rather Ortrud plans, Telramund simply submits) is played before the castle wall. At the beginning of the scene Ortrud and Telramund were placed at either end of this wall. The original pattern of movement envisaged them gradually converging towards the centre and ending up again at each end of the wall, though at opposite ends.

Rehearsals were conducted always with the music (played on a piano), though the singers were not expected to sing with full voice. Since Wieland Wagner disapproves of action echoing the music, it might seem that he could have achieved his aim quicker without a musical accompaniment. But in fact he needs it, not only because it sets the pace at which the action should move, but because it helps the singer consciously to resist the movement which the music urges him to make.

Why should he resist it? Wieland Wagner justifies his objection to what he calls the balletic approach by maintaining that Richard Wagner conceived his music dramas originally in terms of psychology: words and music are the instruments of expression of his psychological ideas, and in consequence the music must follow and not dictate the action. One could question this argument by pointing out that, since Wagner worked in this way, one would expect to find the intended relationship between action and music laid down in the score, and all that a producer need do is to follow the lines which the composer deliberately laid down. This is of course exactly what Cosima Wagner did. However, as we have seen, such meticulous observance runs the danger of defeating its own ends by destroying spontaneity. Wieland Wagner's method, on the other hand, brings certain dramatic advantages. By deliberately discouraging the gesture the music suggests, the producer forces the singer to think about the character he is playing and to interpret it dramatically. The method also allows a much greater flexibility of interpretation. This is a process with which we are more familiar in the theatre where we do not expect, for instance, the Lear of one actor to be exactly like the Lear of another than in the opera house. Such legitimate flexibility of interpretation is permissible in great works of art (it is of course one of the proofs of their greatness) and has been applied to the music dramas with impressive results.

In order to obtain from a singer an interpretation which springs from his own personality, allied with his own view of the character he is playing, the producer must himself be flexible—if not as regards the final goal, at least in the way of reaching it. For a man of such strong ideas Wieland Wagner possesses this quality to an extraordinary degree. Though he had worked out beforehand exactly how he wanted the Ortrud-Telramund scene to unfold, he was always prepared to modify his pattern to suit the feelings of his two singers. First of all he would try to explain why he felt a particular movement or gesture was the right one, not only by translating it into terms of a parallel modern situation, but also by demonstration. Perhaps, however, the gesture did not come naturally to the singer: after a few attempts at imitation he would drop it. Wieland Wagner would then try the opposite course: he would imitate the singer, seeking in his natural gesture a way of conveying the right impression.

Thus with constant repetition, with ideas tried out and discarded, the rehearsal slowly progressed. After a few days nothing at all was left of the original pattern, and so many alternatives had been tried out that one wondered how the singers could possibly remember which was the one currently in favour. Yet after a few more hours of rehearsal a definite form did begin to emerge. It was in complete contrast to the original pattern. Telramund and Ortrud no longer manoeuvred themselves during the scene from one side of the stage to the other: they remained almost completely static and at the end of the scene were in exactly the same positions as at the beginning.

This did not mean that the producer had given up his two singers as a bad job and had decided to let them simply sing and not act. Wieland Wagner explained after the rehearsal that it had taken him some time to realize that Ramon Vinay's very forceful personality emerged best in a static position: movement obscured rather than enhanced the effect. Other singers who had played Telramund had required more movement to make this scene effective, and neither he nor Vinay had immediately seen that this time movement was more a hindrance than a help. This explanation might have appeared a merely tactful excuse if the performance itself had not belied it. The scene, a strong one under any circumstances, emerged with a truly demonic force, and it was abundantly evident that the hours of rehearsal, of experimenting with this idea and that, had had their effect. However much the action may have differed in detail from the original pattern, the basic intention came through intact.

Wieland Wagner's attitude towards scenery can also be illustrated by the Ortrud-Telramund scene. In this production the castle wall before which it is acted consisted of a plain, lightly curved strip without any embellishments beyond a suggestion of stonework construction. Otherwise the stage is bare. As always with Wieland Wagner, there is a strong practical reason behind such scenic conceptions. An elaborate set imposes its own conditions and affects the movement as well as the positioning of the actors.

Wieland Wagner likes to leave himself elbow-room, so that he can obtain different patterns with different singers without having to adapt his set. But there is more behind his thinking than mere practical convenience. He has a horror of the conventional. A gesture or a movement undertaken just because it has always been done that way is for him the unforgivable sin. Every movement on the stage must, to be effective, come straight from the inner conviction of the moment.

It is understandable that Wieland Wagner should guard himself against the conventions of an earlier time which are obviously in conflict with his own style, but in fact he tries to defend himself against his own "clichés" (as he calls them) as well as against those of others. Nothing must be allowed to settle down: everything must be thought out anew every time it arises. It is symptomatic of this restlessness that the *Lohengrin* production that I am using here as an example was already five years old at the time, and this was the last year in which it was to be performed. Wieland Wagner was at the time engaged in a new production of *Tristan und Isolde* and he could have been excused if he had decided to leave his *Lohengrin,* which had been widely praised, exactly as it had been in the previous year. Nevertheless he thought it worth while at that late stage to engage two new singers for the roles of Ortrud and Telramund and to spend fourteen precious hours of rehearsal time with them.

His is the restlessness of the experimenter rather than of the perfectionist. Perfectionism implies a certain narrowness, a clear conception of one's goal and a pre-conceived way of reaching it. In the history of Bayreuth it obviously applies above all to Cosima Wagner. Wieland Wagner certainly uses the methods of a perfectionist: Cosima could not have been a more severe taskmaster than he, yet he always allows scope for his own sudden impulses. Never mind if a new idea which suddenly strikes him during rehearsals makes nonsense of something that has gone before or will come after. With his constant vigilance Wieland Wagner will note the discrepancy and deal with it, either by abandoning the new idea or adapting some of his old ideas to fit in with it.

All this means that Wieland Wagner's rehearsals, particularly in the middle stages, are apt to look chaotic, as Fricke tells us they were apt to look at the same stage in Richard Wagner's rehearsals. Disheartenment is however rare. Wieland Wagner, if he does ever lose his way, never shows any signs of knowing it. And the confidence that he shows in himself is matched by the confidence that his singers show in him. The cordial atmosphere that prevails even when rehearsals are at their most chaotic is due in large measure to his inexhaustible patience and good humour on the stage. This is not to say that he is easygoing. His authority is always complete. But his severity is applied with understanding even when his patience is most sorely tried. In another production I have seen him struggling with a singer who seemed unable to grasp what was required of her or to suggest anything suitable of her own. He could not entirely conceal his inner irritability, though he gave it no conscious outward expression, but patiently discussed the character with the singer, demonstrated movements repeatedly, either in front of her or—an occasional device of his—beside her as she played it. In the final result his persistence was rewarded, for the singer, so wooden in rehearsal, remembered everything in performance.

Inevitably there are times when Wieland Wagner's severity breaks through with some harshness, but such moments—in public at any rate—are reserved for groups rather than for individuals. I have heard him rate the chorus for ragged movement or insist that the brass instruments, after a bout of fluffing, put in some extra practice by themselves. Such outbursts are all the more effective because of their rarity. Wieland Wagner prefers to work in an atmosphere of collegial dedication, and he will strive hard to preserve it when it is threatened by tiredness or by the less tactful intervention of others. At one rehearsal of *Die Meistersinger* the singers were being brought to the point of rebellion by a conductor whose tireless striving for the best equalled the producer's own, but was applied with less respect for individual feelings. The fact that the conductor was invariably right in his objections did not improve the situation: in fact it seemed to make it worse. In this case it was Wieland Wagner who came to the rescue with some light-hearted and soothing remarks. In a subtle way he appeared to place himself among the victims of the conductor's wrath and to alleviate his singers' sufferings by enduring it with them.

Until a late stage acting rehearsals are held without the orchestra, which practises separately in another building. The moment of meeting between singers and conductor can therefore be a perilous one, particularly if the conductor is new to Bayreuth. The singers have up to that point been accompanied on the piano, and the various tempi have been set either by the singer or by the coach at the piano. Wieland Wagner never publicly interferes on the musical side. When the full forces assemble there are bound to be differences concerning the tempi at first, and here Wieland Wagner allows his conductor full authority. This is only logical in view of his axiom that the personality of the performer should be allowed to play a part in the interpretation: what applies to the singer must also logically apply to the conductor. It means in practice that the producer may find it necessary to adapt certain movements to fit the conductor's tempi, and this Wieland Wagner does as a matter of course.

It might seem that such an accommodating attitude on the part of the producer is unlikely to ensure performances of very great authority. In a normal opera house, where contractual obligations make miscastings occasionally inevitable, trouble could of course arise. But for his productions at Bayreuth, Wieland Wagner has his pick of conductors and singers from all over the world, and he is consequently working with people whom he himself has chosen and in whom he has confidence. Sometimes mistakes have been made: a comfortable working relationship has not been established, and in such cases that conductor or singer is not invited again to appear at Bayreuth. This

final weapon of authority, passed on to him by his grand-
parents and his parents, Wieland Wagner wields with a
certain ruthlessness.

The extent of Wieland Wagner's authority is clearly
seen in his handling of large crowd scenes. Though he
works with a bare stage, a minimum of scenery and an
economy of movement, he is acutely conscious of the
importance of the visual element in his productions. In
fact the very simplicity of his means forces him to devote
more attention to grouping and to movement than would
a more ornate and crowded scene, since every detail of it
is visible. His success lies in a meticulous attention to
every component part. He will spend hours on his groupings, surveying them in rehearsal from the middle of the
auditorium and making adjustments through his assistants,
whom he addresses through a microphone. This is merely
a time-saving device: he would prefer, one feels, to do it
all himself, to work directly with each chorus member as
he does with the solo singers, and indeed he makes
frequent excursions to the stage to do so. Either way he
makes it clear to the chorus members that each of them
has something individual to contribute to the production.

This technique he applies even to a scene as necessarily
crowded as the *Festwiese* in the third act of *Die Meistersinger*. I once heard him deliver a lecture to a group of
extras who had placed themselves rather far back in the
wings, where they would scarcely be seen by any of the
audience. Perhaps it would not have mattered very much:
there were so many people on the stage already that the
audience would not have missed them. But Wieland
Wagner would not permit any such laxity. Allowing himself a little more severity than usual, he told the extras
that their place was in sight and not out of it: they had
as much a part to play in the production as anyone else.

In his crowd scenes Wieland Wagner seldom makes use
of exact symmetry. He may start with a symmetrical
conception but in rehearsal, by means of his usual trial
and error method, he makes individual adjustments which
subtly soften the original formality. Chorus members are

required to remember all such deviations from the pattern—no easy matter on a bare unmarked stage. But it makes the tiny role more interesting, both for the audience and for the chorus member, and the extra duty is willingly assumed.

Important as final groupings are, Wieland Wagner regards as equally important the movements that lead up to or dissolve them. This smoothness of development and dissolution is always one of the most striking features of a Wieland Wagner production, and scenes such as the entry of the *Gralsritter* in *Parsifal* and the procession to the church in *Lohengrin* are managed with a simplicity that looks much easier to achieve than it is. Fluidity of this sort is the result of hours of painstaking rehearsal and demands an intense effort of concentration from all participants. It is not only a question of reaching a certain place on the stage but of reaching it at one exact moment. A mistake of positioning or timing on the part of any chorus member or extra is liable to throw out all that follows and upset the carefully thought-out flow. When this happens, Wieland Wagner is liable to lose his temper, as I once saw at a public dress rehearsal of *Tannhäuser*. For most of us the departure of the knights and their ladies from the Wartburg in Act Two had looked acceptable enough, but an angry voice over the microphone brought everything to an abrupt halt. Exhorted vigorously to pay more attention to their job, the chorus members returned sheepishly to their places and made their exit again—this time with a precision that brought no reproaches.

The parade-ground exactitude to which the crowd players are subjected is not so vigorously insisted upon with the solo singers. This is because the producer, more intent on revealing character and remembering no doubt the example of his grandmother Cosima, sees in outward routine a refuge for solo singers equivalent to the wings for the extras. He therefore concentrates his attention more on their minds than their bodies, relying on their understanding to evolve the movement which reveals and convinces.

These two elements, character and movement, can be
regarded as fundamental to Wieland Wagner's method,
and I have dealt with them at length in the belief that
they will remain permanent features of his method, however much he may vary the details of their application.
In discussing his use of scenery and of lighting a certain
caution is necessary, for these are matters in which he has
shown less consistency. His gradual emergence from dim-
ness into light has been indicated in the previous chapter,
and in his 1963 *Meistersinger* he surprised everybody by
throwing overboard all the symbolic ideas with which
he had come to be associated. There was in this action no
doubt an intrinsic artistic purpose, but there was also a
demonstrative one. Changes—whether of detail within an
existing production or within the framework of a different
approach—are evidence of Wieland Wagner's determination never to stand still, but always by the injection of new
ideas to keep himself, his performers and his audience
fresh. The changes from what may have seemed at the time
to be near perfection and the occasional disappointment
that such changes sometimes arouse are the inevitable
price one must pay for the excitement of new experience.
And on the whole one must be grateful for Wieland
Wagner's refusal to rest on his laurels. The "new" Bayreuth style could become as stultifying as the old if it
were allowed to settle down.

Sixteen

Wieland Wagner and Die Meistersinger

THE first Bayreuth *Meistersinger* after the Second World War was a completely conventional production by Rudolf Hartmann. It was approved publicly by Wieland Wagner on the grounds that *Die Meistersinger*, being both historically based and a comedy, stands outside the canon and requires a more realistic approach, as has been already pointed out.

This statement did not prevent Wieland Wagner from bringing out in 1956 *Die Meistersinger* in a new production of his own that swept all the realistic settings aside—the church interior, the Nuremberg street and the festival meadow—and concentrated on the poetic implications of the work, the evocation of a midsummer madness. Within this atmospheric framework he made in successive years some modifications without abandoning the basic conception, which needless to say aroused considerable controversy.

The sharpest criticism was directed against the final scene on the *Festwiese,* in which all popular merrymaking was ruthlessly eliminated. The people of Nuremberg were banished to tribunals ranged in a half-circle round a bare arena in which the song contest took place and in which, before that, the entry of the guilds had been depicted by a solo mime. The tribunals were so constructed that they appeared to be a rounding off of the Festspielhaus auditorium itself, thus drawing the audience

189

into the action—Wagner's own intention fundamentally, though in reverse order.

This sort of formality did what it was intended to do: it brought the music to the forefront and allowed it to bear the main brunt of telling the story, as in the other works of Wagner, and this approach well served the more lyrical parts, particularly in Act Two. But elsewhere the cost was great. The direct visual contrast in the third act —the thrilling transition from the *Tristan*-like introspection of the first scene in Sachs's workshop to the outward-looking brilliance of the *Festwiese*—was lost, and the comedy content of the whole production was low.

There is nothing to be said against playing *Die Meistersinger* once in a while introspectively, for the seriousness that is undoubtedly to be found in it, if only as an antidote against the devastatingly unfunny *buffo* treatment to which it is only too often subjected and in which the serious parts are apt to appear merely sentimental. But no one, and certainly not Wieland Wagner, would claim that such a treatment provides the correct balance at which the composer aimed. Wieland Wagner's first Bayreuth production of this work was a deliberate experiment which proved, however interestingly, the rightness of his earlier statement that *Die Meistersinger* stands outside the canon.

His second new production of 1963 was a more logical attempt to treat the work for what it is, a dramatic comedy; and it appeared at first sight that he had stepped right out of his previous character. Yet had he in fact done so? If there was an unwonted amount of realism in the action and a complete lack of formality, this was projected against an entirely unrealistic background: a semi-circular gallery on two levels which served throughout the work, with only minor changes in the shape and trappings of the balustrades, for church, street and meadow. It was in fact a deliberate copy of the old Shakespearian stage. Only in the first scene of Act Three was there an attempt at scenic realism with a detailed replica of Sachs's cobbler's shop, complete with rows of shoes, tools and (to remind us that Sachs was a poet as well as a shoemaker) books. But the realism of the set was modified by its small size and by the backcloth, which depicted John the Baptist in the river Pegnitz with the contours of old Nuremberg behind him—a motive based of course on David's song in this scene. Consequently, for all the central realism of the set, we were reminded that we were watching not life itself but a comedy of life, and the type of comedy in which the accent is on character and not on situation.

It is this distinction in the type of comedy that made Wieland Wagner's *Meistersinger* so different in flavour from the traditional comic presentation of it and brought it at the same time nearer to his usual line of approach in all the other Wagner works. His main concern in all of these has always been with the psychology of the people involved in the dramas, and the scenic background has been evolved out of the psychology, or rather out of the words and music in which the psychology is given artistic expression. His first production of *Die Meistersinger* might be described as a consistent application of that same principle. His second production took note of the one vital difference between this and all the other works, namely, that *Die Meistersinger* is a comedy, and comedy is an analytical and not a synthetic art form. The audience response to it should be critical and not emotional. In consequence the scenic background can with advantage be contrasted rather than integrated: then the play of character in which the comedy lies becomes even more sharply focused. This is of course a general definition. The question can now be asked whether *Die Meistersinger* is a true comedy in this sense and therefore responsive to a consistent comedy treatment. To answer this question it is necessary to examine Wieland Wagner's approach in detail.

In a conversation following the production he told me that in all the many performances of *Die Meistersinger* that he had seen in his lifetime—and he added that he had seen the first in Bayreuth at the age of six—the master

singers had been presented as patricians: well-dressed
and apparently well-to-do men whom one would not
recognize as bakers, soapmakers, tailors and all the other
trades which Wagner carefully noted beside their names
in his cast list. Yet this was a basic condition of the work
and the one from which his new approach stemmed. As
Hans Sachs points out to Walther von Stolzing, it is these
humble and homely men who have been keeping German
art alive while the noblemen, of whom Walther is one,
have been busy fighting wars. If Germany were to be
militarily vanquished, the German soul would remain
alive through the efforts of its poets. Therefore, he tells
Walther, *verachtet mir die Meister nicht*—do not despise
the masters.

Wieland Wagner's handling of this final scene is interesting in a number of ways. Through having presented
Kothner, Nachtigall, Zorn and all the rest as artisans first
and foremost and as poets in their spare time, he not only
makes dramatic sense of Walther's petulant repudiation
of them (it is the last stirring of his aristocratic snobbery),
but he also removes the taint of nationalism from Sachs's
words, or rather from what Sachs's words are usually
taken to mean. When one remembers how the master
singers have usually looked (and we have all experienced
with Wieland Wagner those pompous elderly gentlemen
with an acute sense of their own importance), it is not
surprising that Sachs's spirited championing of them has
sounded like a piece of political tub-thumping, a prime
example of the spirit of *Deutschland über alles*. And this
is the way it had hitherto always been taken, even to the
extent in Siegfried Wagner's time of the audience rising
for it, as Anglo-Saxon audiences rise for the Hallelujah
chorus in the *Messiah*.

It is for that reason that Germans of today are inclined
to show embarrassment about this particular passage of
Die Meistersinger. Through his subtle adjustment of the
social balance Wieland Wagner has shown that there is
really no need for embarrassment, that Sachs is in fact
propounding a thought of irreproachable liberalism,

Tristan und Isolde, 1952: Act III (Wieland Wagner)

Tristan und Isolde, 1962: Act I (Wieland Wagner)

Der Fliegende
Holländer, 1961:
Scene III
(Wieland Wagner)

almost indeed of pacifism. It is not through its warriors that a nation shows its greatness, he says, but through its artists. And if ever Germany is defeated by foreign might, its spirit will live on in its art.

One might well ask whether this is not a deliberate distortion of Wagner's intention. It is undeniable that Wagner was a firm believer in the supremacy of the German race, and it is thus very probable that he did mean this passage as a stirring call to patriotic feelings. A further proof that this was so lies in the fact that the traditional way of presenting *Die Meistersinger* goes back to Wagner himself, who supervised the first production at Munich in 1868.

However, in order to judge the intent one ought to consider the prevailing conditions. In 1868 Germany still consisted of a number of small states, each of them fully autonomous. Though Bismarck and the Prussian king were busy pursuing their expansionist plans, that major outburst of German nationalism, the Franco-Prussian war, had not yet taken place. Wagner, who shared King Ludwig's antipathy against the Prussian Wilhelm, cannot therefore be accused of having known what German lust for supremacy was later to look like in practice. It is true that he subsequently rejoiced in Prussia's defeat of France, but this was mainly a subjective reaction—pleasure in seeing the nation humbled that in his early days had so cruelly humbled him. And equally, in proclaiming the importance of the ordinary German people through the mouth of Hans Sachs, Wagner might have been venting his spite on all the German princes from the King of Saxony downwards (always excepting of course the King of Bavaria) who had either persecuted or ignored him. Wagner's reactions were always subjective —a contributory factor to his greatness as an artist maybe, but equally a contributory factor to his weakness as a politician.

Seen in this context, it appears probable that Wagner never intended Hans Sachs's words to have the tremendous impact which they later acquired in more nationalistic days. If there was any distortion, it lay far more in the exploitation of a passage which had acquired a never-dreamed-of significance than in Wieland Wagner's attempt to restore the balance by a less traditional presentation of it.

If Wieland Wagner did not himself so much insist on asserting that his main object as a producer is to rescue Richard Wagner's works from the distortions of an over-pious tradition, it would be unnecessary to examine him so closely on the matter. Any producer has the right to present a work in the way he finds best—provided he can make it convincing. Not tradition but the written text is the only thing to which the conscientious producer must hold fast, and in that respect Wieland Wagner is usually beyond reproach. In *Die Meistersinger* he admittedly allows himself liberties with Eva's nurse Magdalene. Wagner certainly meant her to be getting on a bit in years: the apprentices tease David for his devotion to the "old maid" and Walther also refers to her as "the old woman". In making Magdalene a young and lively girl and a con-federate in Eva's pursuit of Walther, Wieland Wagner does deliberately contradict his grandfather—an act which I for one am grateful for, since the relationship with David always seemed rather distasteful and it is, as Wie-land Wagner says, dramatically unnecessary. Perhaps Richard Wagner, like Gilbert in some of the Savoy operas, thought it amusing to make fun of ageing women. Wieland Wagner, in rejecting that idea, might for consistency's sake have adapted the text to fit his conception of a young Magdalene, but he chose to leave that as it was: there is obviously a limit in his mind as to what one dare do in Bayreuth.

Of the master singers only Sachs and Beckmesser are fully characterized by Wagner: Pogner to a lesser extent, but the rest not at all. Wieland Wagner's device of taking note of their trades allows him at any rate to give each a more individual profile than they usually receive, if only in the matter of their clothes. Pogner has a more active role, and here Wieland Wagner has seized the chance to satirize. In place of the usual noble figure we are shown a sort of modern post-war industrialist, a man whose sole aim is self-glorification. His action in "auctioning off his daughter" (the expression is Wieland Wagner's own) is undertaken not—as he tells his fellow master singers—in the interests of art but in the interests of his own social position. He had seen in Beckmesser an acceptable son-in-law (Beckmesser, the town clerk, is after all the only professional man among the artisan master singers) until the nobleman Walther von Stolzing arrives on the scene, and a title for his daughter is not to be sneezed at. So in Act One we find Pogner already engaged in extricating himself from his promise to Beckmesser and transferring his support to Walther. Walther's failure in the trial scene is a considerable embarrassment to him, and he is consequently grateful to Sachs for pleading in Walther's favour. In fact Pogner has reason to be grateful to Sachs for all the successive deeds with which he shields Pogner from the consequences of his absurd and rash decision to auction his daughter, and there is evidence throughout the work of his gratitude, though the true reasons for it may naturally enough not be explicitly stated.

Since Pogner is what he is, it is not surprising that his daughter Eva should turn to Sachs for fatherly advice rather than to Pogner (whose one moment of self-doubt, the question addressed to himself, *Oder war es doch nur Eitelkeit?*—Or was it simply vanity?—is not further pursued by the composer, but in this production is ironically given its value by an ensuing shake of the head).

If one must regard Wieland Wagner's satiric conception of Pogner simply as an interesting speculation, in that the text and the music give no real indications either way of the composer's attitude towards him, his conception of Eva as a strong-willed, thoroughly uninhibited young girl is borne out completely by the text. From the moment that she plants her neckcloth and brooch in the church in order to speak to Walther (if she did not plant them it was a very convenient accident) she is entirely shameless in her determination to have him and no other. Her coquetry with Hans Sachs in Act Two, when she suggests that he himself might care to compete for her hand, can be seen as an instinctive playing for time at an awkward moment. Whichever way she is presented this scene is unpalatable, since it is clear that she would not consider even Sachs as a suitable substitute for the man she really wants. She is therefore simply angling for his support—and with an insensitivity to his true feelings which does her no credit. However, she is young and in love and therefore ruthless. This does not prevent her, once she is sure that Sachs is working on her side and the goal is in sight, from repenting of her cruelty to him and expressing with genuine sincerity her devotion to him as a friend. Peace being restored, she can settle down to the Third Act quintet with all the serenity in the world.

When one considers that Wieland Wagner's presentation of Eva as a tempestuous teenager shows her at the end in as sympathetic a light as the more usual presentation, yet with a great deal more conviction, it may seem strange that it aroused so much protest at its first showing. To me this interpretation of Eva seems as obviously right within its context as the modern way of presenting Desdemona as a self-assured young lady of society. But if the former milk-and-roses Desdemona has now been consigned to the scrapheap, the same cannot unfortunately be said of the sweet little Eva. German audiences, it seems, prefer the traditional view, even at the expense of colour and drama and indeed of truth.

We know that in the character of Beckmesser Wagner portrayed the Viennese critic Hanslick. Perhaps his passionate hatred of Hanslick led Wagner originally to overplay his hand in making Beckmesser appear ridiculous, since by this means the effect of his defeat by Sachs is diminished. The pompous posturing figure which we are usually shown is so obviously a fool that we can only wonder at Sachs resorting to such drastic and indeed unscrupulous methods to overcome him.

However, it is possible to present Beckmesser in a more formidable light (and thereby to restore dramatic balance) without any violent distortion of the text. It is done first of all by remembering that Beckmesser is a city dignitary of some importance: it is hardly likely that a town of the size and significance of Nuremberg in the sixteenth century would tolerate a shambling ape as its town clerk. Wieland Wagner's Beckmesser, though narrow-minded, is no fool in his own sphere: he rather becomes foolish when he is driven by ambition to compete on grounds which are foreign to his nature—in serenades, street brawls and the like. This Beckmesser is a truly dangerous adversary for Sachs, and Sachs's equivocation in the matter of passing off Walther's prize song as his own, which seems unscrupulous when aimed at a fool, becomes more justifiable when aimed at an intelligent rival. It is in fact a healthy respect for Beckmesser's intelligence that leads Sachs to bait his trap so cunningly, and it is Beckmesser's arrogant sense of superior intelligence that leads him to fall into it. He makes no secret of his contempt for the poem which he takes to be Sachs's; its attraction to him is that he knows Sachs to have the popular touch and, however much he may despise such an accomplishment, he realizes that to gain Eva he must gain the support of the public. What he fails to realize is that the popular touch is not so much a matter of finding the right words as of having the personality to put them over.

Why then, if Wagner did not intend Beckmesser to be a farcical fool, did he make him garble the poem? This could be put down perhaps simply to Wagner's unbalanced attitude towards the critic Hanslick (hence to Beckmesser), which led him to exaggerate. However, Wieland Wagner, showing an entirely proper respect for the composer's dramatic skill, finds for Beckmesser's behaviour at this point a convincing explanation. Beckmesser's innate contempt for the popular touch makes it impossible for him to judge it rationally. He knows very well that what he is singing is nonsense, but if that is what the people want, then on this occasion they shall have it from him. It is an attitude quite consistent with Beckmesser's colossal arrogance and the outcome of it, his downfall, gives us satisfaction instead of the usual sneaking feeling of guilt.

In his treatment of character Wieland Wagner, as these examples show, has been convincing if unorthodox. There were other features of his 1963 production, however, which showed a less sure touch, and it is perhaps permissible to dwell on them even though by the time these lines are read Wieland Wagner with his customary restlessness may have eliminated them.

In general the Shakespearian gallery justified itself as a unifying element and conveniently solved the problem of scenery. Nevertheless, it seemed unfair of the producer to defy all laws of probability in the use of it. This was particularly noticeable in the second act, when we found that those parts of the upper gallery which we had come to identify with Sachs's house and with Pogner's house were invaded by the Night Watchman as if they were as much a part of the street as the lower level. The people in the drama saw each other or did not see each other as the action demanded without relevance to actual distance: from one moment to the next the whole stage might be taken for a tiny room or for a vast public square. Apart from a sketchy bower representing the porch before Sachs's house there was no permanent point on the stage at all.

Wieland Wagner had no qualms about making things so difficult for the audience to follow: one is, after all, expected at Bayreuth to have put in some study on the works beforehand. He explained that the second act of *Die Meistersinger* is a sort of comedy of errors like *The Merry Wives of Windsor* or *The Marriage of Figaro*, and thus he felt justified in treating it in the same sort of way. Yet it seems odd that a producer who is so sworn an enemy of convention should justify himself by relying on the conventions of a yet earlier period of comedy, conventions which one can regard—except as applied to these older works—as thoroughly outmoded. The same old comedy conventions were again pressed into service for the final chorus of the opera. This was not addressed, as written, to Hans Sachs but to the audience in the manner of the finale of *Die Entführung aus dem Serail* or *Don Giovanni*, the whole huge company advancing to the front of the stage to deliver it. This seems a perverse idea altogether, and I shall be surprised if it holds the stage for long.

Such blemishes as there were in this production of *Die Meistersinger* seem to me to arise almost entirely from Wieland Wagner's obsessional dislike of clichés, even when it does not drive him, as in the foregoing instances, to take refuge consciously in yet older clichés. It cannot be said that his decision to replace the extended procession of guilds at the beginning of the *Festwiese* scene with a peasant dance was a particularly happy one. True, it provided a very pleasant and characteristic picture in the manner of Breughel, thus further emphasizing the artisan element which the producer was anxious to bring out. On the other hand it fitted at times awkwardly with the music and in addition turned the ensuing procession of the guilds—for, after all, they have to be brought on stage—into a rather mad scramble. This delayed procession was done to the music designed for the entry of the master singers themselves, who then came on in a bunch at the end of it. The chorus launched on the great tribute to Sachs (*Wach' auf*) before the audience was even fully aware of Sachs's presence.

It is not difficult to see why Wieland Wagner chose to present the final scene in this way. His conception of *Die Meistersinger* as a picture of the sixteenth-century working class at play had to be carried through to its logical conclusion. This meant that the procession of guilds should not be beautiful in itself but should be the sort of thing that artisans of that time might feel to be striking and beautiful. In fact, as such public processions usually are, this one (and it was based on contemporary historical pictures) was quite hideous. Most people in the audience, however, failed to grasp the point that what they were seeing was the artisans' and not Wieland Wagner's idea of a beautiful procession, and he was vigorously attacked for his lack of taste. It was a failure of communication, for which the producer must be blamed in that he did not make his intention sufficiently clear.

It is of course a risk that any producer runs, when he decides to be untraditional, that the lovers of tradition will attack him, and it is only when his untraditional reading convinces utterly that he can hope to get away with it. In many ways Wieland Wagner's production was as revealing as it was convincing, particularly in the magnificently handled first act and in the scene in Sachs's workshop. In both these scenes the producer's realistic comedy approach was sharply focused and brought new revelations of character. Act Two might have done the same if Wieland Wagner had not allowed himself to be seduced away from his basic conception by an uncharacteristic devotion to an older comedy convention. The last scene missed fire partly for the same reasons but mainly because the producer imagined that he had defined his general approach to the work sufficiently to carry it through. In doing so he miscalculated the strength of logic: audiences are apt to forget the pattern unless they are constantly reminded of it, and in a mass scene like this, addressed more strongly to the eye than to the powers of reason, there is little opportunity to remind.

The production of 1963 is certainly not Wieland Wagner's last word on *Die Meistersinger*. It is undoubtedly the work which most obstinately defies his efforts to get through to its secrets. But, whatever the deficiencies of detail in this new approach, or that, enough has emerged in his two attempts so far to suggest that there is much more in the work than the traditional way of doing it has found room for. It is fortunate that Wieland Wagner has not kept to his original avowed intention of consigning this work to the museum of tradition. What unorthodox glimpses of it he has so far given us carry exciting implications of future revelations.

Seventeen

The Bayreuth Names of Today

THERE was no particular artistic reason why Wieland and Wolfgang Wagner should not have followed their father's example and engaged for the reopening of the festival in 1951 a number of the singers who had been prominent there before. Max Lorenz, Jaro Prohaska and Margarete Klose, for example, were still in good voice and did indeed continue to sing the big Wagner roles at Berlin and elsewhere for a number of years. However, the political need to disassociate themselves from former times coupled with their wish to work out their new production style untrammelled by tradition led them to make a completely new start.

A few leading singers of the pre-war period have made occasional appearances on the Festspielhaus stage since the reopening, chief among them Max Lorenz, who sang Siegfried in 1952 and Siegmund in 1954. Another distinguished singer of the Thirties, Eugen Fuchs, who was the Bayreuth Beckmesser from 1933 to 1944 and a frequent visitor to Covent Garden, returned to the Bayreuth stage in 1956 as Hans Foltz, one of the master singers, and sang this small role each year until 1961, by which time he had completed nearly half a century as a singer. Ludwig Suthaus, the Stolzing of the wartime productions, sang Loge in the festivals of 1956 and 1957 and also Siegmund in the latter year. Others who appeared in those wartime performances and on occasions since are Erich Kunz

(Beckmesser 1943 and 1951), Paul Schöffler (Sachs 1943–1944, Holländer 1956), Annalies Kupper (Eva 1944, Elsa 1960) and Friedrich Dalberg (Hagen and Pogner 1942–1944, Fafner and Pogner 1951).

In 1951 there was also a complete change of conductors. Hans Knappertsbusch, a famous Wagnerian from Munich, had not previously conducted in Bayreuth, owing no doubt to the traditional rivalry between the two towns—now like much else a thing of the past. Wilhelm Furt-wängler, who conducted Beethoven's Ninth Symphony at the first post-war festival, had of course been associated with Bayreuth in the questionable years, and the grand-sons' invitation was a brave gesture of recognition towards a distinguished conductor whose relations with the Nazi bosses had been anything but untroubled. A similar gesture was made in 1959, when Heinz Tietjen was invited to Bayreuth to conduct some performances of *Lohengrin*.

Sharing the conductor's duties at that first festival with Knappertsbusch was Herbert von Karajan, who though well enough known had not yet attained to international fame. In this and the following festival he established himself as a Wagner conductor in the great tradition, and it is Bayreuth's loss that he has since confined his Wagner activities mainly to Vienna, where he has produced the works (in association with Emil Preetorius) in addition to conducting them.

The continuity of conducting which had been a feature of the festival since its inception has been lost in the post-war years. Only Knappertsbusch has appeared year after year to conduct *Parsifal*, and Wieland Wagner ascribes much of the artistic success of his production to that fact. None of the others, who include Clemens Krauss, Josef Keilberth, Rudolf Kempe, Wolfgang Sawallisch and Karl Böhm, can be described as regular conductors in the traditional Bayreuth sense. The non-German contin-gent, represented in all the preceding years by Toscanini and Victor de Sabata alone, has been larger—the Belgian André Cluytens and the Americans Ferdinand Leitner, Lorin Maazel and Thomas Schippers up to 1963.

It would be wrong to assume that the rapid turn-round of conductors necessarily implies any failure of good relations between them and the grandsons. The plain fact is that the number of international festivals has increased greatly since the war and, as they all take place at more or less the same time, competition for the services of leading conductors and singers is great. Consequently the failure of a conductor or a singer to appear in any one year at Bayreuth may mean no more than that he has already been engaged elsewhere.

It is for competitive reasons of this sort that Bayreuth has now become a yearly festival, abandoning its previous pattern of a complete rest every third year. As Wolfgang Wagner says, in the race for the services of leading artists Bayreuth can simply not afford to drop out of the running every third year. However, though Bayreuth is now only one among many festivals vying for the attention of the holiday-making public (a development that Richard Wagner would certainly have deplored), it does possess a hard core of singers who have remained faithful to it for many years. Names which immediately spring to mind when one thinks back on the opening years are Astrid Varnay, Martha Mödl, Hans Hotter and Wolfgang Windgassen.

No other singer in the history of Bayreuth has equalled the record of the Swedish-born American soprano Astrid Varnay, who has appeared in every single festival since 1951 and has sung all the leading dramatic soprano roles, including Isolde and Brünnhilde, as well as many smaller ones. It is a record not only of fine singing but also of a selfless devotion to a cause in which she wholeheartedly believes. How many other great singers are as ready as she to take over roles at a moment's notice or to relinquish them as readily in order to give newcomers a chance? Certainly Martha Mödl would have matched Astrid Varnay's achievement in full if ill health and consequent voice trouble had not hampered her. Since the festival of 1956 her appearances have been less regular—to the regret of the grandsons and audiences alike.

Wolfgang Windgassen's wide range of heroic roles was almost equalled in the past by Max Lorenz, but, whereas in the Thirties there were a number of fine dramatic tenors to share the burden with him, Windgassen had to carry the whole dramatic tenor department virtually unaided. Much the same can be said of Hans Hotter as far as the role of Wotan is concerned, and, though he seldom sings the role nowadays, there is still no obvious successor to him in sight. Apart from an unexampled range of roles assumed in the Festspielhaus he has carried the Bayreuth influence far outside, not only as a singer but also as a producer, notably of the *Ring* at Covent Garden.

In retrospect the years 1951 to 1958 seem to represent the last flowering of the great Bayreuth singing tradition, in which the major roles were taken year after year by singers of acknowledged authority such as Varnay, Mödl, Hotter and Windgassen, supported in the character parts by a group of equally loyal singers such as Gustav Neidlinger, Ludwig Weber, Joseph Greindl, Hermann Uhde and George London. Since then there has been a rather disquieting lack of continuity which has meant at times that even within a single cycle of the *Ring* some of the main parts have been taken by different singers. Not even Birgit Nilsson, potentially the finest Brünnhilde of our day, has been prepared to sing the whole cycle under the conditions in which the *Ring* has been traditionally presented at Bayreuth: on successive evenings with a rest day between *Siegfried* and *Götterdämmerung*. However, some new singers have emerged out of this interim period who hold out promise of a new blossoming.

Among dramatic tenors hopes rest most securely on the American Jess Thomas, who made his Bayreuth debut as Parsifal in 1961 and has since played Lohengrin and Stolzing with distinction, and on the Austrian Fritz Uhl, who has played Siegmund, Loge and Erik. Among the younger generation of dramatic sopranos is the Finnish singer Anita Välkki, who made her debut in *Die Walküre* at Covent Garden in 1962 and has since sung the role at Bayreuth. A successor for Hotter as Wotan appears more difficult to find. One promising claimant of the younger generation, the Canadian James Milligan, died before having an opportunity to sing more than one very impressive *Wanderer* at Bayreuth in 1961. Present contestants for the role are the American Jerome Hines and the German Theo Adam, who has graduated in the Bayreuth school over the years since 1952 from roles such as Ortel and Reinmar to Wotan in 1963.

It is interesting to note the large number of non-German singers who nowadays appear in the Bayreuth cast list. As we have seen, there has always been a place there for distinguished foreigners, mostly from the Scandinavian countries and to a lesser extent from America, but since the Second World War the list has been very much longer. It cannot be said that the result has always been rewarding, and no doubt this was how the suspicion arose that the Wagner grandsons were lowering their artistic standards in an effort to attract audiences from abroad—a reproach that Wolfgang Wagner has rebutted convincingly enough by showing that only a very small percentage of the audience comes from any one particular foreign country. The increase in the number of foreign singers is due in part to the grandsons' desire to find the best they can (and this leads inevitably to the occasional disappointment), but in the main to the changing conditions of today.

It would need a whole chapter and lead us rather far off course to attempt to trace why in Britain and the United States interest in opera increased so remarkably after the Second World War and led to a rise in the general level of performance in these two countries. The supply of opera singers of a high standard in both countries coincided with a shortage of good voices on the European mainland, due to the vast wartime losses and the slower rate of recovery there. And since opportunities of learning by experience are limited in both Britain and America, it is not really surprising that young British and American singers should have sought engagements in the countries of Europe which required them for their many opera houses (in West Germany alone there are more than fifty). Today there is scarcely an opera house in Germany, Austria and Switzerland which has not an American or a British singer under contract, and it is clear that the best of these are of interest to Bayreuth. In addition to those already mentioned, American singers at Bayreuth who have emerged in this way included Thomas Stewart (Gunther and Amfortas), Grace Bumbry (the "black Venus" of the 1961 *Tannhäuser*) and Grace Hoffman (Fricka, Brangäne and Waltraute).

The list of British and American singers whose experience was gained at home rather than in Germany is shorter but distinguished: at its head stands Astrid Varnay; Irene Dalis has shown herself to be a remarkable Kundry and also an effective Ortrud; whereas the Chilean singer Ramon Vinay has achieved the unusual feat of making his mark both as a dramatic tenor (Tristan, Siegmund and Parsifal) and later as a dramatic baritone (Telramund). Others are the Canadian Jon Vickers, who has sung Parsifal and Siegmund, and the Scotsman David Ward, a pupil of Hans Hotter in the role of Wotan at Covent Garden, who has so far sung only small roles at Bayreuth (Fasolt, Titurel, Night Watchman).

The large number of American, British and Scandinavian soloists has led to the creation of a new post on the Bayreuth staff, that of director of studies for foreign singers. The post is held by Karl Schmitt-Walter, whose outstanding performances as Beckmesser at Bayreuth in the years 1956–61 should not be allowed to obscure the fact that he was before that one of Germany's leading lyric baritones.

It would be wearisome to list the many native German singers who have appeared at Bayreuth since 1951, but a few should be named who have appeared continuously in many different roles, such as Gerhard Stolze, Franz Crass (whose first appearance was as a member of the chorus) and Gottlob Frick. It is in the nature of things that the list should contain predominantly male singers, since the number of female roles in Wagner's works is so much less.

But to the name of Martha Mödl should be added Elisabeth Grümmer (Elisabeth, Elsa and Eva) and Anja Silja,
who almost alone among the female singers can be said to
have made her name primarily at Bayreuth. Chosen by
Wieland Wagner for the role of Senta in 1960, she brought
a striking appearance and a welcome note of youth to that
role and subsequently to Elsa and Eva (she was the
turbulent teenager of the 1963 production).

Since 1951 some well-known singers, though not primarily associated with Wagner's works, have taken on
specific roles, such as Elisabeth Schwarzkopf (Eva and
Rhinemaiden), Gré Brouwenstijn (Elisabeth, Eva and
Sieglinde), Régine Crespin (Sieglinde and Kundry),
Victoria de los Angeles (Elisabeth), Lisa della Casa (Eva)
and Dietrich Fischer-Dieskau (Wolfram and Amfortas).

Both orchestra and chorus are still recruited at Bayreuth in the traditional way from all parts of Germany,
and there are players in the orchestra who have taken part
in all Bayreuth festivals since the time of Siegfried Wagner.
The splendour of the chorus is due in part to an equally
careful selection of singers, some of them soloists in their
own right who take part more modestly at Bayreuth for
the sake of experience, but in the main to the skill of the
chorus master, Wilhelm Pitz, who has directed it in every
work since 1951, thus continuing the tradition of long
service established by Julius Kniese and maintained by
Hugo Rüdel.

Of the third generation of the Wagner family, apart
from the two grandsons themselves, only Wieland
Wagner's wife Gertrud has taken an active part within
the Festspielhaus, most notably with her choreography
for her husband's production of *Tannhäuser* in 1954 and
of *Die Meistersinger* in 1963. In both she has shown a
definite artistic personality of her own and a style which
owes nothing to classical ballet but something to the
Mary Wigman school of character dancing, a style which
blends well with Wieland Wagner's production methods.

Winifred Wagner's elder daughter Friedelind, though
taking no part in the productions, has been a constant

visitor to Bayreuth since the reopening. Now an American citizen, she brings groups of students from the United States to each festival, where they attend rehearsals and study aspects of Wagner production with members of the Bayreuth staff. Another member of the Wagner family who continues to take an active part in the festival is Count Gilbert Gravina, who works as a stage manager and musical assistant. Though belonging in age to the generation of Winifred Wagner, he is in fact a first cousin of Wieland and Wolfgang Wagner, being the son of Cosima's second daughter Blandine.

It is impossible to do more than describe very sketchily the present Bayreuth scene, since it is obviously constantly on the move. It is equally impossible to attempt any comparison between the singers of today and those of former times. It cannot be denied that, with a few notable exceptions, singers nowadays seem to come and go with increasing rapidity, but whether this is due to faults in vocal training, to the rigours of overmuch travel or to increased competition I shall not go into here. What has chiefly distinguished the performances of the Bayreuth singers of today has been the intensity of their acting. The standard of acting which Wieland Wagner manages to coax from most of his singers is certainly no more than Richard Wagner himself demanded but did not always succeed in achieving. In this respect Wieland Wagner enjoys the advantage of having public taste vigorously on his side. What audiences now demand in the way of outward appearance and acting ability is far more exacting than formerly and the price of it—a certain tolerance towards vocal shortcomings—is more willingly paid.

Die Meistersinger, 1956: Act II (Wieland Wagner)

Die Meistersinger, 1963: Act III, Scene 2 (Wieland Wagner)

Four versions of Wotan: Franz Betz,
(*top left*); Karl Braun, 1924 (*top rig*
Rudolf Bockelmann, 1931–41 (*bottom l*
and Hans Hotter, 1952–58 (*bottom rig*

Eighteen

Bayreuth and the Future

THE Bayreuth festival of today is still recognizably the Bayreuth of Richard Wagner's own creation. In outward form and in its administrative machinery it has altered not at all. Conductors and singers are still chosen for their ability and not for their box office appeal and are paid fees which can be regarded as little more than token payment. Members of the chorus and the orchestra are still recruited from all the opera houses of Germany and Austria and still regard an invitation as a signal honour. Young and not so young conductors, chorus masters, coaches and technicians do not find it beneath their dignity to accept junior backstage posts for the sake of the experience to be gained in the production of Wagner's works. The repertoire is still rigidly restricted to the works which Wagner himself considered fit for presentation in the Festspielhaus. No attempt has been made to add curiosity value to the festival by introducing the three early works *Die Feen, Das Liebesverbot* and *Rienzi,* though there must be many among Bayreuth's visitors who would be glad, if only once in a while, to make the acquaintance of Wagner's prentice work. There are even those who suggest that the operas of Siegfried Wagner might occasionally be used to widen the repertoire: after all, Siegfried was a member of the family and he wrote his works according to his father's ideas; one might accord him the benefit of performances on the only existing stage that fulfils all the conditions of Wagnerian production.

It is also remembered that Wagner himself never thought of his "theatre for the people" as being for himself alone: it was to be used for the propagation of German opera, and that included in Wagner's estimation such works as *Die Zauberflöte, Fidelio* and *Der Freischütz*. Why should not these works now be produced at Bayreuth?

Perhaps one day they may be. Who can be so sure of the future to be able to say definitely yes or no to that? Wieland and Wolfgang Wagner, who are naturally as deeply concerned about the future of the festival as about its present, will give no categorical answer to the question, since they do not regard it as urgent yet. And of course they are right. It is remarkable that ninety years have not succeeded in exhausting the appeal of the seven works (or ten if one counts the *Ring* as four) to which the Bayreuth festival is devoted. Empty seats in the Festspielhaus—no uncommon sight in the time of Richard and Cosima Wagner—are nowadays inconceivable.

Such persistent success would not have been possible if Wagner's works had not been great and inexhaustible works of art. And if Bayreuth had ever failed in its task of keeping interest in them alive, this would have been a reflection on the prowess of the successive festival managers and not on the works themselves. The dogmatic approach, right as it was in the time of Cosima Wagner, if persisted in could have killed Bayreuth for ever, but it did and could do no serious damage to the works. Equally the attempts to experiment, cautious in the case of Siegfried Wagner and Heinz Tietjen, bold in the case of the grandsons, could not be seen as expedients, growing gradually more desperate, to inject new life into a dying institution. If anything has ever looked small at Bayreuth it has not been the works but the attempts to interpret them. But in fact none of the attempts has looked small —only incomplete. Wagner's work, like Shakespeare's, has that quality of revealing some fresh and unexpected feature with each new approach to it. But it has never yet revealed all its significance at once, not even when the composer himself tackled it in the role of producer.

It is this elusive quality that makes Wagner's work so infinitely fascinating and at the same time enables Bayreuth to remain the unique place that it is. It is not just a centre for definitive performances, where interest is exhausted by comparing the Brünnhilde of Nilsson with the Brünnhilde of Gulbranson or the *Parsifal* of Knappertsbusch with the *Parsifal* of Muck. There will always be people to do this (and why not?), but in fact such comparisons are irrelevant and incidental. Fundamentally all that matters in Bayreuth is the work itself, and each festival is an expedition, undertaken by producer, performers and audiences alike, to find a way through to its secrets or as many as can possibly be discovered on one single occasion.

The point has been made throughout this book that, the family succession apart, there has been less continuity than diversity in the development of the festival. The "old" Bayreuth style in its pure state lasted at the most thirty years, from 1884 to 1914, which is not long in terms of artistic movements. The "new" Bayreuth has been in existence so far for fourteen years and has shown within itself a considerable diversity of style which should exonerate it from the accusation of being doctrinaire. And what lay in the forty years between these two most easily identifiable stylistic conceptions had its own particular character and formed only very indirectly a connecting link.

Bayreuth has a quaint habit of recording the performance times of certain of the works, and one could perhaps expect to see in these some sign of logical change to match the changing view of Wagner's works over the years. Would one not expect Levi's *Parsifal* to have been more ponderous than Knappertsbusch's? It was not. Levi got through the work (excluding intervals) in four hours and eighteen minutes, whereas Knappertsbusch takes four hours and forty minutes. The slowest *Parsifal* on record was Toscanini's in 1931—five hours and five minutes; the fastest was in 1953, when Clemens Krauss negotiated it in three hours and fifty-six minutes. Richter's *Rheingold* of 1876 (two hours and thirty-one minutes) was slightly faster than Furtwängler's in 1936 (two hours and thirty-six minutes). With *Tristan und Isolde* Mottl and Karajan finished up only three minutes apart, Toscanini again bringing up the rear more than twenty minutes later. Variations of tempo as pronounced as these (more than an hour between the *Parsifal* of Toscanini and that of Krauss) suggest a fascinating field of study on the differing interpretations of various conductors and on the consequence of Wagner's deliberate refusal to provide metronome markings. However, I am here making the general rather than the individual point that Wagner's works allow great diversity of approach on the musical as well as on the scenic side and that tempo is no measurement of old-fashionedness or otherwise.

Obvious as such a conclusion may seem, it is nevertheless important to state it, if only because it does call into question the necessity for a festival at Bayreuth at all. If there is no such thing as a definitive performance of a Wagner work, if every new production is simply to be regarded as an attempt, why should Bayreuth be more important than any other opera house which is prepared to devote an equal amount of time and thought to the production of Wagner's music dramas? The question partly answers itself, since it is in the nature of things that no other opera house has an equal amount of time to spare, but it is only a very small part of the answer. More important is the fact that in Bayreuth producers, singers, conductors, coaches, orchestral players and technicians still spend endless hours rehearsing their functions in accordance with the methods laid down by the composer himself. The necessity for complete integration of the aural and visual elements in the music dramas is fully recognized, however much the relationship of any one element to the others may alter in emphasis. There are consequently standards against which everything can be measured, and any deviation from these is preceded by deep heart-searchings and undertaken only in a spirit of conscious deliberation. This is what Wieland Wagner means when he speaks ruefully of the difficulty of trying to move forwards while looking backwards.

One can see the difficulty and yet be glad that it is there. The discipline that it imposes on him certainly plays an important part in the depth and authority of his achievements. And one feels that he and his brother Wolfgang fully appreciate the artistic value of this discipline, however much they may profess to deplore it. If this were not so, they would be less concerned to preserve intact Bayreuth's greatest technical asset of all: the Festspielhaus itself.

As a building the Festspielhaus has no claims to be regarded as a model of architectural beauty. If the grandsons were to pull it down and replace it with a more permanent and outwardly more beautiful building, they would in fact be acting in accordance with Richard Wagner's own wish. He considered the theatre which he himself erected as only a temporary structure and left it to future generations to replace it with something more solid and expensive. No doubt he would be surprised and possibly even hurt to find his flimsy structure still in existence nearly a century after it was put up: what would he have thought of the deliberate decision of his grandsons to keep it intact in its present shape and, by replacing its crumbling parts with carefully matched materials of greater strength, to prolong its life indefinitely?

The decision to retain the building is based not only on consideration of its unique acoustics. Important as these are, it would not be entirely impossible to reproduce them in another building, though acoustics are notoriously elusive and resistant to measurement by scientific means. But though one could in theory and probably in practice construct an interior which would conform in every way with Wagner's special requirements, something that the grandsons are not willing to relinquish would be lost for ever—the direct physical link with the composer which the present Festspielhaus keeps most effectively alive.

This may sound sentimental, but it is an aspect of Bayreuth that has to be taken into account even by those who measure the success of festivals only by the money they earn. Bayreuth owes its uniqueness—and hence its drawing power—not only to the knowledge that it was created by the composer himself, but also to the knowledge that he incorporated in it all the conditions under which alone in his estimation the music dramas can make their full effect. The Festspielhaus as it exists is the one permanent reminder of these conditions.

It is true that the town of Bayreuth as festival visitors know it today is still very much the Bayreuth that Richard Wagner chose. It is still small, still quiet (at any rate by the standards of today), still surrounded by woods and meadows, and it still offers its visitors no cultural alternative to the music dramas, except what television and radio bring in from the outside world. None of this could have been preserved without a deliberate policy, and indeed the town of Bayreuth has made considerable sacrifices to retain its other-worldliness in the interests of the festival. In common with other German towns it could have profited from the post-war *Wirtschaftswunder* and become a centre of industry, offering its own inhabitants better chances of employment and entertainment. But so far such temptations have been resisted, and the festival remains the town's main occupation. Since this is mainly a matter of room-letting and catering, confined at that to a few weeks of the year, it is not surprising that Bayreuth's own citizens, and particularly the young, find life rather dull. Out of the festival season the town has little to offer beyond a certain picturesqueness to which its inhabitants have long become immune, and even the festival offers them little, since their role is to wait on the hordes of visitors and not to share with them its artistic delights.

There is obviously a dangerous artificiality in these efforts to keep Wagner's own Bayreuth atmosphere intact, and who can say how long it will be possible to maintain them against the inevitably growing opposition within the town itself? The grandsons are not blind to the dangers: in fact their festival policy is shaped to a very large extent by awareness of them. If they had matched the praiseworthy historical conservatism of the town with a similar historical conservatism within the Festspielhaus itself, one could safely predict the beginning of the end. One day the still sizeable crowd of Wagner traditionalists, with their roots in the Bayreuth of Cosima, must die out, and if once the Festspielhaus were to begin to empty, the battle would be lost. There would no longer be any compulsion to preserve artificially the traditional atmosphere of the town, which can be justified only on account of the very real contribution that it makes to the success of the festival. Quite apart from artistic considerations there is therefore a harsh practical necessity behind the grandsons' efforts to keep interest in their work alive and to spread it over the widest possible field: if the uniqueness of Bayreuth is to be preserved, the interest of new generations must be captured and held.

It would be a hopeless task if Wagner had been simply a product of his own time with nothing new to say to later generations. But all the evidence points the other way. Wagner's works remain a matter of passionate interest to people of all ages, now as before. But the emphasis has shifted. Among today's audiences fewer come steeped in the texts and the theories behind the works. The majority are content with the music alone, which is to say that they take Wagner on their own terms and no longer on his. For these he has become just one of the composers of opera. And if he remains, as he does, the most compelling of them all, fewer people are conscious just why this is so or what part Bayreuth and the Festspielhaus play in making it so.

Thus, as a result of this changing attitude, the future of the Bayreuth festival depends on a curious paradox, which can be defined as an attempt to preserve its active authority by abandoning its inherent claim to be regarded as authoritative. The grandsons themselves know exactly how important a role the Festspielhaus and its surroundings play in the festival, even if many in the audience do not. They know that all the artistic ideals that led Wagner to create it in the form he did are as valid today as they were at the beginning. And they know that their task as producers is to take all these ideals into account. In doing so, they have rejected the traditional form of production on the grounds that it no longer corresponds with the taste of today, but equally they have resisted the temptation to accept the easy modern view that the music alone matters. Their decision to regard Bayreuth as an experimental workshop rather than as a shrine is a measure of their sense of responsibility towards the works for which it was built and on which its future depends. Richard Wagner's injunction to his followers to create something new (*Kinder, schafft Neues!*) was an invitation to think imaginatively and to use the weapons which he had put into their hands critically, not dogmatically. His own tradition was the result of experiment and he saw, as his grandsons see, that experiment alone can keep it alive.

PRODUCTIONS AND CONDUCTORS 1876–1964

RICHARD WAGNER 1876–1882

1876   *Ring:* Hans Richter.
1882   *Parsifal:* Franz Fischer, Hermann Levi.

COSIMA WAGNER 1883–1906

1883   *Parsifal:* Franz Fischer, Hermann Levi.
1884   *Parsifal:* Franz Fischer, Hermann Levi.
1886   *Parsifal:* Hermann Levi. *Tristan und Isolde:* Felix Mottl.
1888   *Parsifal:* Felix Mottl. *Die Meistersinger:* Hans Richter.
1889   *Parsifal:* Hermann Levi. *Die Meistersinger:* Hans Richter. *Tristan und Isolde:* Felix Mottl.
1891   *Parsifal:* Hermann Levi. *Tristan und Isolde* and *Tannhäuser:* Felix Mottl.
1892   *Parsifal:* Hermann Levi. *Tristan und Isolde* and *Tannhäuser:* Feli Mottl. *Die Meistersinger:* Hans Richter, Felix Mottl.
1894   *Parsifal:* Hermann Levi. *Tannhäuser:* Richard Strauss. *Lohengrin:* Felix Mottl.
1896   *Ring:* Felix Mottl, Hans Richter, Siegfried Wagner.
1897   *Parsifal:* Felix Mottl, Anton Seidl. *Ring:* Hans Richter, Siegfried Wagner.
1899   *Parsifal:* Franz Fischer. *Ring:* Siegfried Wagner. *Die Meistersinger:* Hans Richter.
1901   *Parsifal:* Karl Muck. *Ring:* Hans Richter, Siegfried Wagner. *Der Fliegende Holländer:* Felix Mottl.
1902   *Parsifal:* Karl Muck. *Ring:* Hans Richter, Siegfried Wagner. *Der Fliegende Holländer:* Felix Mottl.
1904   *Parsifal:* Karl Muck, Michael Balling. *Ring:* Hans Richter, Franz Beidler. *Tannhäuser:* Siegfried Wagner.
1906   *Parsifal:* Karl Muck, Michael Balling, Franz Beidler. *Ring:* Hans Richter, Siegfried Wagner, *Tristan und Isolde:* Michael Balling, Felix Mottl.

SIEGFRIED WAGNER 1908–1930

1908   *Parsifal:* Karl Muck, Michael Balling. *Ring:* Hans Richter. *Lohengrin:* Siegfried Wagner.

217

1909   *Parsifal:* Karl Muck, Siegfried Wagner. *Ring:* Michael
       Balling. *Lohengrin:* Karl Muck, Siegfried Wagner.
1911   *Parsifal:* Karl Muck, Michael Balling. *Ring:* Michael
       Balling, Siegfried Wagner. *Die Meistersinger:* Hans
       Richter.
1912   *Parsifal:* Karl Muck, Michael Balling. *Ring:* Michael
       Balling, Siegfried Wagner. *Die Meistersinger:* Hans
       Richter.
1914   *Parsifal:* Karl Muck. *Ring:* Michael Balling. *Der Flie-
       gende Holländer:* Siegfried Wagner.
1924   *Parsifal:* Karl Muck, Willibald Kaehler. *Ring:* Michael
       Balling. *Die Meistersinger:* Fritz Busch.
1925   *Parsifal:* Karl Muck, Willibald Kaehler. *Ring:* Michael
       Balling. *Die Meistersinger:* Karl Muck.
1927   *Parsifal:* Karl Muck. *Ring:* Franz von Hoesslin. *Tristan
       und Isolde:* Karl Elmendorff.
1928   *Parsifal:* Karl Muck. *Ring:* Franz von Hoesslin, Sieg-
       fried Wagner. *Tristan und Isolde:* Karl Elmendorff.
1930   *Parsifal:* Karl Muck. *Ring:* Karl Elmendorff. *Tristan
       und Isolde* and *Tannhäuser:* Arturo Toscanini.

WINIFRED WAGNER 1931–1944

(Productions from 1933 Heinz Tietjen)

1931   *Parsifal* and *Tannhäuser:* Arturo Toscanini. *Ring:* Karl
       Elemendorff. *Tristan und Isolde:* Wilhelm Furtwängler.
1933   *Parsifal:* Richard Strauss. *Ring:* Karl Elmendorff. *Die
       Meistersinger:* Karl Elmendorff, Heinz Tietjen.
1934   *Parsifal:* Richard Strauss, Franz von Hoesslin. *Ring* and
       Die Meistersinger: Karl Elmendorff, Heinz Tietjen.
1936   *Parsifal:* Wilhelm Furtwängler. *Ring* and *Lohengrin:*
       Wilhelm Furtwängler, Heinz Tietjen.
1937   *Parsifal* and *Ring:* Wilhelm Furtwängler. *Lohengrin:*
       Heinz Tietjen.
1938   *Parsifal:* Franz von Hoesslin. *Ring:* Heinz Tietjen.
       Tristan und Isolde: Karl Elmendorff.
1939   *Parsifal:* Franz von Hoesslin. *Ring:* Heinz Tietjen.
       Tristan und Isolde: Victor de Sabata. *Der Fliegende
       Holländer:* Karl Elmendorff.
1940   *Ring:* Franz von Hoesslin. *Der Fliegende Holländer:*
       Karl Elmendorff.
1941   *Ring:* Heinz Tietjen. *Der Fliegende Holländer:* Karl
       Elmendorff.
1942   *Ring:* Karl Elmendorff. *Der Fliegende Holländer:*
       Richard Kraus.

1943 *Die Meistersinger:* Wilhelm Furtwängler, Hermann Abendroth.
1944 *Die Meistersinger:* Wilhelm Furtwängler, Hermann Abendroth.

WIELAND AND WOLFGANG WAGNER 1951–1964

1951 *Parsifal*[1]*:* Hans Knappertsbusch. *Ring*[1] and *Die Meistersinger*[2]*:* Herbert von Karajan, Hans Knappertsbusch.
1952 *Parsifal*[1] and *Die Meistersinger*[2]*:* Hans Knappertsbusch. *Ring*[1]*:* Joseph Keilberth. *Tristan und Isolde*[1]*:* Herbert von Karajan.
1953 *Parsifal*[1]*:* Clemens Krauss. *Ring*[1]*:* Joseph Keilberth, Clemens Krauss. *Tristan und Isolde*[1]*:* Eugen Jochum. *Lohengrin*[3]*:* Joseph Keilberth.
1954 *Parsifal*[1]*:* Hans Knappertsbusch. *Ring*[1]*:* Joseph Keilberth. *Lohengrin*[3] and *Tannhäuser*[1]*:* Eugen Jochum, Joseph Keilberth.
1955 *Parsifal*[1]*:* Hans Knappertsbusch. *Ring*[1]*:* Joseph Keilberth. *Tannhäuser*[1]*:* André Cluytens, Joseph Keilberth. *Der Fliegende Holländer*[3]*:* Joseph Keilberth, Hans Knappertsbusch.
1956 *Parsifal*[1]*:* Hans Knappertsbusch. *Ring*[1]*:* Joseph Keilberth, Hans Knappertsbusch. *Der Fliegende Holländer*[3]*:* Joseph Keilberth. *Die Meistersinger*[1]*:* André Cluytens.
1957 *Parsifal*[1]*:* Hans Knappertsbusch, André Cluytens. *Ring*[1]*:* Hans Knappertsbusch. *Die Meistersinger*[1]*:* André Cluytens. *Tristan und Isolde*[3]*:* Wolfgang Sawallisch.
1958 *Parsifal*[1] and *Ring*[1]*:* Hans Knappertsbusch. *Tristan und Isolde*[3]*:* Wolfgang Sawallisch. *Die Meistersinger*[1] and *Lohengrin*[1]*:* André Cluytens.
1959 *Parsifal*[1]*:* Hans Knappertsbusch. *Tristan und Isolde*[3] and *Der Fliegende Holländer*[1]*:* Wolfgang Sawallisch. *Die Meistersinger*[1]*:* Erich Leinsdorf. *Lohengrin*[1]*:* Heinz Tietjen, Lovro von Matacic.
1960 *Parsifal*[1] and *Die Meistersinger*[1]*:* Hans Knappertsbusch. *Ring*[3]*:* Rudolf Kempe. *Lohengrin*[1]*:* Ferdinand Leitner, Lorin Maazel. *Der Fliegende Holländer*[1]*:* Wolfgang Sawallisch.

[1] Production by Wieland Wagner.
[2] Production by Rudolf Hartmann.
[3] Production by Wolfgang Wagner.

1961 *Parsifal*[1]: Hans Knappertsbusch. *Ring*[3]: Rudolf Kempe.
Der Fliegende Holländer[1] and *Tannhäuser*[1]: Wolfgang
Sawallisch. *Die Meistersinger*[1]: Josef Krips.

1962 *Parsifal*[1]: Hans Knappertsbusch. *Ring*[3]: Rudolf Kempe.
Tristan und Isolde[1]: Karl Böhm. *Lohengrin*[1] and *Tannhäuser*[1]: Wolfgang Sawallisch.

1963 *Parsifal*[1]: Hans Knappertsbusch. *Ring*[3]: Rudolf Kempe.
Tristan und Isolde[1]: Karl Böhm. *Die Meistersinger*[1]:
Thomas Schippers.

1964 *Parsifal*[1]: Hans Knappertsbusch. *Ring*[3]: Berislav Klobu-
car. *Tristan und Isolde*[1]: Karl Böhm. *Die Meistersinger*[1]: Karl Böhm, Robert Heger. *Tannhäuser*[1]:
Otmar Suitner.

PRINCIPAL SINGERS AND THEIR ROLES

1876–1964

Roles are shown in the chronological order in which they were assumed by the singer.

Adam, Theo	1952–64: Ortel, Gralsritter, Steuermann (*Tristan*), Reinmar, Titurel, Fasolt, König Heinrich, Wotan.
Ahna, Pauline de	1891–4: Elisabeth, Blumenmädchen.
Aldenhoff, Bernd	1951–7: Siegfried.
Alexander, Carlos	1963–4: Beckmesser.
Alvary, Max	1891: Tristan, Tannhäuser.
Andersson, Frans	1958–9: Alberich, Kurwenal.
Andrésen, Ivar	1927–36: Gurnemanz, Marke, Landgraf, Hunding, Titurel, Fasolt, Pogner.
Anthes, Georg	1892: Stolzing.
Armster, Karl	1914: Amfortas.
Bachmann, Hermann	1892–6: Kothner, Heerrufer, Wotan, Donner.
Bader, Willi	1924–5: Gurnemanz, Pogner.
Bahr-Mildenburg, Anna von	1897–1914: Kundry, Ortrud.
Bary, Alfred von	1904–14: Siegmund, Parsifal, Tristan, Lohengrin, Siegfried.
Baumann, Paula	1942: Senta.
Beirer, Hans	1958–64: Parsifal, Tristan, Tannhäuser.
Berger, Rudolf	1901–8: Amfortas, Klingsor, Gunther.
Berglund, Joel	1942: Holländer.
Bertram, Theodor	1892–1906: Nachtigall, Wotan, Holländer, Amfortas.
Bettaque, Kathi	1888: Eva, Blumenmädchen.
Betz, Franz	1876–89: Wotan, Marke, Kurwenal, Sachs.
Birrenkoven, Willi	1894: Parsifal, Lohengrin.

Bitterauf, Richard	1944: Beckmesser.
Björling, Sigurd	1951: Wotan.
Blanc, Ernest	1958–9: Telramund.
Blankenheim, Toni	1954–60: Donner, Biterolf, Klingsor, Beckmesser, Kothner.
Blass, Robert	1901: Gurnemanz, Hagen, Titurel.
Blauwaert, Emil	1889: Gurnemanz.
Blomé, Olga	1924–5: Brünnhilde.
Bockelmann, Rudolf	1928–42: Gunther, Kurwenal, Wotan, Sachs, Holländer.
Böhme, Kurt	1952–64: Pogner, Fafner, Klingsor, Titurel.
Borkh, Inge	1952: Freia, Sieglinde.
Born, Claire	1925: Eva, Gutrune.
Brandt, Marianne	1876–82: Ortlinde, Waltraute (*Gött.*), Kundry.
Branzell, Karin	1930–1: Fricka, Waltraute (*Gött.*).
Braun, Karl	1906–31: Fafner, Titurel, Gurnemanz, Fasolt, Hagen, Pogner, Wotan, Hunding.
Brema, Marie	1894–7: Kundry, Ortrud, Fricka.
Breuer, Hans	1894–1914: Knappe, Mime, David, Zorn.
Brouwenstijn, Gré	1954–6: Elisabeth, Gutrune, Eva, Freia, Sieglinde.
Buchner, Paula	1939–42: Kundry, Brünnhilde.
Bumbry, Grace	1961–2: Venus.
Bunlet, Marcelle	1931–3: Kundry, Woglinde, Schwertleite, Blumenmädchen.
Burg, Robert	1933–42: Kothner, Alberich, Klingsor.
Burgstaller, Alois	1894–1909: Heinrich der Schreiber, Gralsritter, Siegfried, Froh, Siegmund, Parsifal, Erik.
Burrian, Karl	1908: Parsifal.
Carlsson, Carin	1934: Erda, Helmwige.
Casa, Lisa della	1952: Eva.
Challis, Bennet	1912–14: Klingsor, Holländer, Hagen.
Clewing, Karl	1924–5: Parsifal, Stolzing.
Cornelius, Peter	1906: Siegmund.
Correk, Josef	1925–8: Sachs, Gunther, Wotan.
Crass, Franz	1960–3: Holländer, Biterolf, König Heinrich, Fasolt.

Crespin, Régine	1958–61: Kundry, Sieglinde, 3. Norn.
Dalberg, Friedrich	1942–51: Hagen, Pogner, Fafner.
Dalis, Irene	1961–3: Kundry, Ortrud.
Dalmorès, Charles	1908: Lohengrin.
Dawison, Max	1906–9: Alberich, Telramund, Klingsor.
Dehmlow, Herta	1909: Erda, Waltraute (*Wal.*), 1. Norn.
Demuth, Leopold	1899: Sachs, Gunther.
Destinn, Emmy	1901–2: Senta, Waldvogel.
Doeme, Zoltan	1894: Parsifal.
Döring, Georg	1891–4: Marke, Landgraf, Gurnemanz, König Heinrich.
Dressler, Lilli	1889: Eva, Blumenmädchen.
Dyck, Ernest van	1888–1912: Parsifal, Lohengrin.
Edelmann, Otto	1951–2: Sachs.
Eipperle, Trude	1952: Eva.
Elschner, Walter	1924–8: Mime, Vogelgesang, Knappe.
Enderlein, Erik	1925: Stolzing.
Engel, Werner	1911–12: Amfortas.
Ericson, Barbro	1964: Kundry, Venus.
Fischer-Dieskau, Dietrich	1954–61: Wolfram, Heerrufer, Amfortas, Kothner.
Flagstad, Kirsten	1933–4: Helmwige, 3. Norn, Sieglinde, Gutrune.
Fleischer-Edel, Katharina	1904–8: Elisabeth, Brangäne, Sieglinde, 3. Norn, Elsa.
Focke, Ria	1939–41: Erda, Waltraute (*Wal.*). Mary, Ortlinde, 2. Norn.
Forti, Helena	1914: Sieglinde.
Frick, Gottlob	1957–64: Pogner, Hagen, Hunding, Fasolt.
Friedrichs, Fritz	1888–1902: Beckmesser, Alberich, Klingsor.
Fritz, Walter	1951: Loge, Gralsritter.
Fuchs, Anton	1882–9: Klingsor, Gralsritter, Titurel, Marke, Kurwenal.
Fuchs, Eugen	1933–60: Beckmesser, Foltz.
Fuchs, Marta	1933–42: Kundry, Isolde, Brünnhilde.
Gadski, Johanna	1889: Eva.
Geisler, Walter	1957: Stolzing, Gralsritter.

Höffgen, Marga   1960–4: Erda, 1. Norn.

Hoffman, Grace   1957–64: Brangäne, Siegrune, 2. Norn, Waltraute (*Gött.*), Fricka.

Hofmann, Hubert   1964: Wotan (Wanderer), Biterolf.

Hofmann, Ludwig   1928–42: Gurnemanz, Marke, Fafner, Hunding, Hagen, König Heinrich, Daland.

Höngen, Elisabeth   1951: Fricka, Waltraute (*Gött.*).

Hopf, Hans   1951–64: Stolzing, Siegfried, Froh.

Hotter, Hans   1952–64: Wotan, Kurwenal, Amfortas, Holländer, Gunther, Sachs, Pogner, Gurnemanz, Titurel, Marke.

Huesch, Gerhard   1930–1: Wolfram.

Ilosvay, Maria von   1951–64: Erda, Schwertleite, 1. Norn.

Jachnow, Hildegarde   1942: Erda, Schwertleite, 2. Norn, Mary.

Jäger, Ferdinand   1882: Parsifal.

Jaide, Luise   1876: Erda, Ortlinde, Waltraute (*Gött.*).

Janssen, Herbert   1930–7: Wolfram, Amfortas, Gunther, Donner, Kothner, Heerrufer.

Jost-Arden, Ruth   1930: Venus.

Jurinac, Sena   1957: Eva.

Karén, Inger   1936–8: Erda, Waltraute (*Wal.*).

Kaschmann, J.   1892–4: Amfortas, Wolfram.

Kelemen, Zoltan   1964: Alberich, Ortel.

Kemp, Barbara   1914–27: Senta, Helmwige, Kundry.

Kernic, Beatrix   1899: Eva.

Kipnis, Alexander   1927–33: Gurnemanz, Marke, Landgraf, Pogner, Titurel.

Kirchhoff, Walter   1911–14: Stolzing, Froh, Siegfried, Parsifal.

Kittel, Hermine   1902–8: Ortlinde, Blumenmädchen, Knappe, Erda, Helmwige, 1. Norn.

Klaus, Erich   1962–4: Mime.

Klose, Margarete	1936–42: Fricka, Helmwige, 1. Norn, Waltraute (*Gött.*), Ortrud, Brangäne, Erda.
Knüpfer, Paul	1901–12: Gurnemanz, Titurel, Daland, Landgraf, Hunding, Marke, Pogner.
Konya, Sandor	1958–64: Lohengrin, Froh, Stolzing.
Kraus, Ernst	1899–1909: Siegfried, Stolzing, Siegmund, Erik.
Kraus, Felix von	1899–1909: Gurnemanz, Hagen, Titurel, Landgraf, Marke.
Kraus, Herold	1960–1: Mime.
Kraus, Otakar	1960–3: Alberich.
Krollmann, Karl	1942–4: Mime, Steuermann (*Holländer*), Moser.
Krüger, Emmy	1924–30: Sieglinde, Kundry, Isolde.
Kuën, Paul	1951–7: Mime.
Kunz, Erich	1943–51: Beckmesser.
Kupper, Annelies	1944–60: Eva, Elsa.
Larsen-Todsen, Nanny	1927–31: Brünnhilde, Kundry, Isolde.
Leffler-Burkard, Martha	1906–9: Kundry, Sieglinde, Ortrud.
Lehmann, Lilli	1876–96: Woglinde, Siegrune, Waldvogel, Brünnhilde.
Leider, Frida	1928–38: Brünnhilde, Kundry, Isolde.
Leisner, Emmi	1925: Erda, Waltraute (*Wal.* and *Gött.*), 1. Norn.
Liebenberg, Eva	1927–8: Erda, 1. Norn.
List, Emanuel	1933: Gurnemanz, Titurel, Fafner, Hunding, Hagen, Pogner.
London, George	1951–64: Amfortas, Holländer.
Lorenz, Max	1933–54: Siegfried, Parsifal, Stolzing, Lohengrin, Siegmund, Tristan.
Los Angeles, Victoria de	1961–2: Elisabeth.
Lubin, Germaine	1938–9: Kundry, Isolde.
Ludwig, Hanna	1951–2: Fricka, Flosshilde, Siegrune, Knappe, Blumen-mädchen.
Lustig, Rudolf	1954–5: Loge, Erik.
Mailhac, Pauline	1891–2: Kundry, Venus.

Malaniuk, Ira	1951–3: Fricka, Siegrune, 2. Norn, Magdalene, Brangäne, Waltraute (*Gött.*),
Malten, Therese	1882–94: Kundry, Isolde, Eva.
Manowarda, Josef von	1931–42: Gurnemanz, Marke, Landgraf, Fafner, Hunding, Hagen, Pogner, König Heinrich, Titurel, Fasolt, Daland.
Materna, Amalie	1876–91: Brünnhilde, Kundry.
Matray, Desider	1904: Tannhäuser.
Mayr, Richard	1902–24: Hagen, Gralsritter, Gurnemanz, Pogner.
Melchior, Lauritz	1924–31: Siegmund, Parsifal, Siegfried, Tristan, Tannhäuser.
Metzger, Ottilie	1901–12: Flosshilde, Siegrune, Schwertleite, 2. Norn, Erda, Waltraute (*Gött.*),
Meyer, Kerstin	1962–4: Brangäne.
Meyfarth, Jutta	1962–4: Freia, Sieglinde, Gutrune.
Milinkovic, Georgine von	1954–7: Fricka, Siegrune, 2. Norn, Magdalene.
Mill, Arnold van	1951–60: Hunding, Titurel, Daland, Fafner, Fasolt, Marke Nachtwächter.
Milligan, James	1961: Wotan (Wanderer).
Mödl, Martha	1951–62: Kundry, 3. Norn, Gutrune, Isolde, Brünnhilde, Sieglinde.
Mulder, Luise	1891–7: Hirte, Eva, Knappe, Blumenmädchen.
Müller, Maria	1930–44: Elisabeth, Sieglinde, Eva, Gutrune, Elsa, Senta.
Nawiasky, Eduard	1904: Alberich.
Neate, Ken	1963: Loge.
Nebe, Karl	1892: Beckmesser.
Neidlinger, Gustav	1952–64: Alberich, Kurwenal, Nachtwächter, Sachs, Telramund, Klingsor, Kothner.
Neumann, Karl-August	1933: Beckmesser.
Niemann, Albert	1876: Siegmund.
Nilsson, Birgit	1954–64: Elsa, Siegrune, Sieglinde, 2. Norn, Isolde, Brünnhilde.
Nissen, Hans Hermann	1943: Sachs.
Nordica, Lilian	1894: Elsa.
Nôrdmo-Loevberg, Aase	1960: Elsa, Sieglinde, 3. Norn.

Ohms, Elisabeth	1931: Kundry.
Onegin, Sigrid	1933–4: Fricka, 1. Norn, Waltraute (*Gött.*),
Perron, Karl	1889–1904: Amfortas, Wotan, Gunther.
Pflanzl, Heinrich	1951–2: Beckmesser, Kothner, Alberich.
Pilinski, Sigismund	1930–1: Tannhäuser.
Pistor, Gotthelf	1925–31: Froh, Parsifal, Tristan, Siegmund, Siegfried.
Plank, Fritz	1884–97: Klingsor, Kurwenal, Sachs, Pogner.
Popovici, Demeter	1894–9: Telramund, Alberich, Klingsor.
Prohaska, Jaro	1933–44: Wotan, Gunther, Sachs, Amfortas, Donner, Telramund, Kurwenal, Holländer.
Ralf, Oskar	1927: Siegmund.
Ranzenberg, Maria	1925: Fricka.
Ranzow, Maria	1927–8: Fricka, 2. Norn, Waltraute (*Gött.*).
Reicher-Kindermann, Hedwig	1876: Erda, Rossweisse.
Reichmann, Theodor	1882–1902: Amfortas, Sachs, Wolfram.
Reinmar, Hans	1939–41: Amfortas, Donner, Gunther.
Rémond, Fritz	1904: Parsifal.
Rennyson, Gertrude	1909–11: Elsa, Grimgerde, Siegrune, Knappe, Blumenmädchen.
Resnik, Regina	1953–61: Sieglinde, 3. Norn, Fricka.
Reuss-Belce, Luise	1882–1912: Blumenmädchen, Knappe, Eva, 3. Norn, Gutrune, Helmwige, Fricka, 2. Norn.
Ritter, Rudolf	1924–30: Siegfried, Tannhäuser
Roemer, Matthias	1909: Parsifal.
Rohrbach, Hermann	1951: Sachs.
Rooy, Anton van	1897–1902: Wotan, Sachs, Holländer.
Rösler-Keuschnigg, Maria	1930: Kundry.
Roswaenge, Helge	1934–6: Parsifal.
Rysanek, Leonie	1951–64: Sieglinde, Elsa, Senta, Elisabeth.

Saedén, Erik	1958: Donner, Kurwenal, Heerrufer.
Saltzmann-Stevens, Minnie	1911–12: Sieglinde, Kundry.
Scaria, Emil	1882–4: Gurnemanz.
Schefsky, Josephine	1876: Sieglinde, 2. Norn.
Scheidemantel, Karl	1886–92: Amfortas, Klingsor, Kurwenal, Sachs, Wolfram.
Scheidl, Theodor	1914–30: Klingsor, Donner, Amfortas, Kurwenal.
Scheppan, Hilde	1937–58: Woglinde, Helmwige, Rossweisse, Knappe, Blumen-mädchen, Eva.
Schlosser, Karl	1876: Mime.
Schlusnus, Heinrich	1933: Amfortas.
Schmedes, Erik	1899–1906: Siegfried, Parsifal.
Schmitt-Walter, Karl	1956–61: Beckmesser.
Schock, Rudolf	1959: Stolzing.
Schöffler, Paul	1943–56: Sachs, Holländer.
Schöpflin, Adolf	1924: Gurnemanz, Pogner.
Schorr, Friedrich	1925–31: Wotan.
Schultz, Heinrich	1911–25: Beckmesser.
Schumann-Heink, Ernestine	1896–1914: Erda, Waltraute (*Gött.*), Grimgerde, 1. Norn, Magdalene, Mary, Rossweisse.
Schütz, Hans	1899–1902: Amfortas, Donner, Klingsor.
Schützendorf-Bellwidt, Alphons	1908–12: Klingsor, Donner, Telramund.
Schwarzkopf, Elisabeth	1951: Eva, Woglinde.
Siehr, Gustav	1876–89: Hagen, Gurnemanz, Marke.
Siewert, Rut	1951–60: Erda, Grimgerde, 1. Norn, Waltraute (*Gött.*), Fricka.
Silja, Anja	1960–4: Senta, Blumen-mädchen, Elsa, Elisabeth, Eva.
Soomer, Walter	1906–25: Donner, Kurwenal, Wotan, Amfortas, Sachs, Fasolt, Hunding, Hagen, Gurnemanz.
Stahmer-Andriessen, Pelagie	1886: Brangäne.
Staudigl, Gisela	1886–1912: Brangäne, Magdalene.
Steber, Eleanor	1953: Elsa.
Stern, Jean	1943: Sachs.

Stewart, Thomas	1960–4: Amfortas, Donner, Gunther.
Stolze, Gerhard	1951–64: Moser, Hirte, Froh, Heinrich der Schreiber, David, Mime, Loge, Vogelweide, Knappe.
Sucher, Rosa	1886–99: Isolde, Kundry, Eva, Venus, Sieglinde.
Suthaus, Ludwig	1943–57: Stolzing, Loge, Siegmund.
Svanholm, Set	1942: Siegfried, Erik.
Szantho, Enid	1930–7: Erda, Grimgerde, 1. Norn, Blumenmädchen, Waltraute (*Gött.*), Rossweisse, Knappe.
Ternina, Milka	1899: Kundry.
Thomas, Jess	1961–3: Parsifal, Lohengrin, Stolzing.
Töpper, Herta	1951–60: Flosshilde, Helmwige, 3. Norn, Knappe, Blumen- mädchen, Fricka.
Traxel, Josef	1954–8: Froh, Vogelweide, Gralsritter, Steuermann (*Holländer*), Stolzing.
Treptow, Günther	1951–64: Siegmund, Eisslinger.
Trundt, Henny	1927–8: Sieglinde, Kundry.
Uhde, Hermann	1951–7: Gunther, Klingsor, Wotan, Telramund, Donner, Holländer, Titurel.
Uhl, Fritz	1957–64: Melot, Vogelgesang, Loge, Gralsritter, Erik, Siegmund.
Ulmer, Wilhelm	1914: Froh, Siegmund, Parsifal.
Unger, Georg	1876: Froh, Siegfried.
Urlus, Jakob	1911–12: Siegmund.
Välkki, Anita	1963–4: Brünnhilde, 3. Norn.
Varnay, Astrid	1951–64: Brünnhilde, Isolde, Ortrud, Sieglinde, Gutrune, Senta, 3. Norn, Kundry.
Vickers, Jon	1958–64: Siegmund, Parsifal.
Vinay, Ramon	1952–62: Tristan, Siegmund, Parsifal, Tannhäuser, Telramund.
Vogelstrom, Fritz	1909: Parsifal, Lohengrin, Froh.
Vogl, Heinrich	1876–97: Loge, Tristan, Parsifal, Siegmund.

Völker, Franz	1933–42: Siegmund, Lohengrin, Parsifal, Erik.
Wachter, Ernst	1896–9: Fasolt, Hunding, Gurnemanz.
Waechter, Eberhard	1958–64: Amfortas, Heerrufer, Kothner, Wolfram, Kurwenal.
Walker, Edyth	1908: Kundry, Ortrud.
Weber, Ludwig	1951–61: Gurnemanz, Fasolt, Hagen, Marke, Pogner, König Heinrich, Daland, Titurel, Kothner.
Weil, Hermann	1911–25: Sachs, Amfortas, Gunther.
Westphal, Elisabeth	1924: Erda, Rossweisse.
Whitehill, Clarence C.	1894–1909: Wolfram, Amfortas, Gunther.
Wiborg, Elisa	1891–4: Elisabeth, Blumenmädchen.
Wiedemann, Paul	1928: Siegmund.
Wiegand, Heinrich	1886–91: Gurnemanz, Marke, Pogner, Landgraf.
Wiener, Otto	1957–63: Sachs, Gralsritter, Gunther, Holländer, Wotan.
Wilfert, Herta	1954–5: Venus, Freia, Rossweisse.
Windgassen, Wolfgang	1951–64: Parsifal, Froh, Siegfried, Lohengrin, Tannhäuser, Erik, Siegmund, Stolzing, Tristan.
Winkelmann, Hermann	1882–91: Parsifal, Stolzing, Tannhäuser.
Wissmann, Lore	1951–6: Blumenmädchen, Eva, Woglinde.
Witte, Erich	1943–53: David, Loge.
Wittich, Marie	1901–9: Sieglinde, Kundry, Isolde.
Wittrisch, Marcel	1937: Lohengrin.
Wolff, Fritz	1925–41: Loge, Gralsritter, Eisslinger, Parsifal, Melot, Stolzing.
Zeller, Heinrich	1891–2: Tannhäuser, Knappe, Heinrich der Schreiber, Melot.
Zimmermann, Erich	1925–44: David, Knappe, Mime, Steuermann (*Holländer*), Loge.

Bibliography

Appia, Adolphe: *La mise en scène du drame wagnerien* (Paris, 1895)
  Die Musik und die Inszenierung (Munich, 1899)
Bahr-Mildenburg, Anna: *Erinnerungen* (Vienna, 1921)
Bergfeld, Joachim: *Die Probleme der Bühnengestaltung bei Richard Wagner* (MS, Richard Wagner-Gedenkstätte, Bayreuth)
Damrosch, Walter: *My Musical Life* (Allen and Unwin, 1924)
Eichner, Walter (Editor): *Weltdiskussion um Bayreuth* (Gesellschaft der Freunde von Bayreuth, 1952)
Fricke, Richard: *Bayreuth vor dreissig Jahren* (Dresden, 1906)
Geissmar, Berta: *The Baton and the Jackboot* (Hamish Hamilton, 1944)
Gregor, Joseph: *Kulturgeschichte der Oper* (Vienna, 1950)
Herzfeld, Friedrich: *Das Neue Bayreuth* (Berlin, 1960)
Hey, Julius: *Richard Wagner als Vortragsmeister* (Leipzig, 1911)
Joy, Charles R. (Editor): *Music in the Life of Albert Schweitzer* (Black, 1953)
Klein, Hermann: *Thirty Years of Musical Life in London* (Heinemann, 1903)
Lehmann, Lilli: *Mein Weg* (Leipzig, 1913)
Leider, Frida: *Das war mein Teil* (Berlin, 1959)
Leiser, Clara: *Jean de Reszke* (Howe, 1933)
Lorenz, Alfred: *Das Geheimnis der Form bei Richard Wagner* (Berlin, 1924–33)
Millenkovich-Morold, Max: *Cosima Wagner* (Leipzig, 1937)
Neumann, Angelo: *Erinnerungen an Richard Wagner* (3rd ed., Leipzig, 1907)
Neupert, Käte (Editor): *Die Besetzung der Bayreuther Festspiele 1876–1960* (Bayreuth, 1961)
Newman, Ernest: *The Life of Richard Wagner*, 4 vols. (Cassell, 1933–47)
Pfitzner, Hans: *Werk und Wiedergabe* (Augsburg, 1929)
Preetorius, Emil: *Richard Wagner: Bild und Vision* (Godesberg, 1949)
Puttkamer, Albert von: *50 Jahre Bayreuth* (Berlin, 1927)

Riess, Curt (translated by Margaret Goldsmith): *Wilhelm Furtwängler* (Muller, 1955)

Rühlmann, Franz: *Richard Wagners theatralische Sendung* (Brunswick, 1935)

Shaw, G. B.: *Music in London 1890–94* (Constable, 1932)

Siegfried, Walter: *Frau Cosima Wagner* (Stuttgart, 1930)

Söhnlein, Kurt: *Bayreuther Arbeit 1924–31* (MS, Richard Wagner-Gedenkstätte, Bayreuth)

Wagner, Friedelind (with Page Cooper): *The Royal Family of Bayreuth* (Eyre and Spottiswoode, 1948)

Wagner, Richard: *My Life* (authorized English translation, Constable, 1911, reissued 1963)
Collected works and letters

Wagner, Siegfried: *Erinnerungen* (Stuttgart, 1923)

Wagner, Wieland (Editor): *Richard Wagner und das neue Bayreuth* (essays by various authors) (Munich, 1962)

Weingartner, Felix (translated by Marguerite Wolff): *Buffets and Rewards* (Hutchinson, 1937)

Westernhagen, Curt von: *Vom Holländer zum Parsifal* (Freiburg, 1962)

Wood, Henry J.: *My Life of Music* (Gollancz, 1938)

Bayreuther Blätter (various years)

Bayreuther Festspielführer (various years)

Bayreuth-Hefte (1951–64)

Der Fall Bayreuth (essays by various authors, including E. Stadler on Appia) (Basel, 1962)

Index

235

Wagner, Winifred, 9, 11–12, 15, 16, 17, 110, 137–46, 156–7. For productions under her regime see *Lohengrin; Meistersinger von Nürnberg, Die; Ring des Nibelungen, Der* (all Heinz Tietjen)

Wagner, Wolfgang, *passim.* Attitude to tradition, 157, 162–4, 168, 176, 212–3. As producer, 165–6. Views on acting, 170; scenery, 170–1, 173. Productions: see *Ring des Nibelungen, Der*

Ward, David, 206

Weingartner, Felix von, 51, 65, 74–75, 110

Wildermann, Hans, 131, 134

Williams, Winifred Marjorie, see Wagner, Winifred

Windgassen, Wolfgang, 203, 204

Winkelmann, Hermann, 57, 67

Wolzogen, Ernst von, 72